IMAGES
of America

PISCATAWAY TOWNSHIP

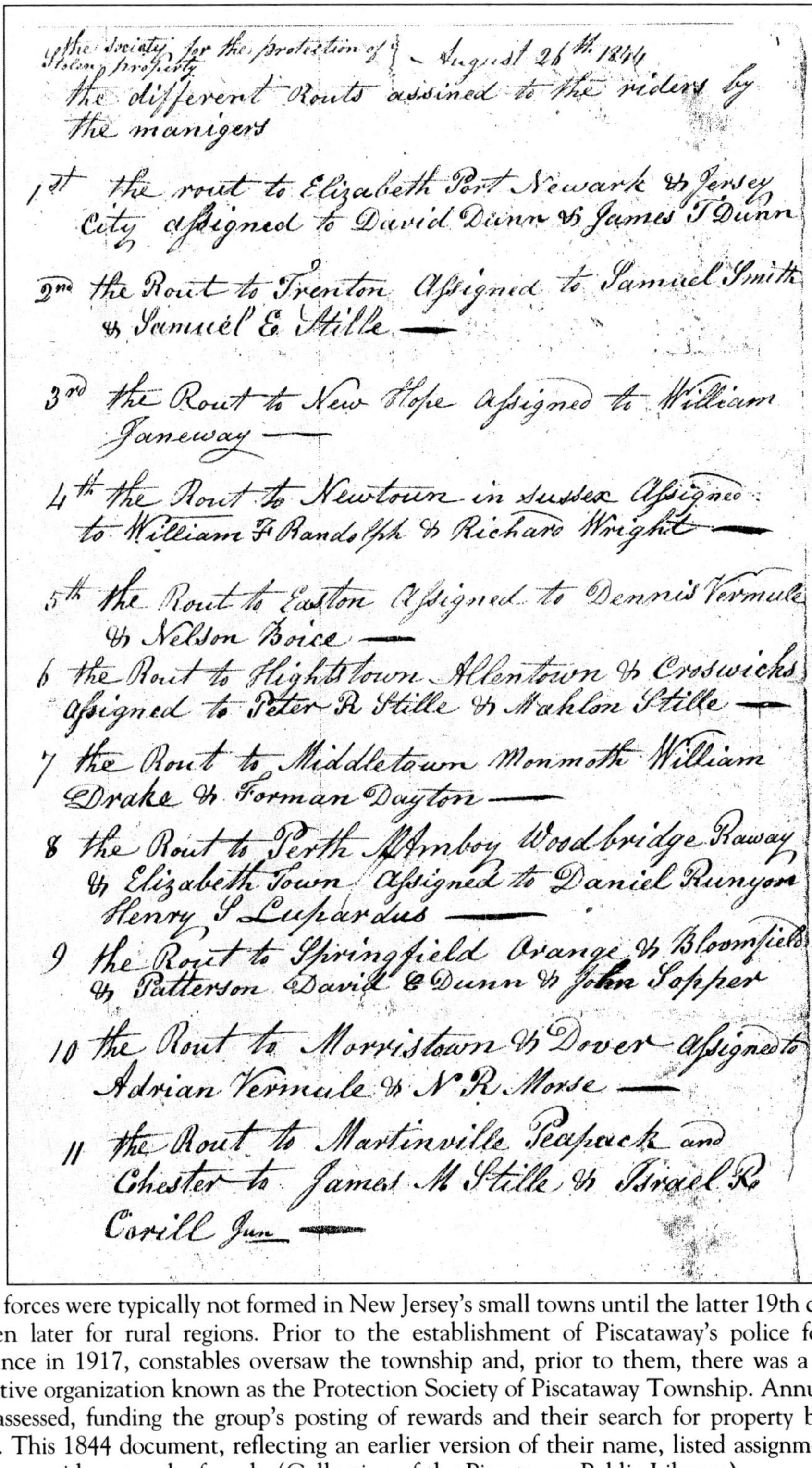

the society for the protection of Stolen property } — August 26th 1844

the different Routs assined to the riders by the manigers

1st the rout to Elizabeth Port Newark & Jersey City assigned to David Dunn & James T Dunn

2nd the Rout to Trenton Assigned to Samuel Smith & Samuel E Stille —

3rd the Rout to New Hope Assigned to William Janeway —

4th the Rout to Newtown in Sussex Assigned to William F Randolph & Richard Wright —

5th the Rout to Easton Assigned to Dennis Vermule & Nelson Boice —

6 the Rout to Hightstown Allentown & Croswicks Assigned to Peter R Stille & Mahlon Stille —

7 the Rout to Middletown Monmoth William Drake & Forman Dayton —

8 the Rout to Perth Amboy Woodbridge Raway & Elizabeth Town Assigned to Daniel Runyon Henry S Lupardus —

9 the Rout to Springfield Orange & Bloomfield & Patterson David E Dunn & John Sopper

10 the Rout to Morristown & Dover Assigned to Adrian Vermule & N R Morse —

11 the Rout to Martinville Peapack and Chester to James M Stille & Israel R Corill Jun —

Police forces were typically not formed in New Jersey's small towns until the latter 19th century, or even later for rural regions. Prior to the establishment of Piscataway's police force by ordinance in 1917, constables oversaw the township and, prior to them, there was a private protective organization known as the Protection Society of Piscataway Township. Annual dues were assessed, funding the group's posting of rewards and their search for property believed stolen. This 1844 document, reflecting an earlier version of their name, listed assignments for covering a wide network of roads. (Collection of the Piscataway Public Library.)

IMAGES
of America

PISCATAWAY TOWNSHIP

Randall Gabrielan

ARCADIA
PUBLISHING

ISBN 978-0-7385-0439-1

Published by Arcadia Publishing
Charleston, South Carolina

Printed in the United States of America

Library of Congress Catalog Card Number: 00-104052

For all general information contact Arcadia Publishing at:
Telephone 843-853-2070
Fax 843-853-0044
E-mail sales@arcadiapublishing.com
For customer service and orders:
Toll-Free 1-888-313-2665

Visit us on the Internet at www.arcadiapublishing.com

On the cover: See page 125.

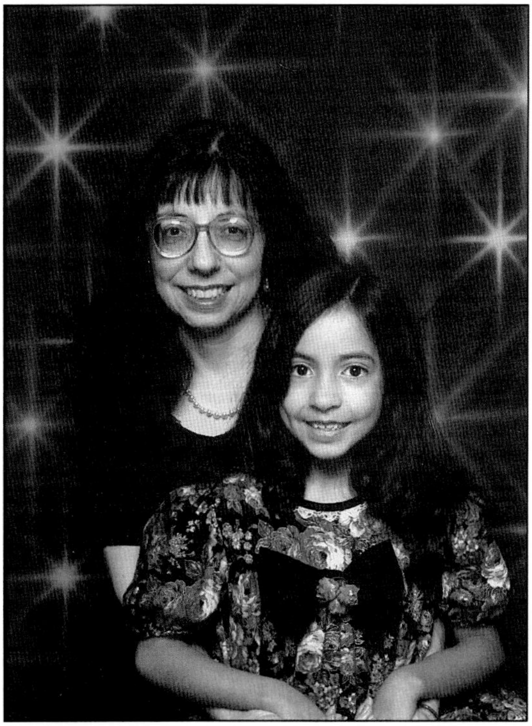

This book is dedicated to Cynthia Tosatto Harris, a dedicated collector who shares her fine material with exemplary generosity. A Jersey City native who taught for many years in that city's schools, Cynthia needed to develop a second career. She is currently completing library studies and is preparing for additional public service in her new professional capacity. Her courage and enthusiasm merit special recognition. She is pictured with daughter Brittany.

Contents

Acknowledgments

Carol Natorelli has performed admirably as a project assistant, having served as my key person around Piscataway with a high degree of charm, graciousness, cooperation, and productivity. A big thanks to Carol.

Constance O'Grady has collected, preserved, and photographed Piscataway history for many years. Her files and storehouse of information were invaluable to the writing. Thanks for doing so much for so long a period, Connie, and for sharing your knowledge. Junelynn Sadlowski, curator of the Metlar House, was present at the origin of this project and was a source of images and help throughout. Indeed, the book began with a contest in which June and the author provided mutual encouragement for the other to write the book. Obviously, June won. Thanks to both June and the Metlar House. Anna Ashkenes and the Middlesex County Cultural and Heritage Commission operate the Cornelius Low House as a museum. It is one of the finest houses in Middlesex County. Thanks to Hillary Murtha, Low House curator. Jeanette Randolph Duryea, a member of one of Piscataway's earliest families, contributed some of the oldest and finest images. They merit this special thanks. Cynthia Harris, one of New Jersey's most generous postcard collectors, makes history come alive through that medium. Many thanks for your early and important help, Cynthia. Rebecca Yamin is an archeologist who performed a crucial role in both the 1979 and 2000 Raritan Landing projects. I thank her not only for two fine images of the digs but also for sharing her pioneering studies on Raritan Landing. The Piscataway Public Library maintains a local history room with a rich collection of printed and pictorial material. Thanks to their staff for liberal access to the collection. The New Jersey Room of the Rutgers Special Collections is one of the state's great local history resources. Its and the staff's contributions, especially those of Edward Skipworth, to this book were considerable and merit this major thank-you.

My heartfelt thanks to all the lenders of pictures, who are in a real respect the coproducers of this volume: Bobby Giarretta, Vincent Gulbin, Jean Kolva, Margaret Kruse, Janice Perrine Kuhn, Bob and Sue Lachenmayer, Robert La Costa, Ed Marsh, Caroline Meuly, Skip Moore, Jeanne Neilson, Cheryl Pedersen, the River Road Fire Company, Rutgers University Special Collections and University Archives, Betty Scott, Nancy Bakker Sheasley, the Sisters of Mercy, New Jersey Regional Community, Thomas Smith, Goldie Sudzin, Union Carbide (a division of Dow Chemical), Donald Wayne, Ruth Morris Williams, and Warren Williams. There has been a sharing of vintage photographs in the Piscataway historic community that has probably resulted in my receiving images from some who obtained them from others. My thanks, too, to the unnamed and unknown-to-me owners of those original pictures.

Introduction

Piscataway was settled in 1666 under the authority of the English owners Berkeley and Carteret. As this land, long occupied by the Lenape Indians, was organized, Middlesex became one of four original counties of East Jersey province. The 12 Articles of Agreement of 1666 outlined terms of settlements in a vast tract that in 1668 was divided between Woodbridge and Piscataway. Piscataway was organized formally in 1693 and incorporated in 1798.

Eighteenth-century municipalities, nearly all of them townships, were few and often vast. Local administration was hardly developed in the early years of the republic, but (although administrative responsibilities devolved locally) the townships were inconveniently large. The history of mid-19th-century township division is fascinating and relates to the present make-up of Piscataway Township. The large original (or at least pre–American independence) townships were divided. Many of the divisions occurred in the 1840s, but Piscataway's occurred relatively late—in 1870, when Raritan Township was sectioned off.

Lesser division occurred as smaller areas sought to administer themselves. These separations include Dunellen in 1887, Middlesex borough in 1913, and South Plainfield in 1926. The past of these newer municipalities is tied to that of their earlier homes. Indeed, the village of Piscatawaytown, one of the township's historic cores, was placed in Raritan (now Edison) Township. Most of the historical picture collections in town embrace these departed areas. This book uses some of those illustrations more to denote municipal separation than to expropriate the newer towns' histories.

The name Piscataway comes from the Piscataqua River, which separates Maine and New Hampshire near the Atlantic Ocean, a region that had been home to some original 17th-century Piscataway settlers. Since place nomenclature goes back only one step, it is proper to say that Piscataway was named for the river rather than the Native Americans who gave their name to that body of water. One other Piscataway, in Maryland, exists in America; it is near a known home of Native Americans.

Piscataway's early significance comes from a river port. The importance of Raritan Landing has only recently been revealed through archeology. The near-total obliteration of this major settlement is one of the great mysteries of New Jersey history. It is told in the first chapter without the imagery one hopes would have survived.

Although Piscataway became so important so early in its history, its present character was not shaped until the latter 20th century. The township had long been a farming community but also had the opportunity to attract some industry in the first half of the century. One signal event shaped the second half: the opening of Interstate 287, a road that bisected the township east and west and initiated a change ethic that paved over much of the farmland. Although the commercial ratables are clean and attractive, the great quantity of housing that was built at the time took much of the suburban and rural character. New roads and patterns of travel can leave many residents, as well as visitors, unaware that Piscataway has an old and historic past.

Piscataway appears to have less of that history than other similarly aged and important developing municipalities. There is a tendency for historians to compare relative preservation fortunes along their travels. (The author is from Middletown and does most of his work in Monmouth County.) Piscataway appears to have lost more than its share of its historic patrimony, as the development climate is too prone to permit destruction of historic properties when former farms must be built upon. The township would do well with a strong preservation law with enforcement powers to help save what remains.

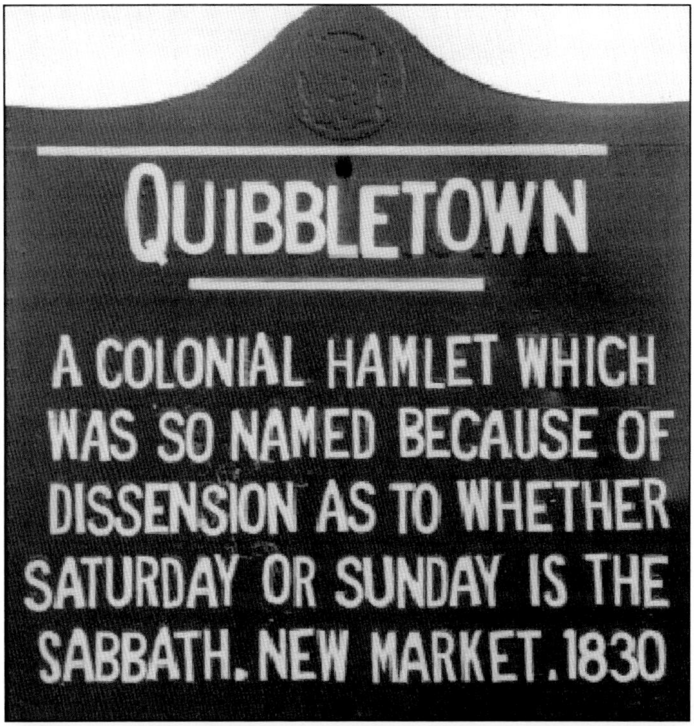

There is more than one attribution to the name Quibbletown, but far be it from the author to quibble.

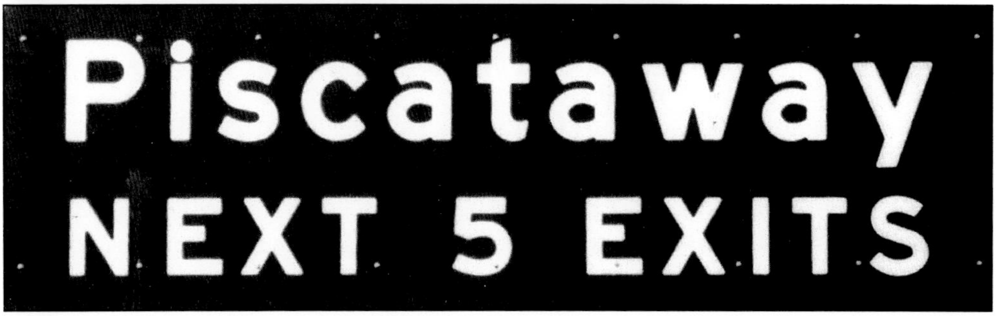

Well, the next nine chapters, actually.

One

Raritan Landing

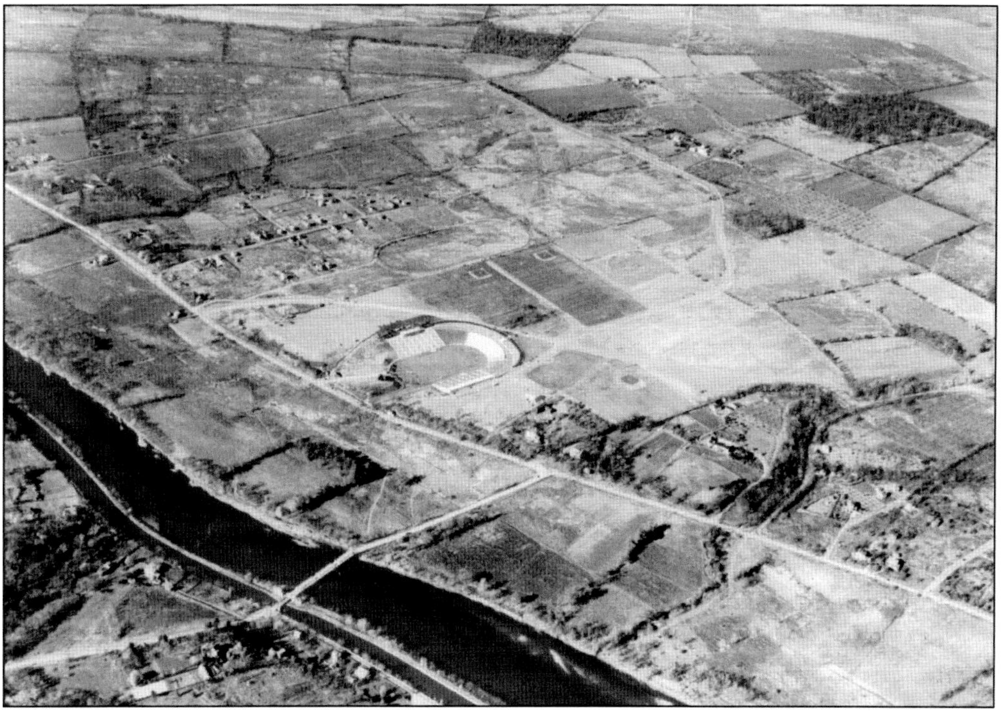

Piscataway's early importance stemmed from its port at the head of deep-water navigation on the Raritan River, a port established near the *c.* 1675 apportionment of lands to its New England settlers. The settlement, large for its time, embraced both banks but was primarily on the Piscataway northern shore. Deep-draft vessels ducked at about the point where the river was first bridged in 1772, the same spot as is located the later span visible in this *c.* 1940 aerial photograph. River Road, the white band bisecting the middle of the image, began as a Native American path and was known in the late 17th century as the Road up Raritan. Rutgers built the stadium in 1938. Now much of the land on all sides of it is occupied by their Busch campus, which includes the University of Medicine and Dentistry of New Jersey, west of Metlars Lane. East of Metlars Lane is the Livingston campus.

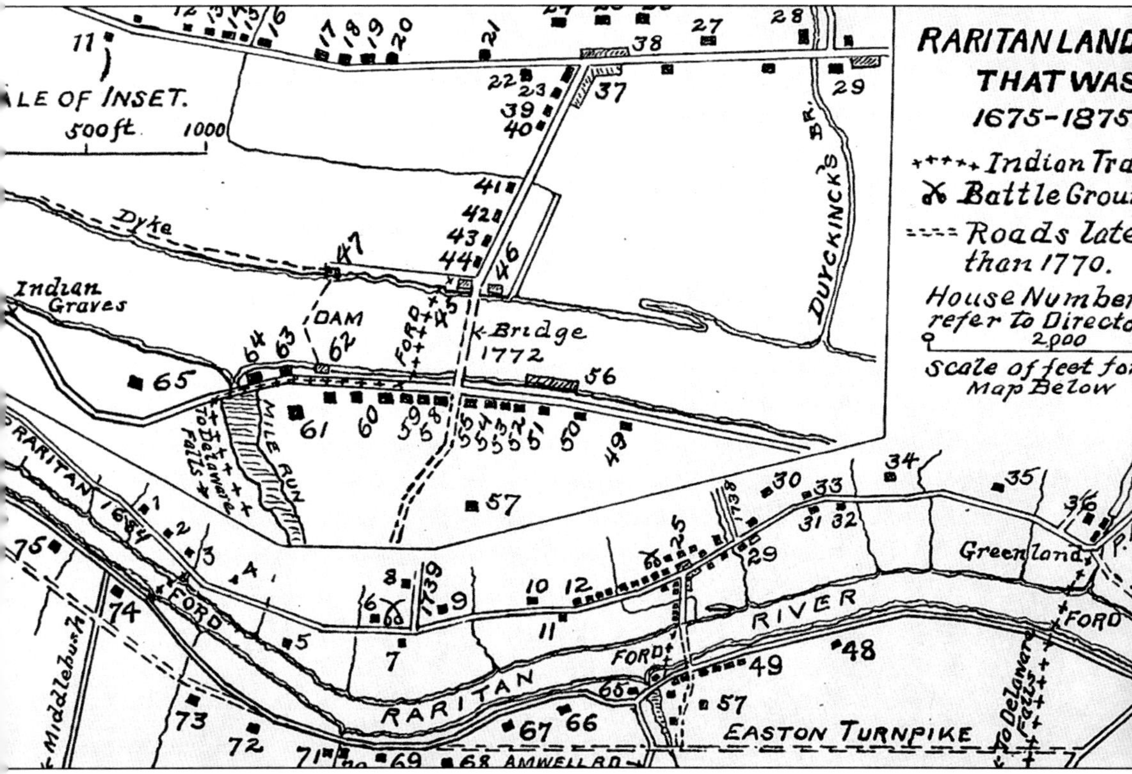

Cornelius Clarkson Vermeule, born in 1895, grew up on River Road overlooking the then-green pastures once filled by an extensive commercial settlement that survived only in the memories of his elders. He expanded his relatives' stories to a major study, *Raritan Landing That Was: The History of a River Port from 1675–1875*, which was presented to the New Brunswick History Club in 1930 and, in April 1936, was expanded and published by the New Jersey Historical Society. This map, the most telling visual of the place in existence, was published with his paper. The large-scale inset can be placed within the small-scale map by comparing placement of the bridge. Later scholars have corrected a few of Vermeule's claims; for example, the large L-shaped building at 37 did not exist. However, the map is substantially accurate. In its earliest years, the place was known as Herdenbrooks Landing. The landing's decline was rapid after the 1834 opening of the Delaware & Raritan Canal. The settlement had disappeared by 1875, and much of the grounds became Johnson Park.

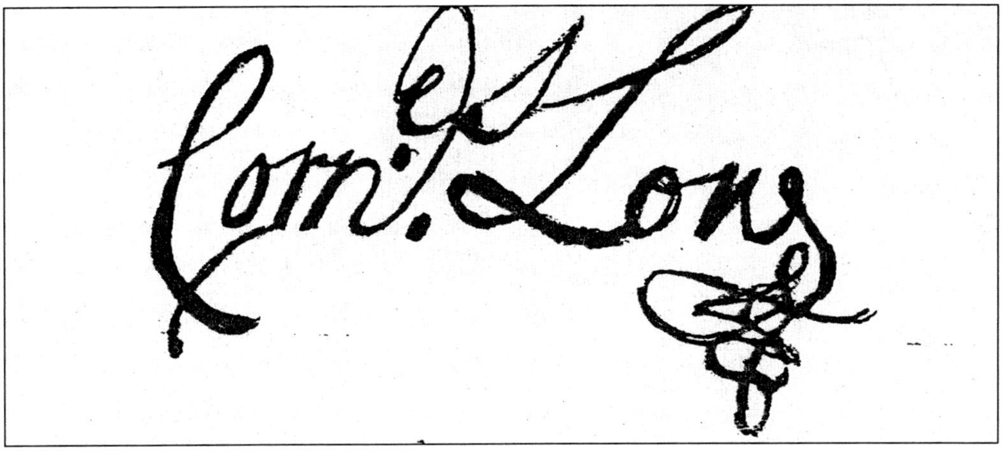

Cornelius Low, born in 1700 in New York, was one of Raritan Landing's most important merchants. He arrived there from Kingston, New York, in 1730, one year after marrying Johanna Gouverneur, the daughter of a prominent New York merchant. He was as prolific as he was influential; the couple had almost one child each year until 1748, when their last daughter was born. Four girls and six boys survived. Low died in 1777 and his estate remained unsettled for years. During this period, his son Cornelius III's widow and their daughter Mary Margaret lived there. No image of Low exists, but he is represented by this impressive signature from his will—and even that may not be from his hand.

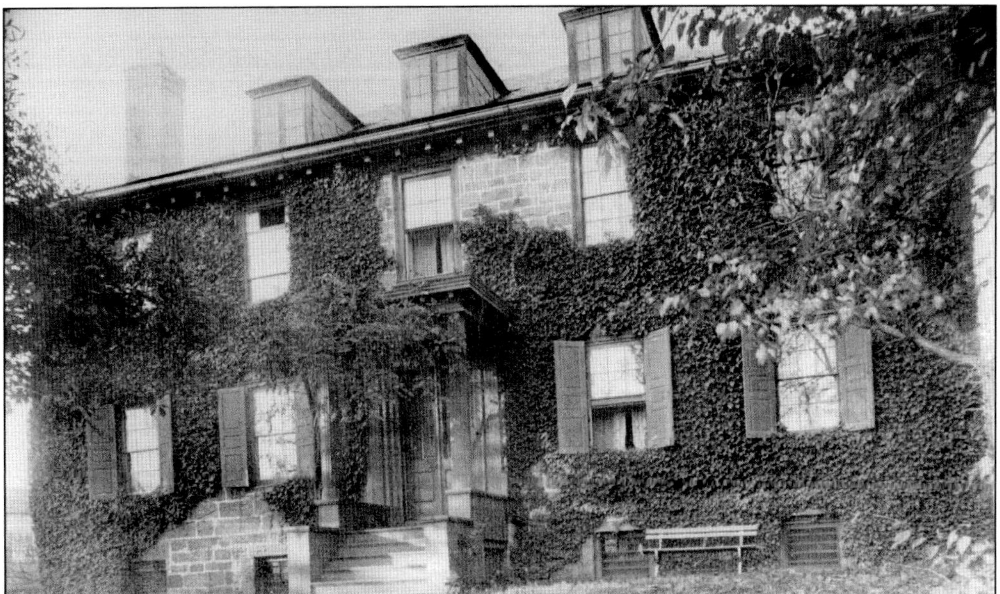

Cornelius Low initially lived close to the Raritan River, which then, as now, overflows. After his house was hit by the 1738 freshet (a charming euphemism that lacks the impact of the word *flood*), he decided to build on the bluff over the Road up Raritan. In 1741, he erected the most substantial house in Raritan Landing, reportedly the largest and costliest in East Jersey province. It remains today one of the most important houses in Middlesex County. This undated picture of a virtually unchanged west facade was taken during the lengthy spell that the place was covered with the weed ivy, giving it the nickname Ivy Hall. (Rutgers Special Collections and University Archives.)

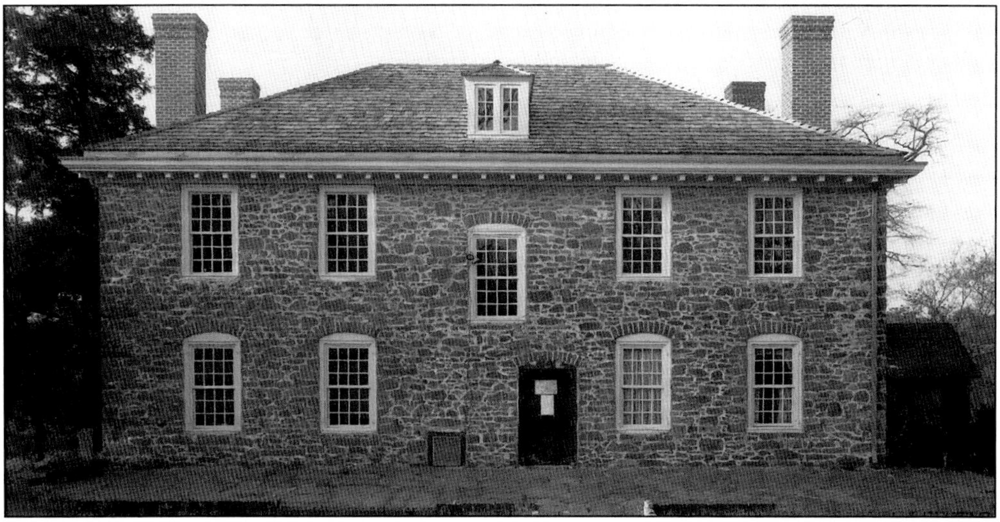

A later picture, perhaps from the late 1970s, of the east elevation shows the Georgian-style house's sandstone blocks, which were quarried west of Bound Brook. Large, costly, square-cut blocks make up the front of the house at 1225 River Road; the rear and sides are made of randomly shaped stone. Other families that have occupied the house include the Pool, Metlar, Voorhees, and Strong families. (Middlesex County Cultural and Heritage Commission, Low House Collection.)

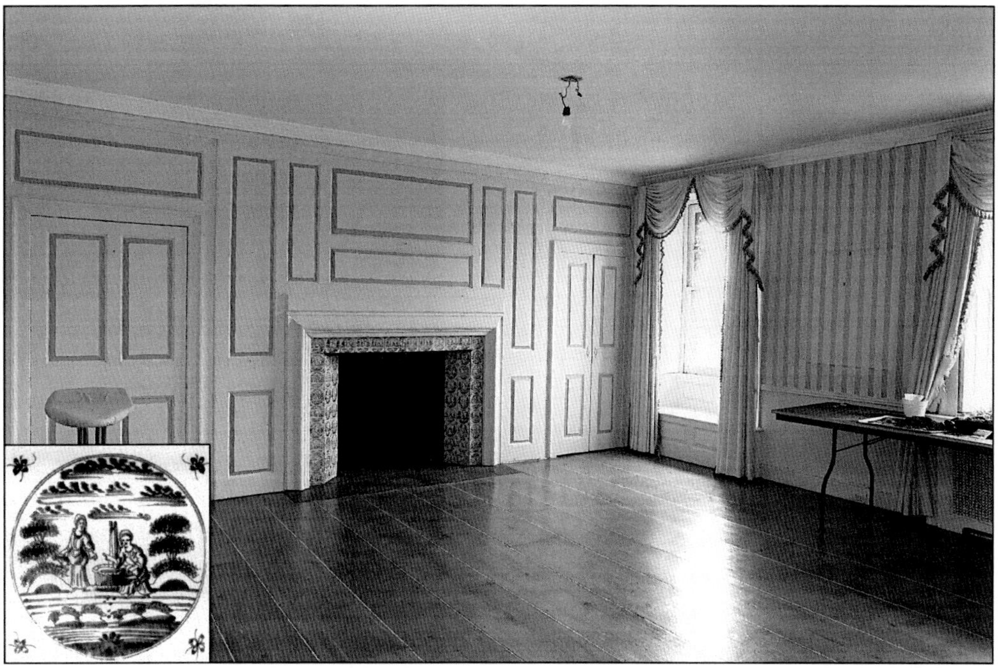

This room, in the northeast corner of the second story, possesses the most intact Georgian features, although the window seat is a reconstruction. The fireplace retains its original box shape, admittedly not the most efficient for heating; its surrounding molding and attractive Delft tiles are original. Notice the width of the floorboards. The Low House was recorded in the Historic American Buildings Survey and was listed on the National Register of Historic Places in 1971. (Middlesex County Cultural and Heritage Commission, Low House Collection.)

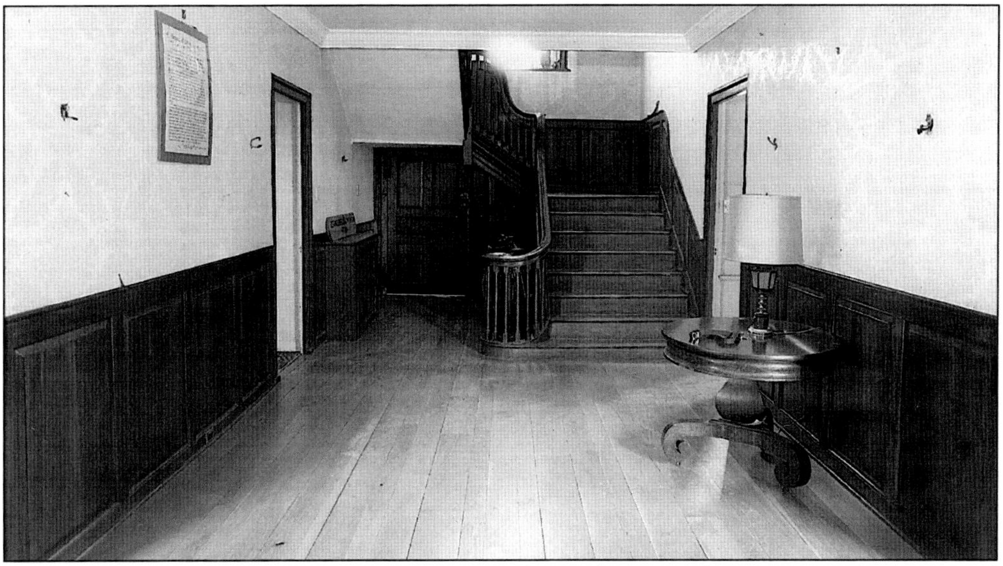

The large center hall of a Georgian house was often as large as other rooms in the house and would have been used for entertainment. Four rooms branch off from the Low House hall, seen in this view looking toward the original rear staircase. The wainscoting is also original. The County of Middlesex bought the Low House from Stephan Van Rensselaer Strong in 1979 and, following an extensive restoration program by architects Ford, Farewell, Mills, & Gatsch, operates the facility as a museum. (Middlesex County Cultural and Heritage Commission, Low House Collection.)

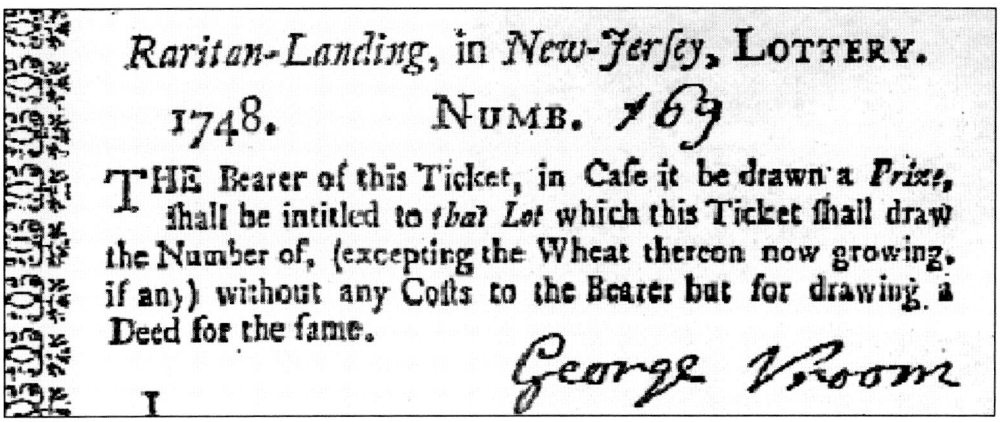

Raritan-Landing, in *New-Jerſey*, LOTTERY.

1748. NUMB. 169

THE Bearer of this Ticket, in Caſe it be drawn a *Prize*, ſhall be intitled to *that Lot* which this Ticket ſhall draw the Number of, (excepting the Wheat thereon now growing, if any) without any Coſts to the Bearer but for drawing a Deed for the ſame.

I George Vroom

Johannes Tenbrook sought to raise 1,400 pounds by lottery—a common Colonial fund-raising scheme—by selling 2,000 tickets at 14 shillings apiece. His choice prizes, located adjacent to his house, were the following: first, a lot of ground 100 feet square with a good storehouse right opposite it; second, a good dwelling house with a fine shop and good kitchen, a good well, and a fine garden; third, a new storehouse and barn, as well as ground at the front to build a large dwelling house. The winners may be unknown, but the original ticket is a prized document in the Rutgers Special Collections and University Archives. (With acknowledgment, *Voices from Raritan Landing*, Rebecca Yamin.)

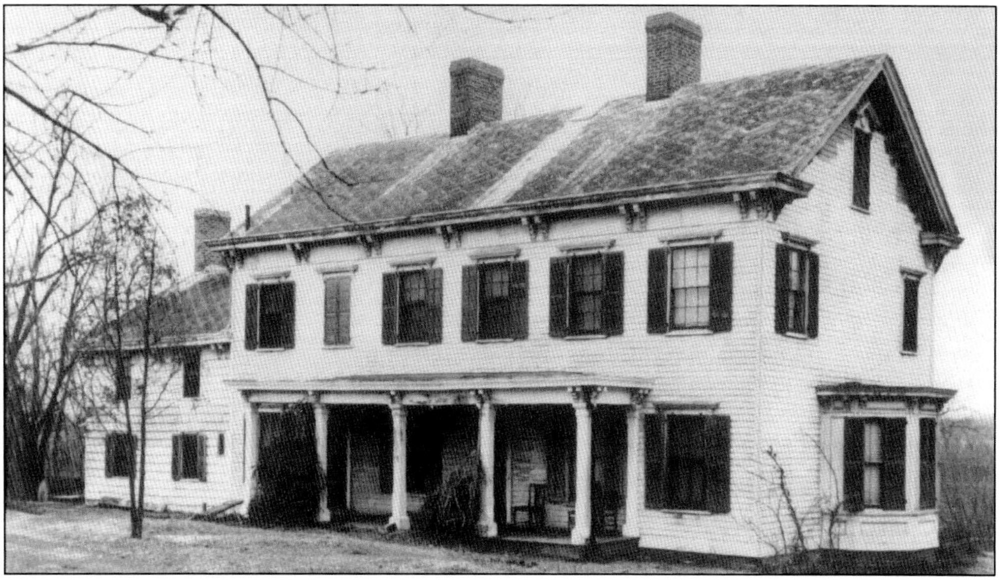

The *c.* 1740 original section of Terrace Hill (left) served as a kitchen wing when the house was photographed *c.* 1950. The house was the seat of Adrian Vermeule's farm of about 100 acres. Around 1853, he added the main block, which is pictured showing the rear elevation but omitting the view of its tall front gable. Rutgers University purchased 91 acres of the farm in 1934 for a stadium and other athletic facilities. The university bought the remainder in 1958 and razed it about two years later. (Collection of the Metlar House.)

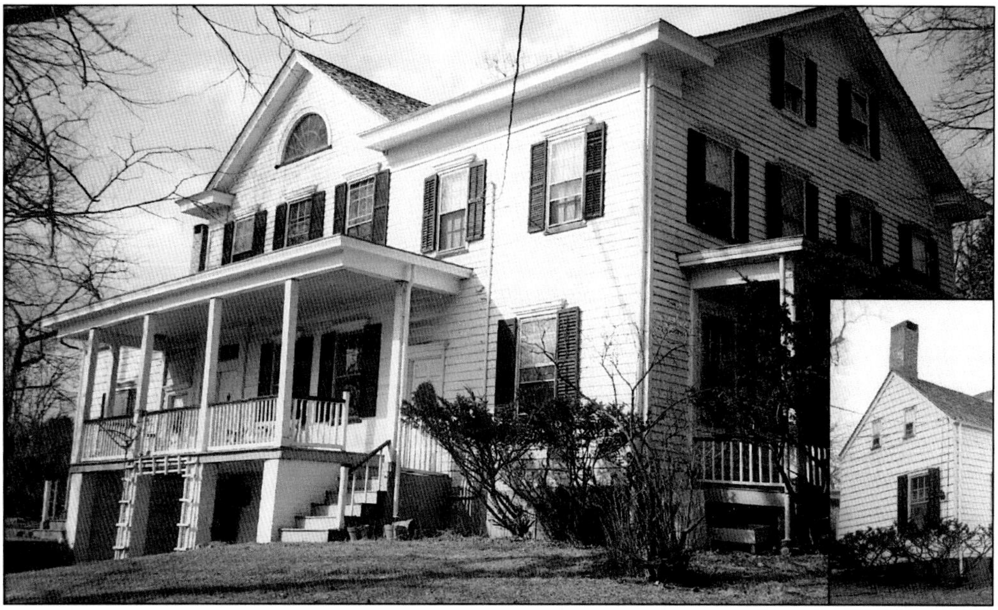

The Metlar-Bodine House, at 1281 River Road, claims a 1728 origin for the one-and-a-half-story section on the north (inset). The three-bay main block is a *c.* 1840 Greek Revival addition; the two-bay wing at the right dates from the late 19th century. The house, which was saved from a road project in the late 1970s, is owned by the State of New Jersey and is operated by the Fellowship for the Metlar House as a museum specializing in Piscataway. (Collection of the Metlar House.)

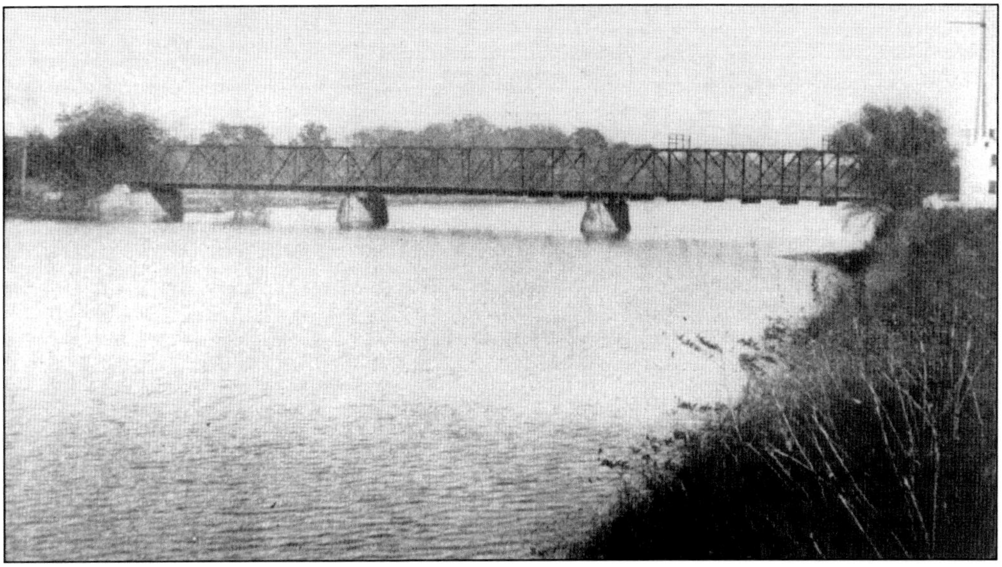

The Raritan River at Landing Lane was originally spanned by a covered bridge that was maintained for more than a century. Middlesex County replaced it in 1895 with this steel-truss bridge erected by the Pennsylvania Bridge Company; George H. Blakeley was the consulting engineer. Time and traffic took the expected toll, necessitating replacement of this bridge (pictured *c.* 1905) with the present 390-foot span, which opened in 1992. Commemorative and date plaques from the 1895 bridge stand near the Piscataway entrance. (Collection of the Metlar House.)

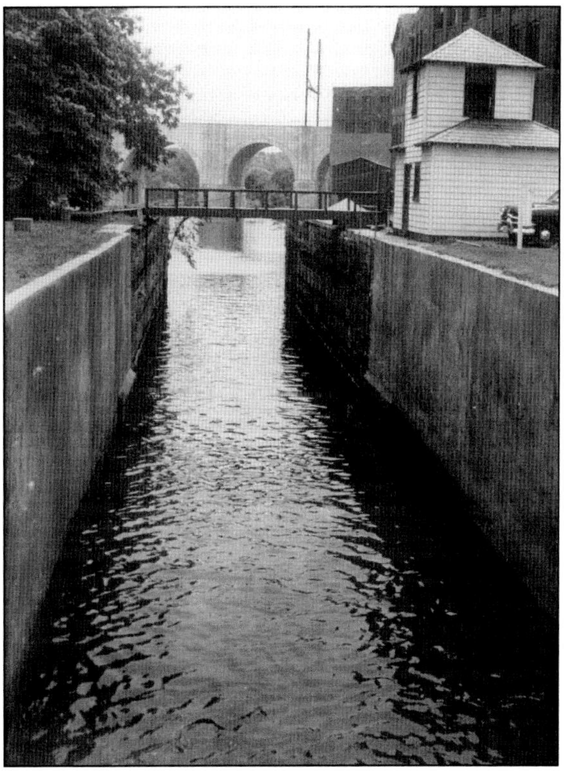

A case can be made for Raritan Landing as a port on both banks. However, Piscataway was its principal side and the New Brunswick shore was at times referred to as "opposite Raritan Landing." More effective means and patterns of transportation have shaped the development of the region from its beginnings. Two are depicted here, including the first lock of the 1834 Delaware & Raritan Canal on the New Brunswick side and the 1903 stone (partially concrete-covered) arch railroad bridge built by the Pennsylvania Railroad. The latter is still the crossing of the region's most important rail line, the New York–Washington stem of the Northeast Corridor. (Rutgers Special Collections and University Archives.)

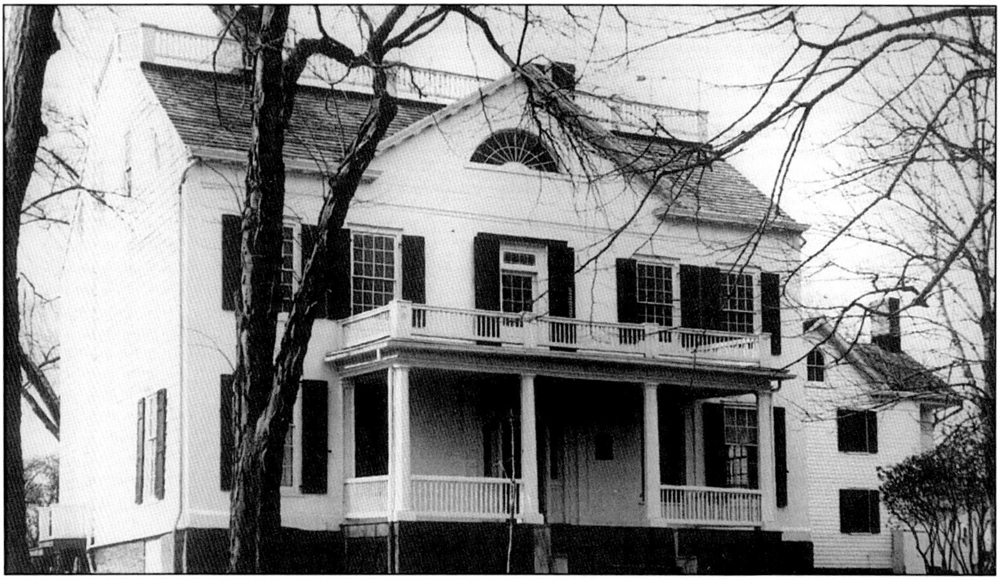

Anthony White built this *c.* 1739 Georgian house on the southern shore of Raritan Landing, or New Brunswick. The large, clapboard main block measures 50 by 41 feet; attached at the right is a 19th-century addition. Note the appealing fanlight in the center gable and the roof balustrade. Revolutionary-era owners included British general William Burton; the Commissioners of Forfeited Estates; and Col. Charles Stewart, the commissary general of Washington's army. (Rutgers Special Collections and University Archives.)

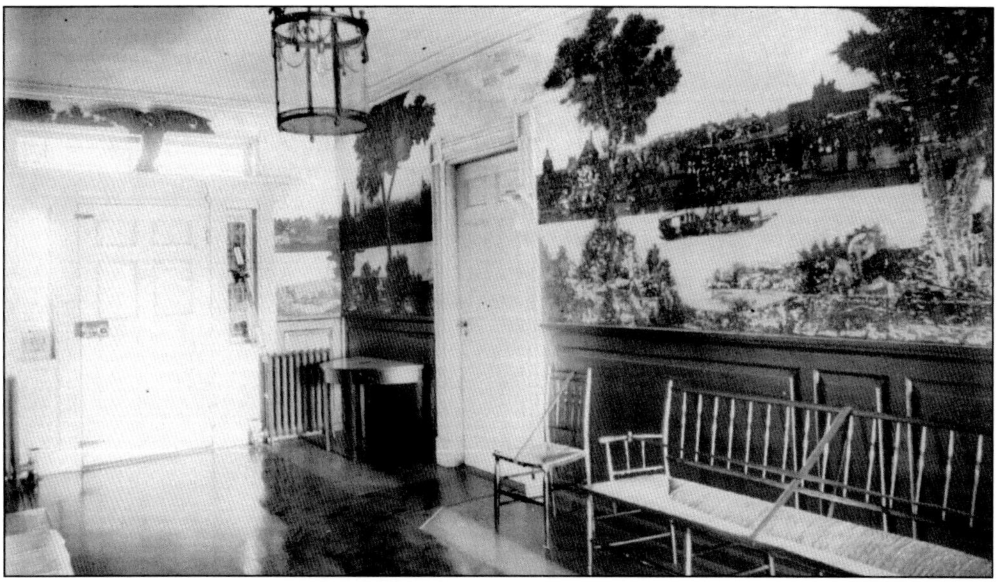

Col. Joseph Warren Scott bought the place in 1821 and named it Buccleuch (pronounced *buck-clue*) in honor of his Scottish ancestor the Duke of Buccleuch. A Scottish grandson, Anthony Dey, purchased the house in 1865 and gave it and the surrounding grounds to the City of New Brunswick in 1911. The Anthony White house is now widely known as the Buccleuch Mansion, a museum operated by the Daughters of the American Revolution. Its famed wallpaper was printed in Paris in 1815 by Du Four of Macon. The design in the downstairs hall is Monument of Paris. (Rutgers Special Collections and University Archives.)

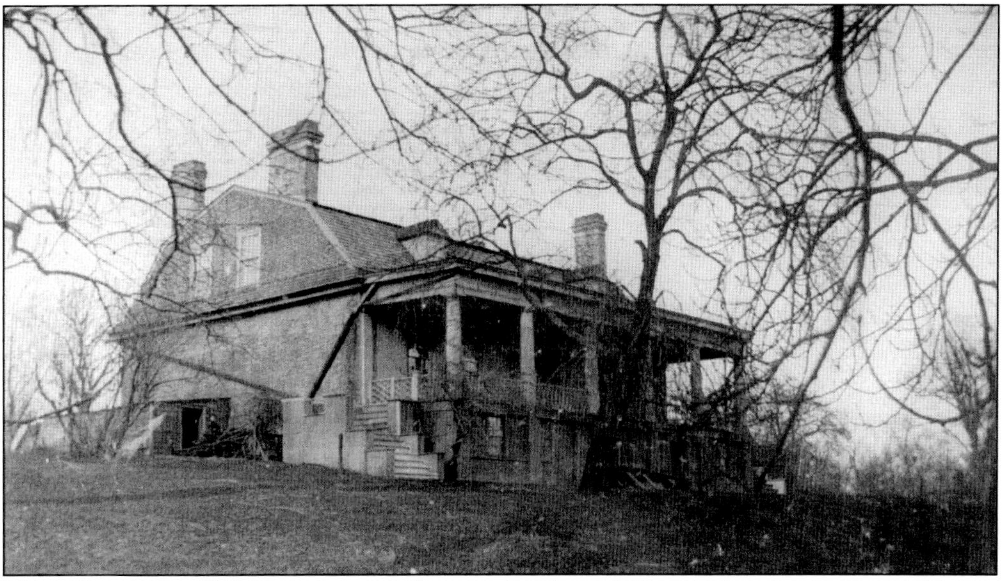

The Edward Antill house, Ross Hall, is a five-bay, 56-by-39-foot, brick and fieldstone house. The one-and-a-half-story structure was built in 1740 and stood on the northeast corner of River Road and Ross Hall Boulevard. Antill's daughter Anna was married to Colonial governor Lewis Morris. The place is named for its second owner, Alexander Ross. The Greek Revival–style porch was added some time in the mid-19th century. (Rutgers Special Collections and University Archives.)

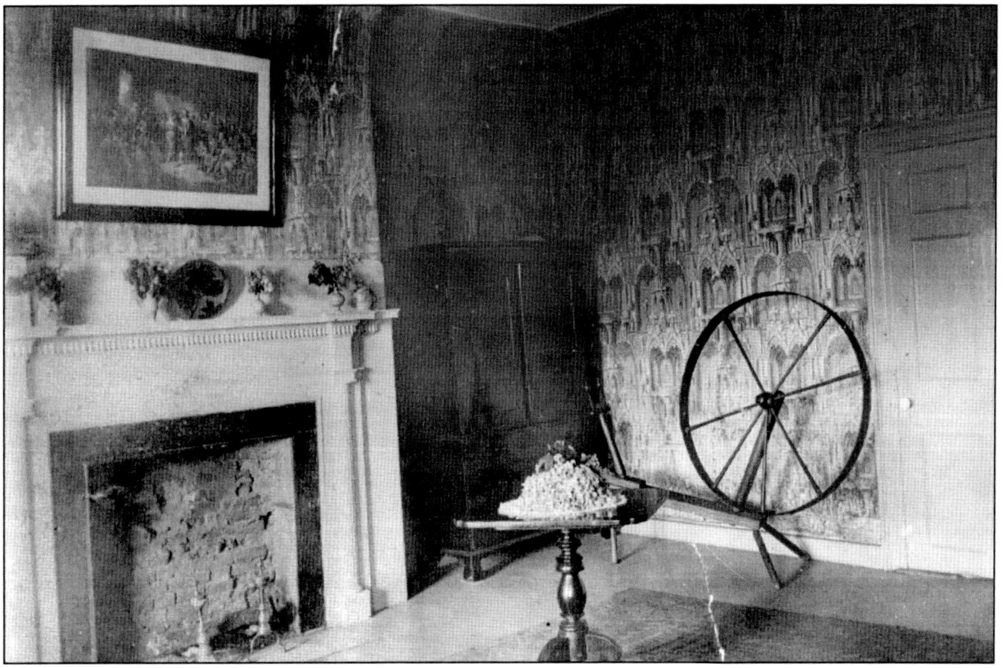

The place served for a while as a clubhouse for the New Brunswick Country Club. After a bitter preservation fight, the house was demolished in the late 1950s by Rutgers University. One wall, preserved by the New Jersey Historical Society, is planned to be returned to the area for installation at the Metlar House. (Rutgers Special Collections and University Archives.)

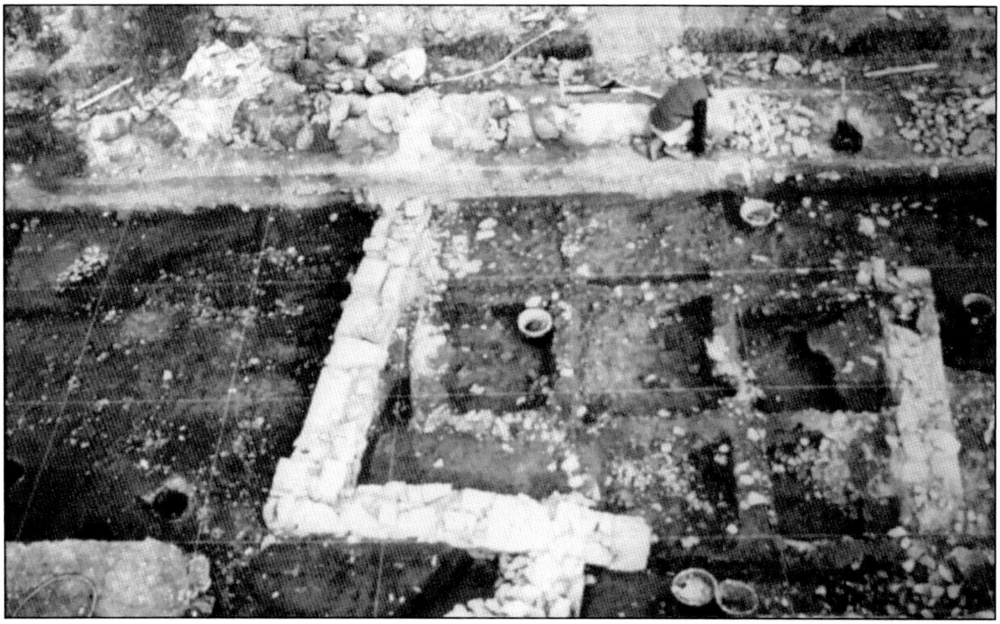

Two archeological projects have uncovered the Raritan Landing settlement. This house foundation—dug as part of the 1979 Middlesex County Sewerage Authority project's mitigation plan—probably belonged to John Bodine, a trader here in the 1730s and 1740s. (Courtesy of Rebecca Yamin.)

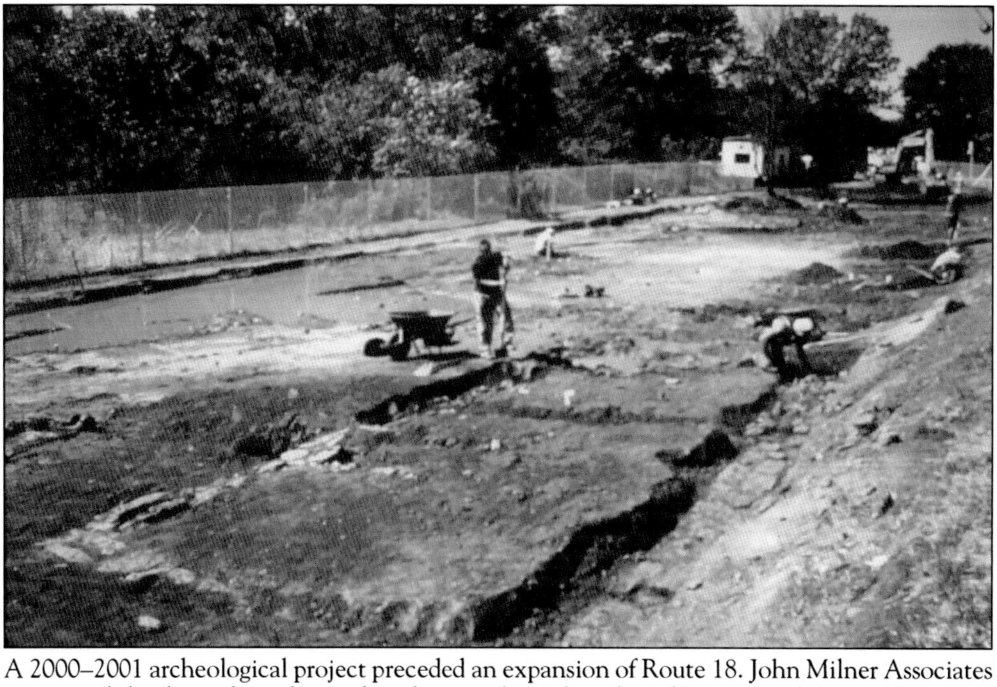

A 2000–2001 archeological project preceded an expansion of Route 18. John Milner Associates uncovered this line of warehouse foundations along the edge of River Road, beginning at the corner of Landing Lane. Although little domestic material was found associated with the warehouses, the size of the buildings reflected the substantial extent of the trading operation. (Courtesy of Rebecca Yamin.)

Two

FARM AND DOMESTIC LIFE

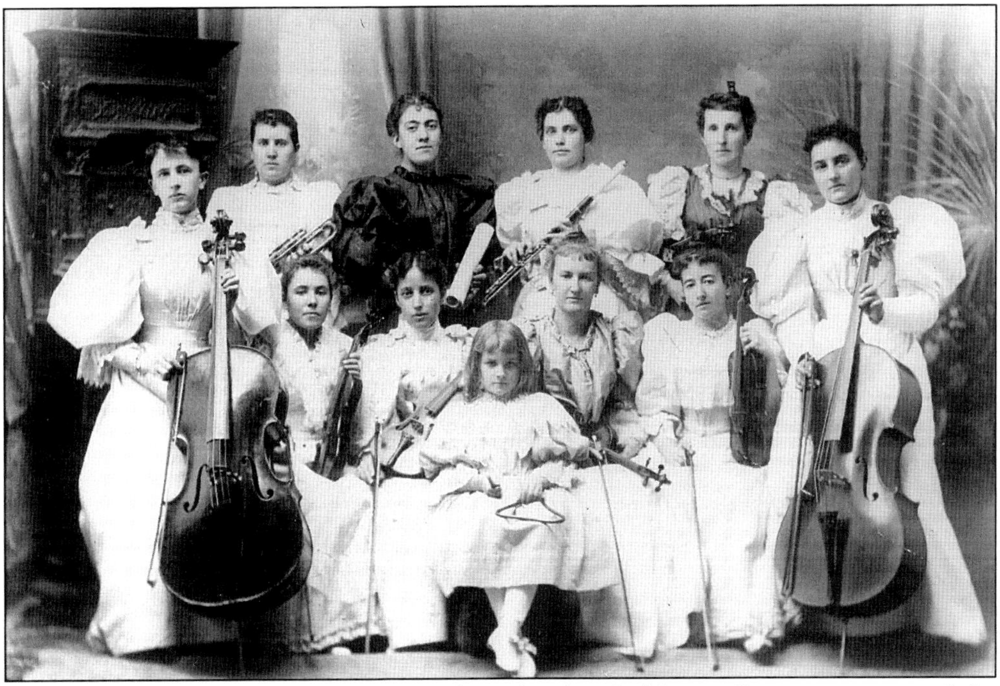

The 11 female musicians shown here reflect the dignified but stiff posing practice of the photograph's likely *c.* 1900 date. Some subjects bear strong family resemblance, but their identities are regrettably unknown. (Collection of the Metlar House.)

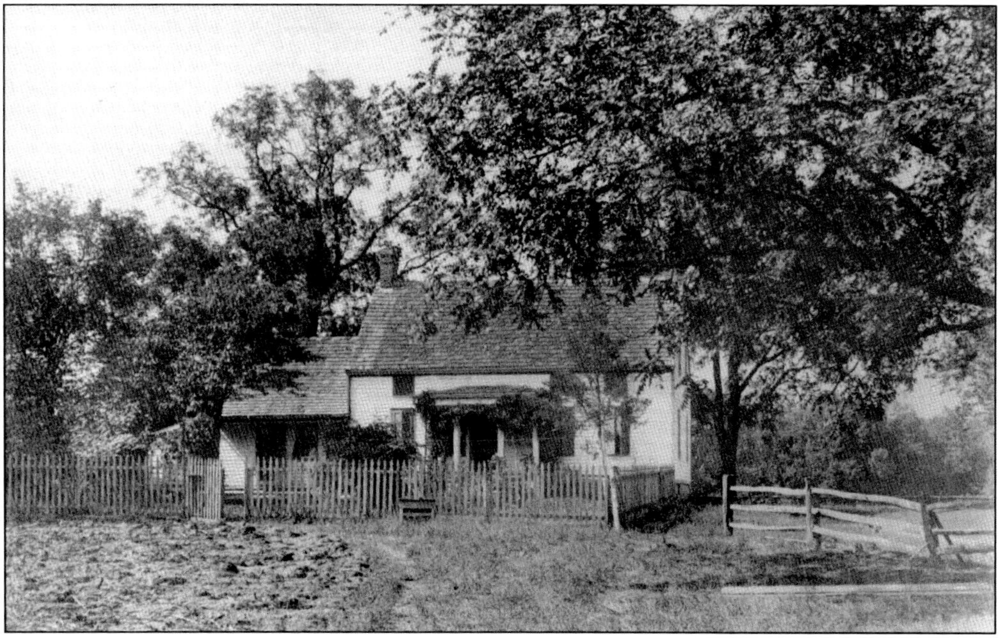

The first Fitzrandolph house in Piscataway—a town where that ancient family's presence placed the locality name Randolphville on the map—is a one-and-a-half-story, rectangular, traditional-style house at 470 Sidney Road, at its juncture with Behmer Road. Its date is attributed to 1740; the picture is likely from the early 20th century.

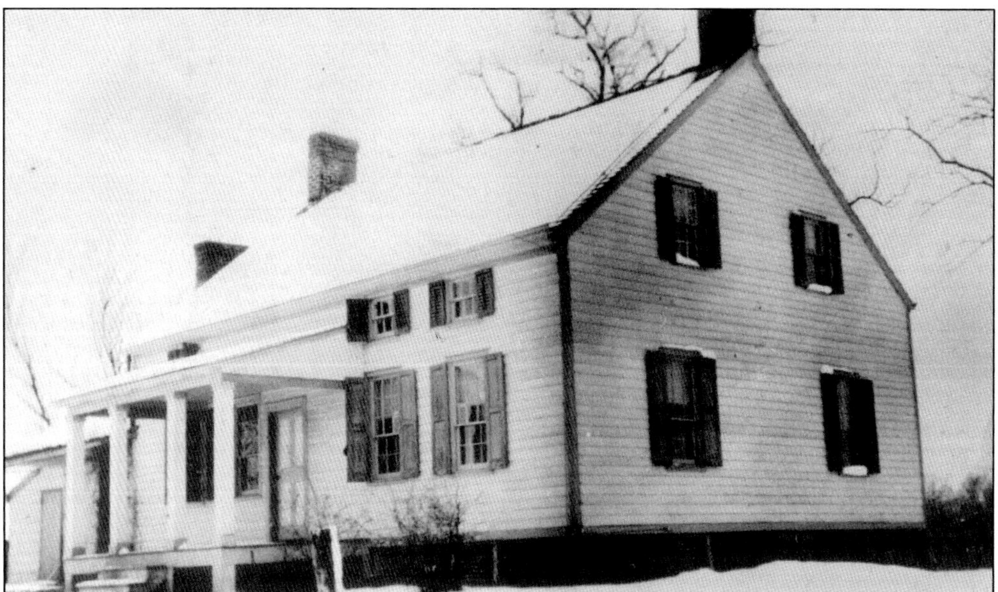

The house is known locally as the Ruene Fitzrandolph house. Ruene was possibly a builder. The house's name distinguishes it from the perhaps nine others that the family built in the area. The well-preserved house, pictured perhaps in the late 1950s, stands little changed.

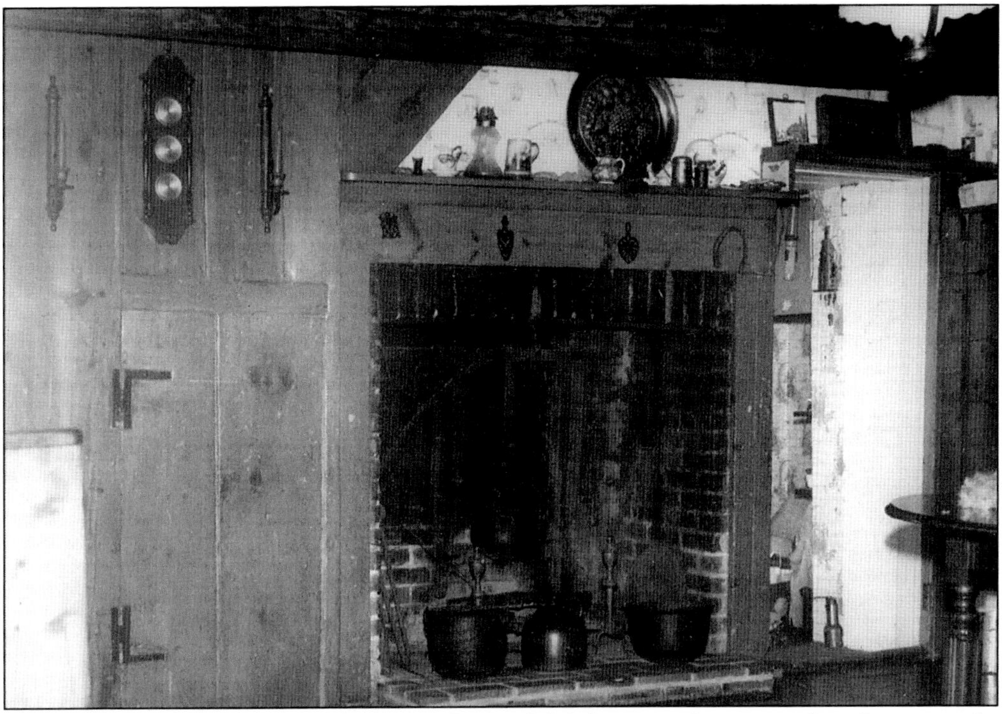

This early fireplace remains in the Ruene Fitzrandolph house with crane and cooking utensils. Various spellings of the Fitzrandolph name were used. One branch of the family abbreviated the *Fitz* to the letter *F*.

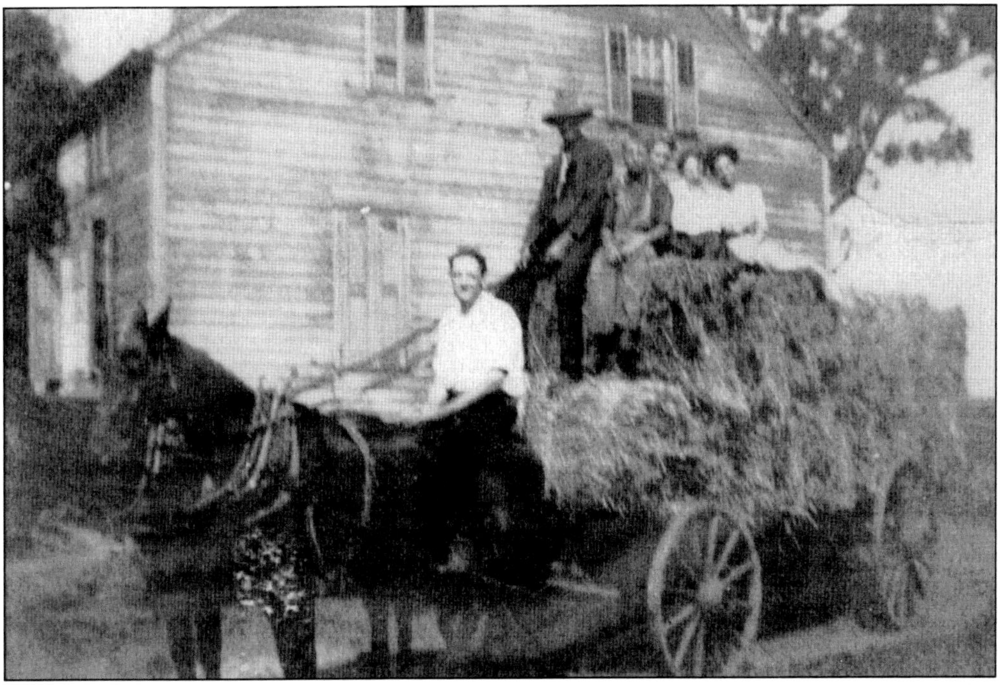

Willard Fitz-Randolph is pictured with friends on a wagon of baled straw at his Sidney Road home.

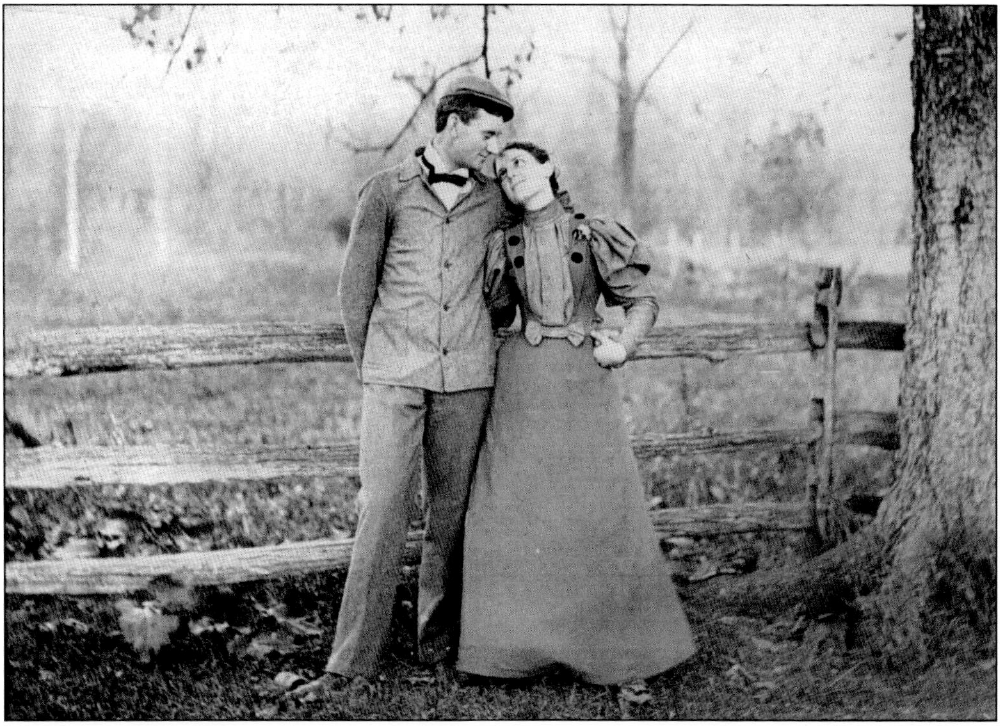

Willard Fitz-Randolph is pictured with Edna Boice on the Boice Hoes Lane farm, the future site of the American Telephone and Telegraph (AT & T) building shown on page 74. Their affectionate pose suggests closeness—closer than one might expect from cousins.

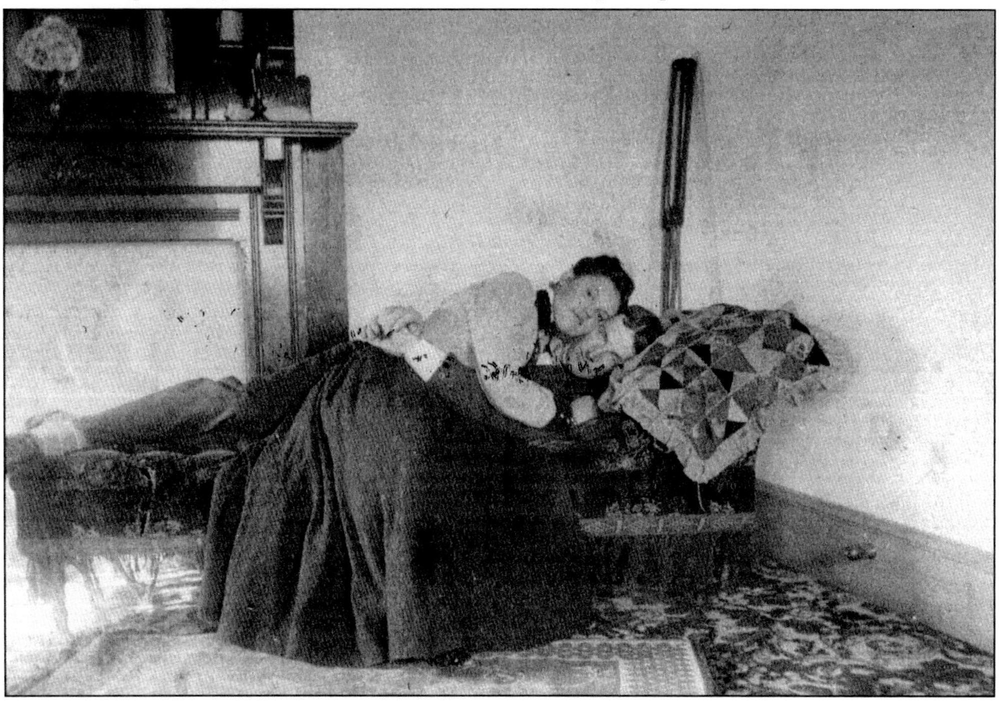

Willard Fitz-Randolph strikes an even closer pose with Lillie Brandt, his wife.

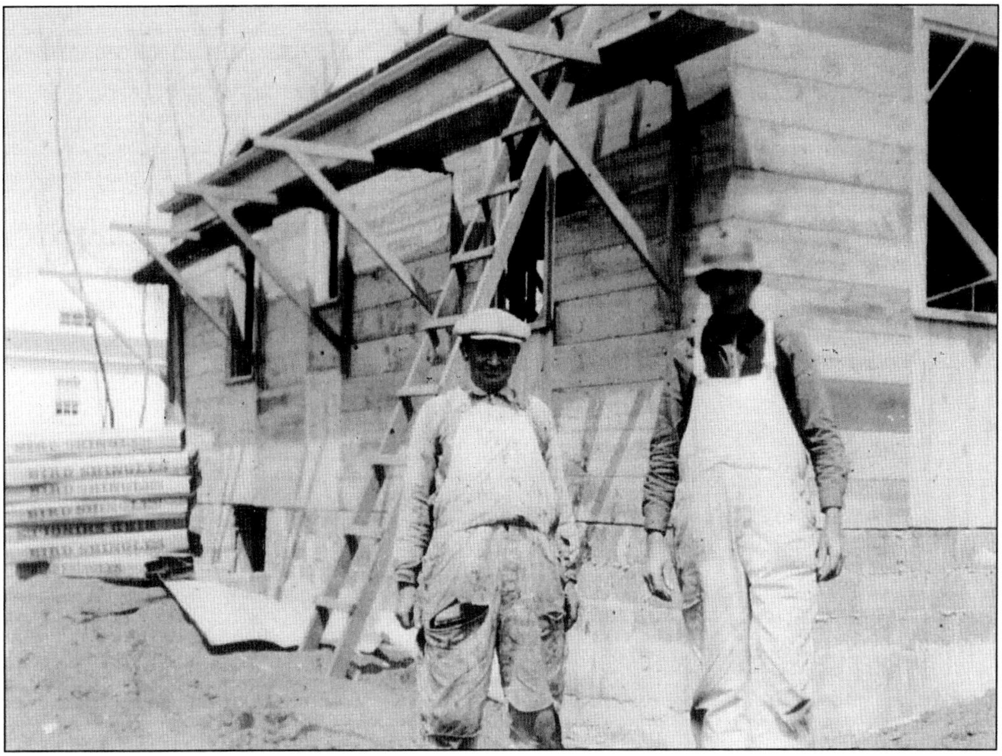

Henry Smalley (left) is descended from the Fitz-Randolph family. Earle F. Randolph raised and butchered hogs among his agricultural pursuits. His branch of the family changed *Fitz* to the initial *F*.

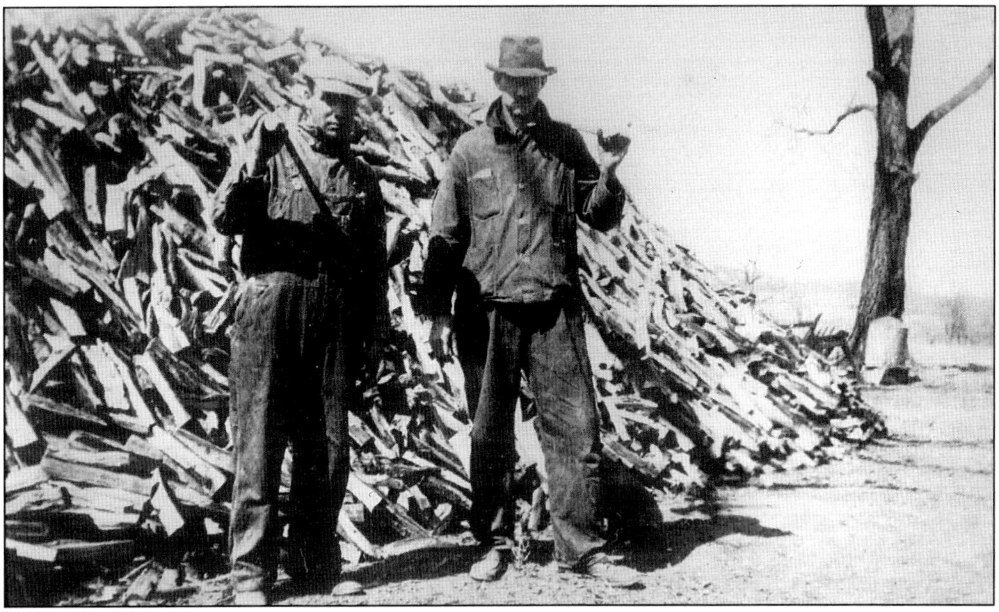

Orson Randolph (left) is pictured perhaps *c.* 1930 with Earle Randolph, the two apparently having just contributed to the massive wood pile. The annotator of the original photograph let future viewers know that the family burned all of it in the kitchen stove.

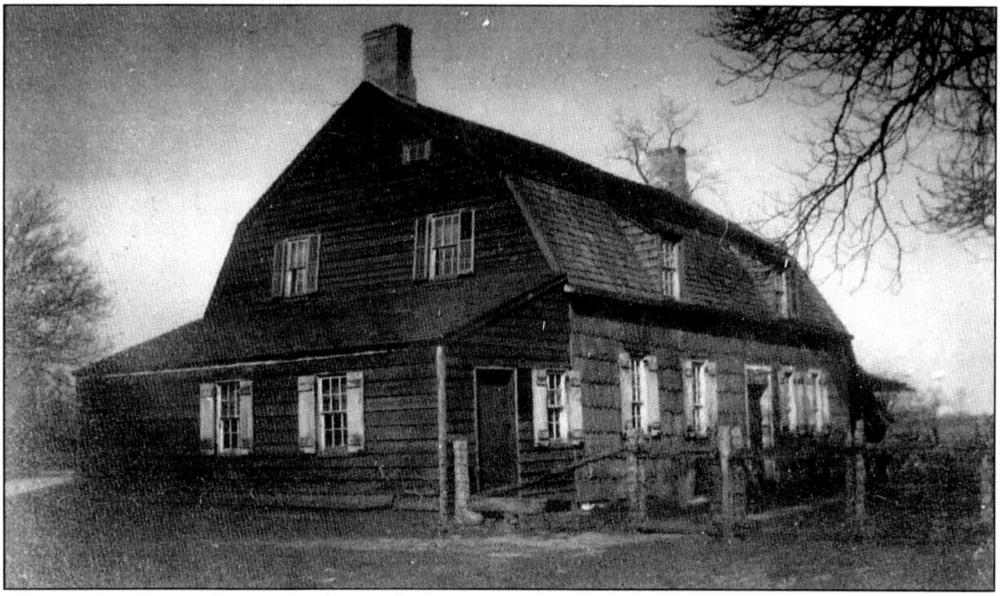

The Walter Dunn house, built in the mid-18th century, stood well behind the street on Old New Brunswick Road, near Hoes Lane. The house was extensively remodeled in the 20th century, prior to its c. 1969 demolition for a commercial building.

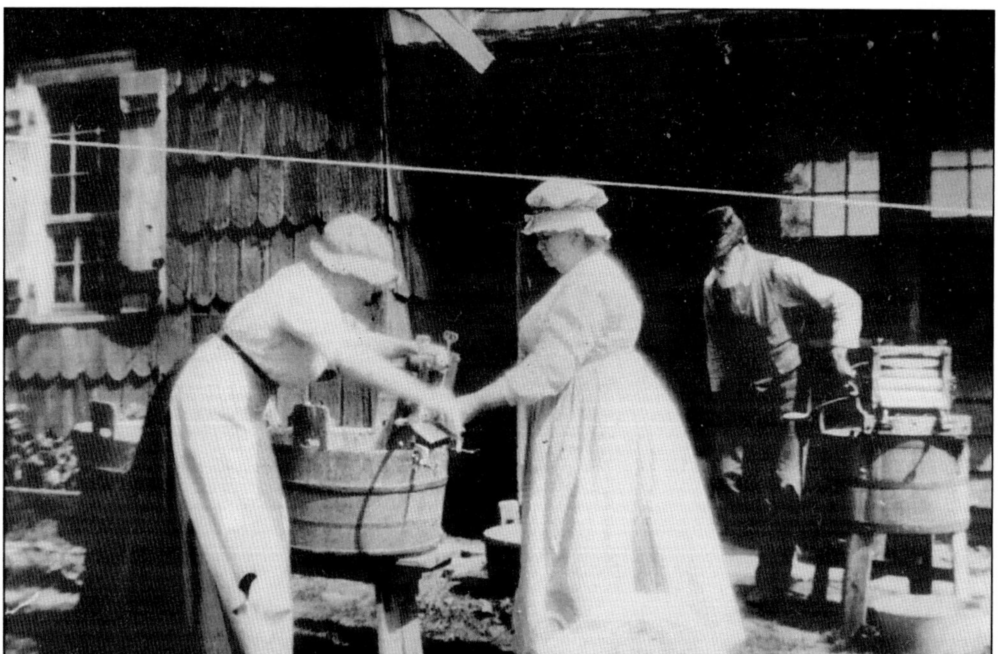

Marjorie Dunn (left) and Ella Larkin Dunn work at a washing machine at the Dunn house as George Larkin looks on. The wringer could readily grab the fingers of a careless user, who was unprotected by guards.

Four generations of the Dunn family offer a striking, serious bearing for the photographer. Walter G. Dunn stands over his father, Louis, and Louis's mother. The three daughters of Walter (and wife Ella) are, from left to right, Jennie, Myrta, and Margorie.

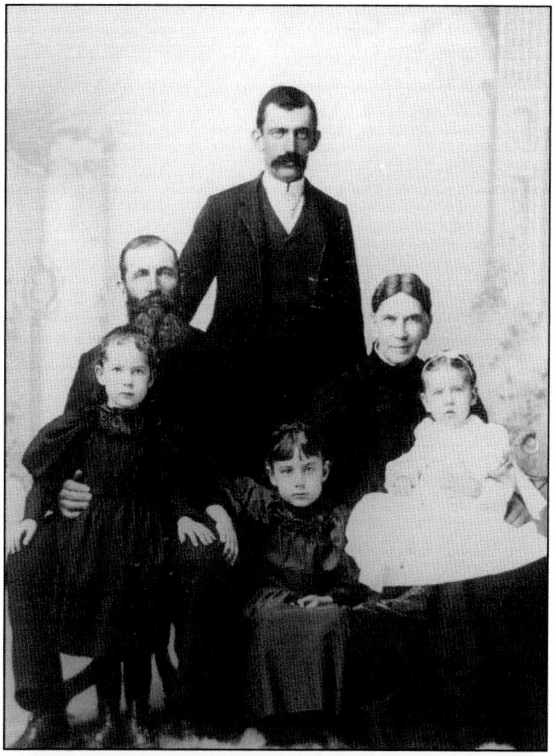

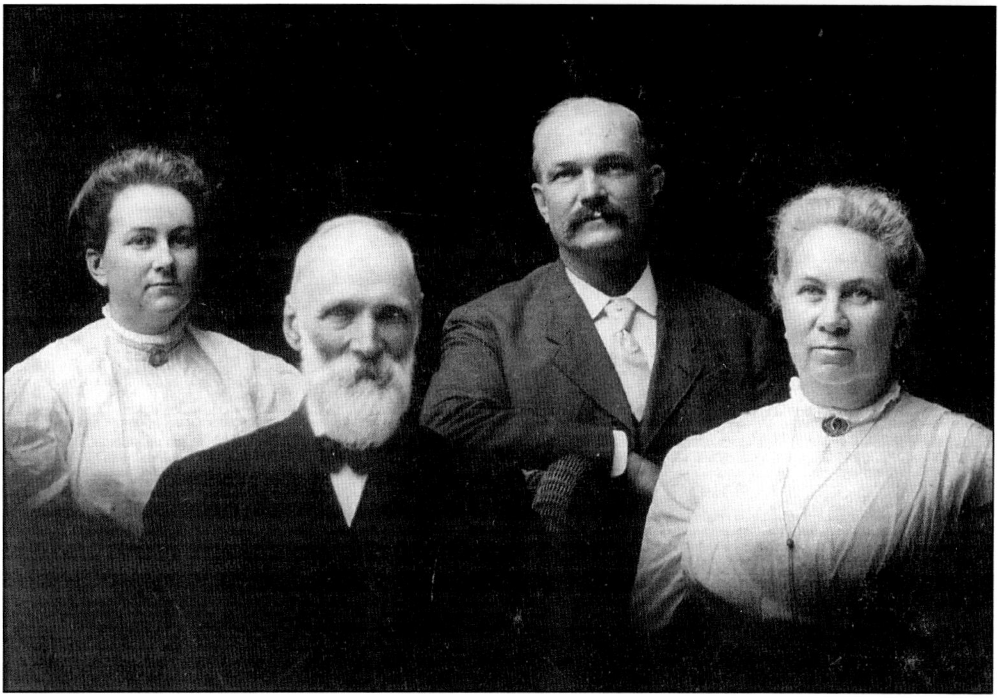

Ella Larkin Dunn, grandmother of Jeanette Randolph Duryea (lender of this and some of the finest vintage photographs in this volume), is on the left with, proceeding to the right, George S. Larkin, O. Eugene Larkin, and Hannah Larkin Crofoot. They are pictured in 1907.

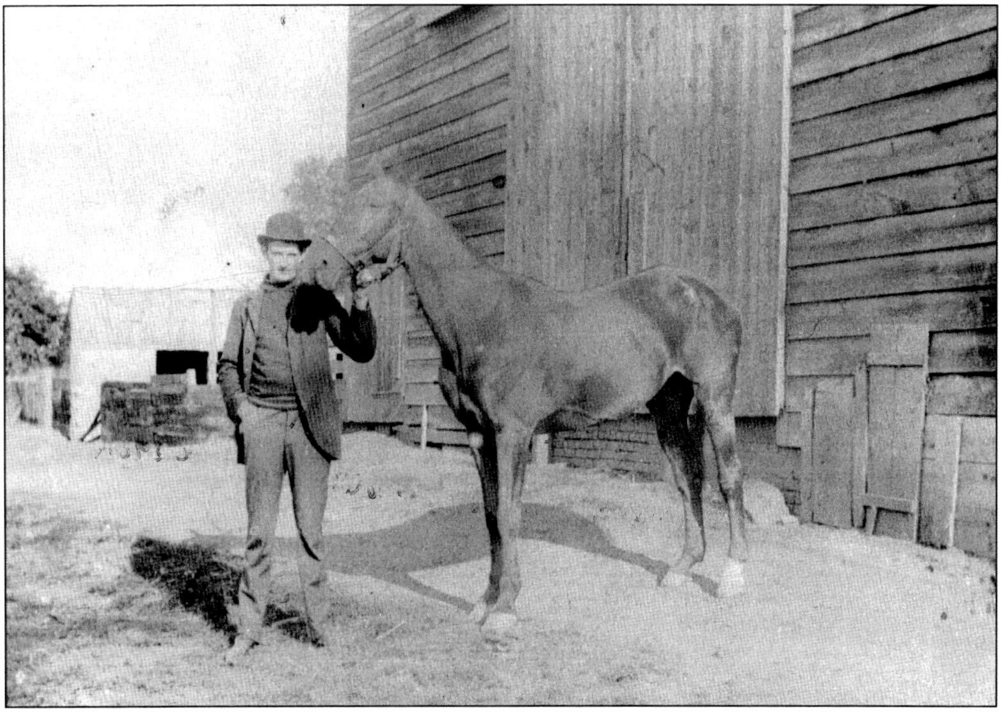

Willard Fitz-Randolph is posing with a magnificent steed, perhaps his finest horse. Willard loved horses and racing, visited the track at Goshen, New York, each year, and was proud to have made a trip to see the Kentucky Derby.

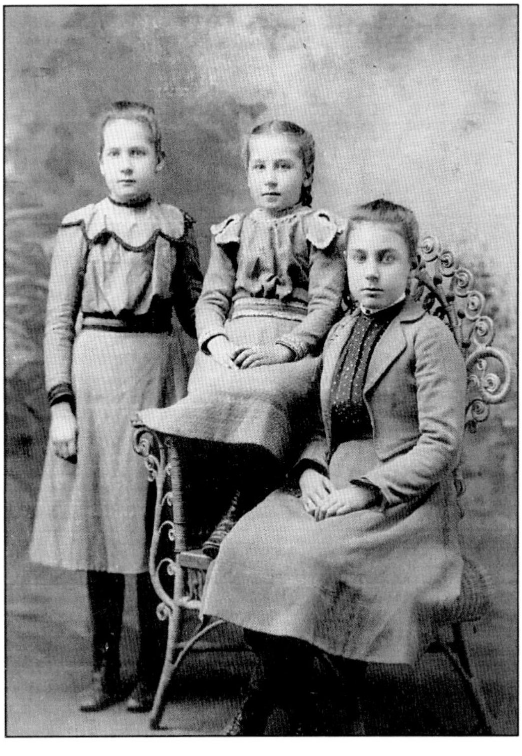

Three Dunn sisters are pictured c. 1904 while attired in attractive dresses. They are, from left to right, Jennie, Marjorie, and Myrta.

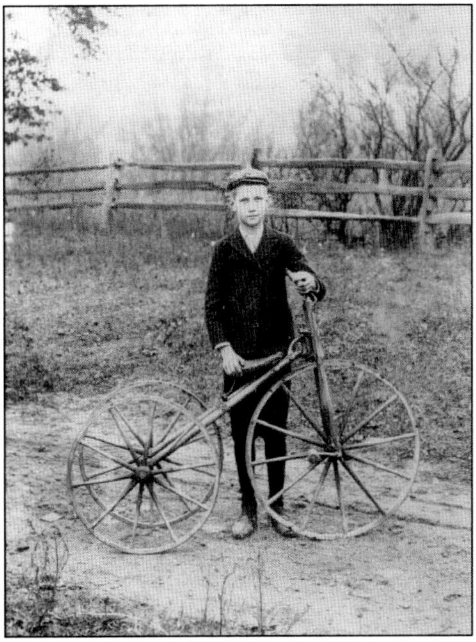
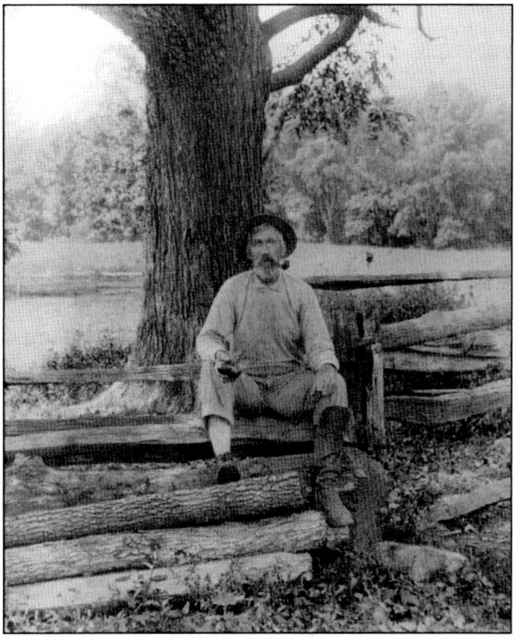

Earle Hayne Randolph is pictured at the upper left in 1897 with a now ancient-looking tricycle. At the upper right, Calvin Fitzrandolph pauses on a split-rail fence, his right hand suggesting it would be a bumper tomato crop that summer. Jennie Dunn, posing with Herbert Dunham at the lower left, bears a marked resemblance to the young girl she was in the photograph on page 25. Roger Dunham is pictured at the lower right in the 1920s holding his teddy bear.

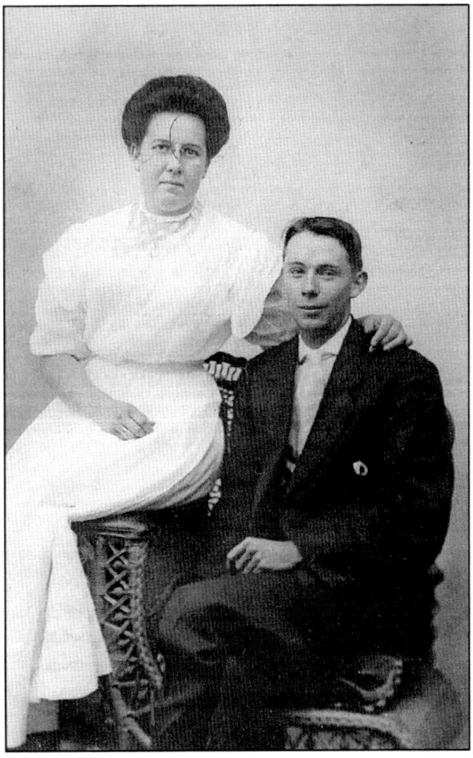
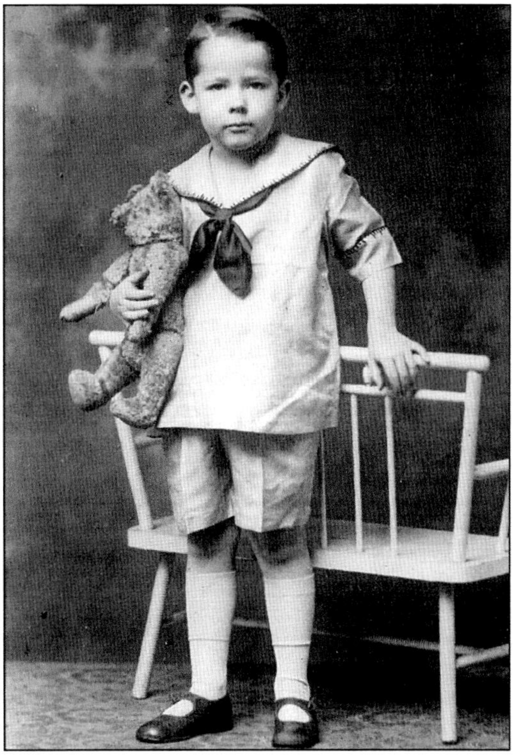

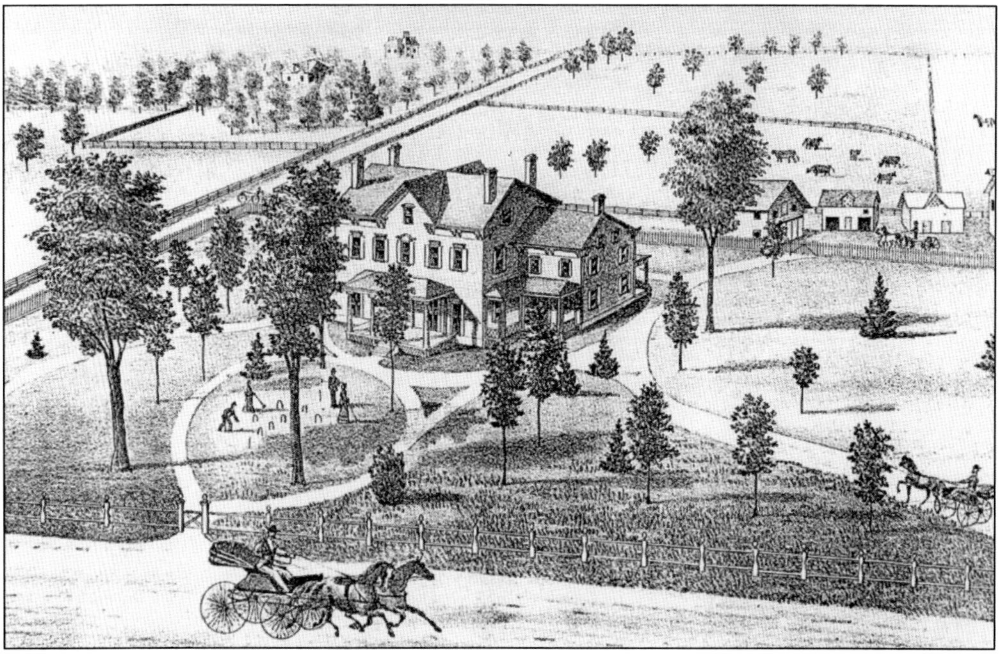

The Charles Sudyam house at 857 Hoes Lane is attributed to the mid-18th century, although the main block appears to be a major expansion from about a century later. The Sudyams were early mill owners near Raritan Landing. This house was later occupied by Mahlon Runyon, the owner when this illustration was first published in the 1876 Evarts and Stewart *Atlas of Middlesex County*.

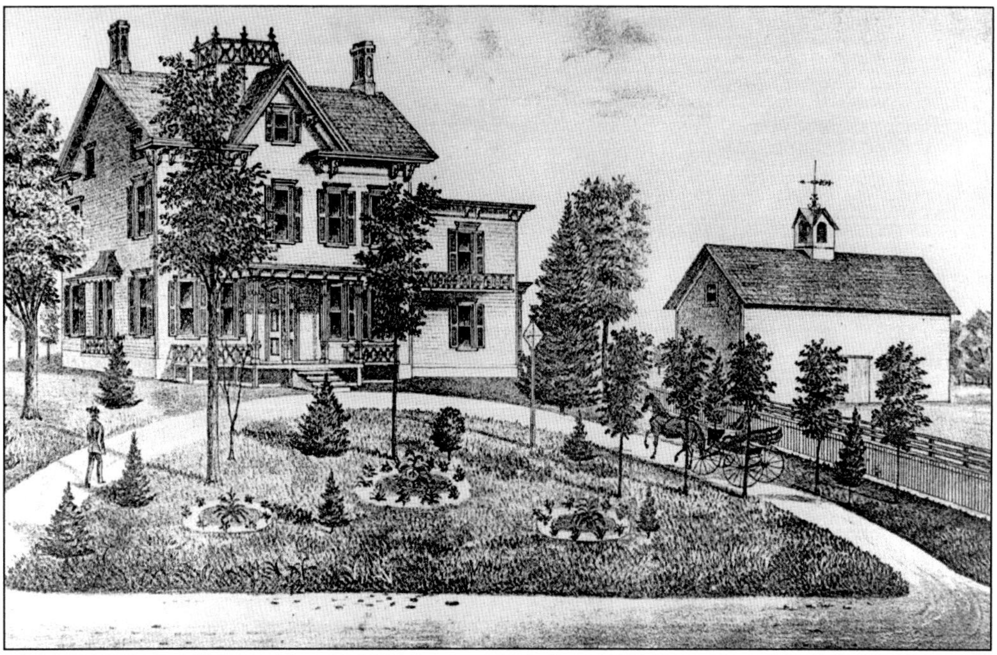

The A.L. Runyon house, a large Italianate, rectangular-plan house, appears to date stylistically from c. the 1850s, but the wing may be older. It was also illustrated previously in the 1876 Evarts and Stewart *Atlas of Middlesex County*.

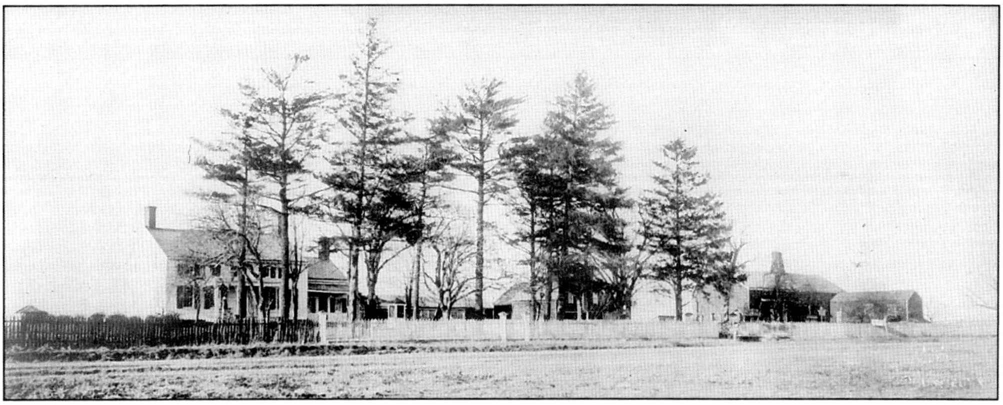

Evergreen Farm, one of the best known in the South Plainfield section of the township, was located on the road to New Market, adjacent to the Port Reading Railroad. Samuel R. Manning purchased the farm in 1865. Pictured in the early 1900s, the place was also illustrated in the 1876 Evarts and Stewart *Atlas of Middlesex County*.

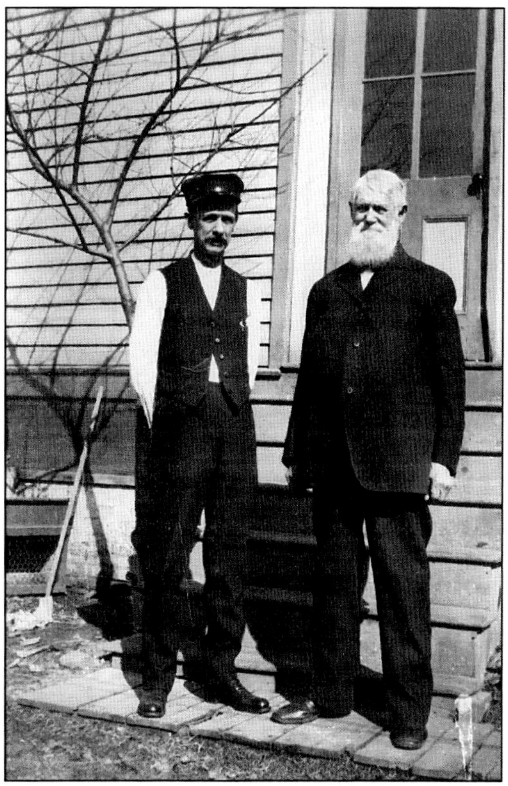

Samuel R. Manning is pictured c. 1912 at Evergreen Farm with Marcus Ward, one of three sons from his first wife, the former Rebecca A. Williamson, whom he married in 1860. After Samuel, born in 1835, was raised in Piscataway, he learned the carriage maker's trade in Newark, in which he worked until he purchased the farm. He was the township road commissioner for many years and was credited with beginning improvements in an era of poorly kept roads. Manning died in 1915, apparently of exertion from fighting a brush fire believed to have been started by a passing locomotive.

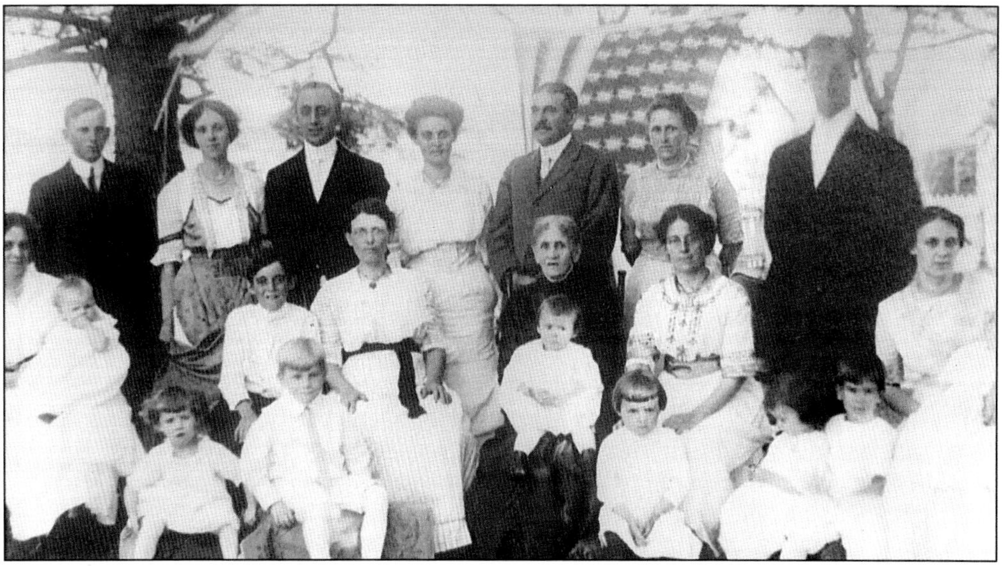

Members of the old Piscataway Boice and Nelson families are seen in 1914 at the Boice Hoes Lane farm, perhaps at a holiday celebration. Seated are Dorothy Barrett Nelson holding Genevieve, with Margaret under the baby. Frank Touzeau is seated under Fred Nelson, who is rubbing shoulders with Edna Boice. Isabella FitzRandolph Boice is holding Lula Belle Chapman; to her left is Lulu Belle Boice, with a hand on the shoulder of Dalton Chapman. Enola Beatrice Nelson Touzeau is holding daughter Selina May; at her feet are Isabel and James. Standing, from left to right, are Albert Boice Nelson; Cyranthia Nelson and her husband, Albert Muller; Verdelle Nelson Chapman; Frank Nelson and his wife, Jennie Boice Nelson; and Frederick Touzeau.

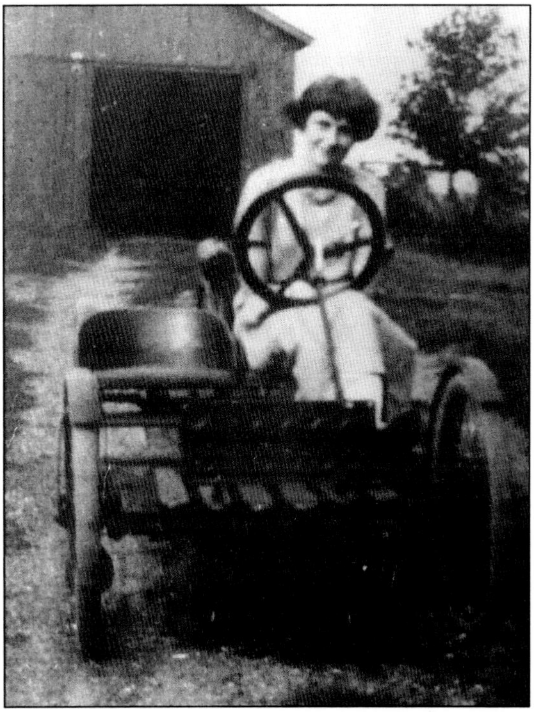

Howell Day used this car, actually a motorized buckboard, to travel to Plainfield High School. It was a lightly powered vehicle, as evidenced by Day's efforts to avoid a particular corner where he would encounter a would-be passenger whose great weight slowed progress to a near crawl. The girl driving appears sufficiently light to be transported up a 10-percent grade.

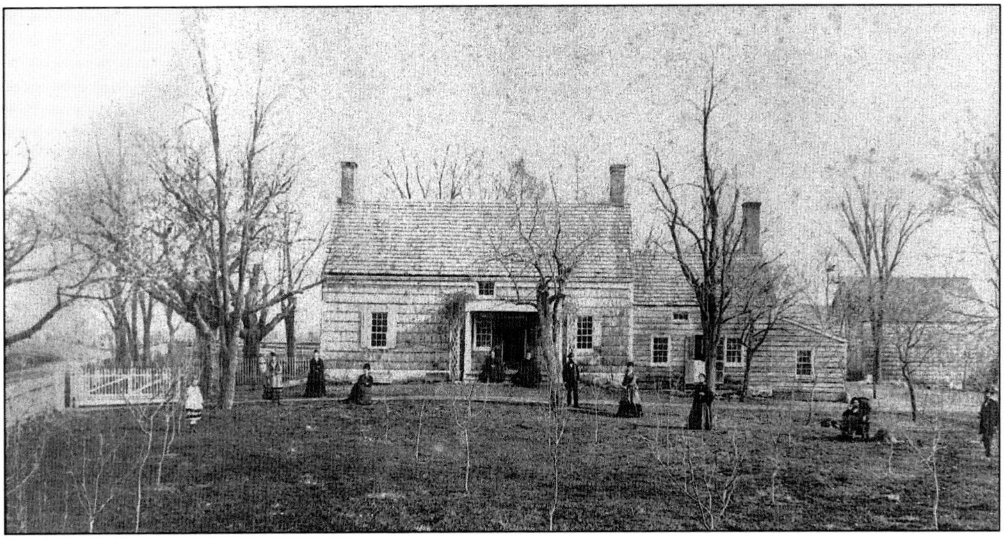

A foundation stone etched with Richard Field's initials and the year 1724 confirms the oldest part of his Fieldville house at 260 River Road. The once vast Field family holdings have been reduced to a few surviving houses. Removal to East Jersey Olde Towne was planned for this one, but it was saved by realtor Michael Santini, whose offices are now located here. Expansions have made the north facade, shown in this *c.* 1870 image, unrecognizable. The main block was raised to two and a half stories, and a wing was added to the left, near River Road. The lean-to on the far right is gone, while the shorter, old section was raised to one and a half stories. The old barns survive.

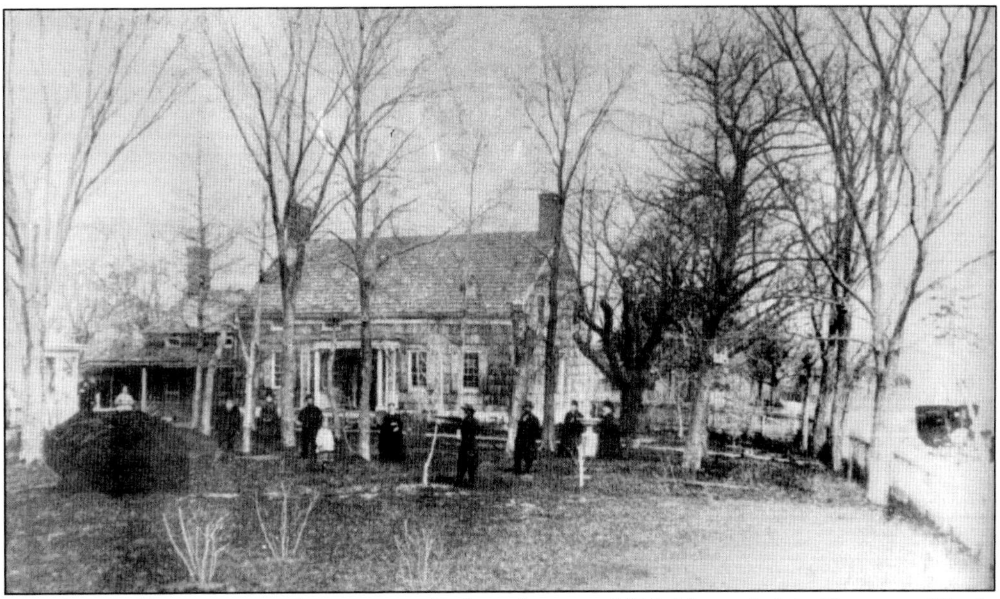

The first Field to come to America was Robert, born in 1610. He settled in Newport, Rhode Island, in 1638. His grandson John came to New Jersey, acquiring in 1695 a 1,055-acre tract that stretched about two and one-half miles. Changes described at the top of the page can be seen in this view of the south facade. The house stands on a bluff, close to the Raritan River; the visitor can readily imagine the appeal of the site to its original builder. The lot was zoned for apartments, but Santini obtained a variance to make the office conversion.

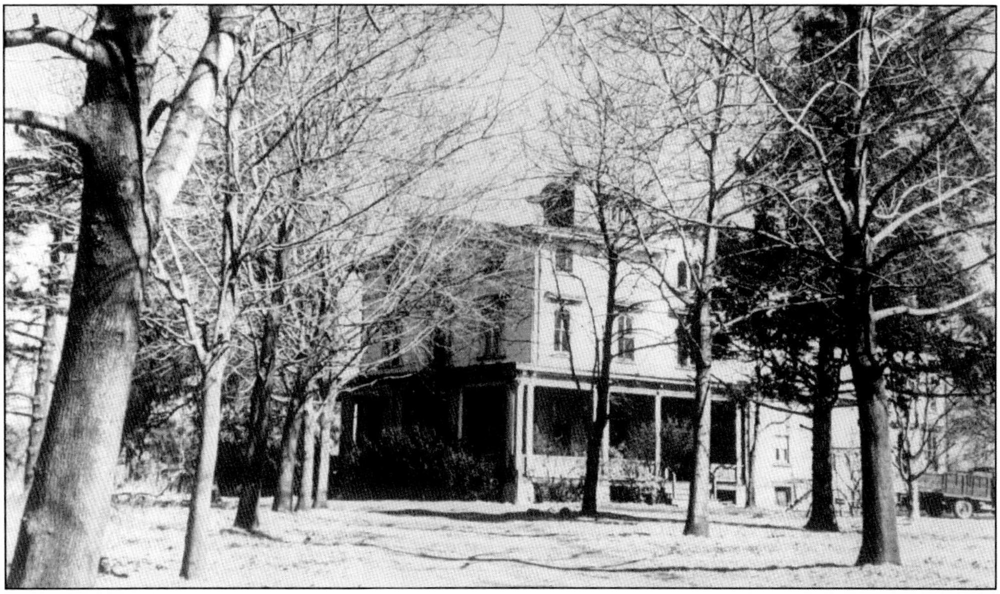

River Rest, a three-story, 24-room Italianate mansion, was built in 1861–1865 on River Road, near Maplehurst Lane. Look through the trees to spot its appealing arched cornice and tall, paired arched windows. Its builder, Richard R. Field, was a supplier to the Union army (a great source of mid-19th-century wealth). Field built two elaborate houses during the Civil War. This home, which had been a nursery in its final years, was razed by Union Carbide in 1965. (Rutgers Special Collection and University Archives.)

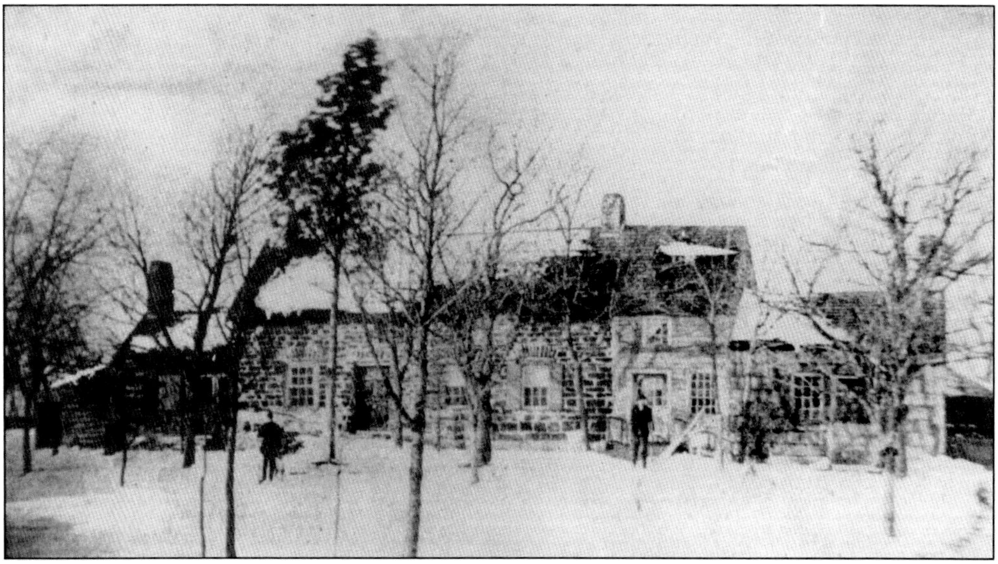

The fieldstone, 17-by-30-foot center section was the original 1743 portion of the John Field house at 625 River Road. The frame section on the right, since expanded to two stories, was a mid-19th-century addition. The house, which faces southwest, lacks windows on its northeast elevation. The section at the left was removed and the stone covered with stucco. The house was later owned by the Boices and was, for many years, the home of the Perrine family (page 92). The house is the southernmost of the significant property in the National Register Road up Raritan Historic District.

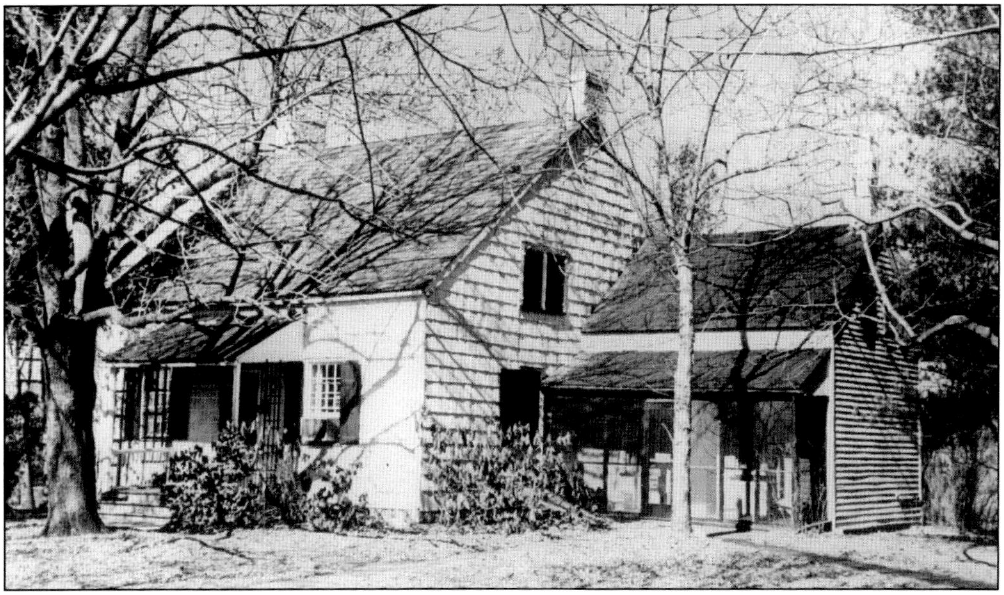

The Jacob Van Deventer house on the east side of River Road, north of the present Interstate 287, was built sometime after 1740. By this time, he was married to Margaret Field, daughter of Judge Jeremiah Field. The roof of the traditional-style house has a Dutch influence. Pictured in 1963, the Fieldville house and barn were demolished by Union Carbide in 1968. (Rutgers Special Collections and University Archives.)

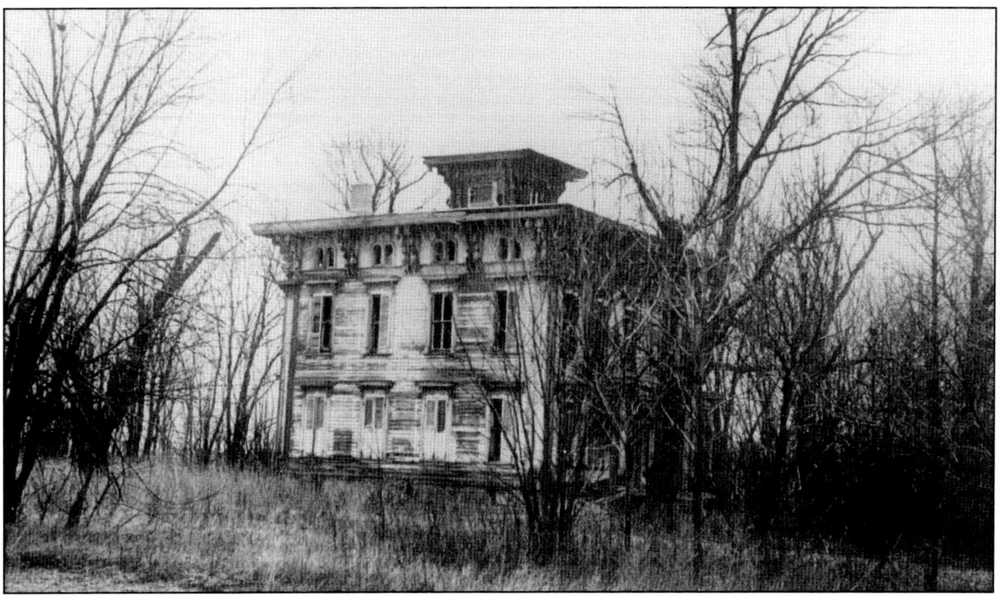

The Italianate John R. Field house, built in 1865 on Maplehurst Lane, appears to have been modeled after a Samuel Sloan pattern book design. This c. 1950s photograph, showing the house in run-down condition, also depicts typical Italianate characteristics—tall, narrow windows; a low-pitched roof with overhanging eaves supported by decorative brackets; a square cupola; and paired, arched windows in the upper story. The house was later converted to multiple occupancy before it was demolished by a developer in 1997. (Rutgers Special Collections and University Archives.)

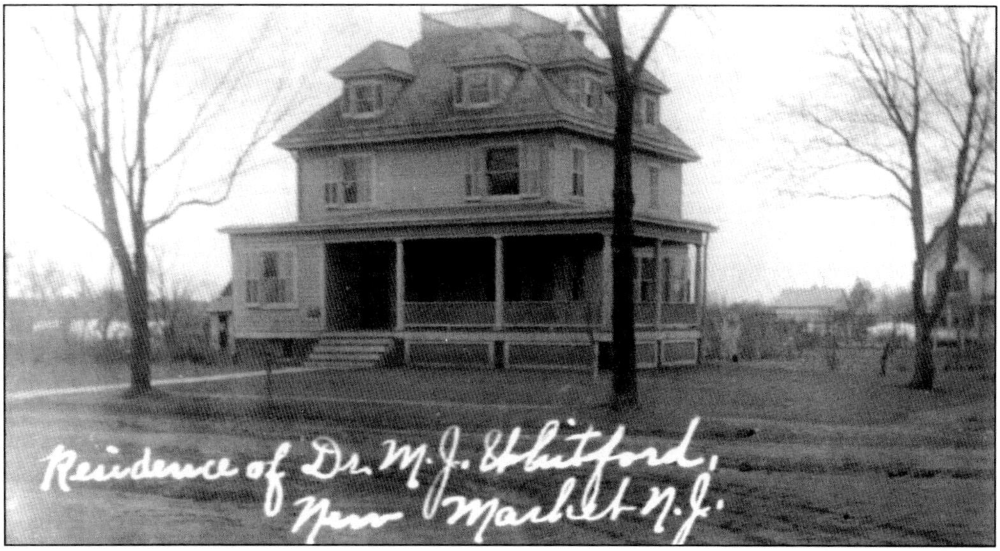

Two similar *c.* 1905 photographic postcards provide a clue to the pictorial richness of the 1905–1915 decade. The international mania of postcard collecting was met primarily by printed cards, notably from German lithographers. Local photographers made cards in small quantities, printing actual photographs on paper marked as postcards. Homes of the prominent, such as Dr. Myron Whitford's, were typical subjects. Identifying them later can be elusive, as in this instance, because the cards often lacked addresses. Whitford's house is believed to have been at an unspecified New Market Road location. (Collection of Cynthia Harris.)

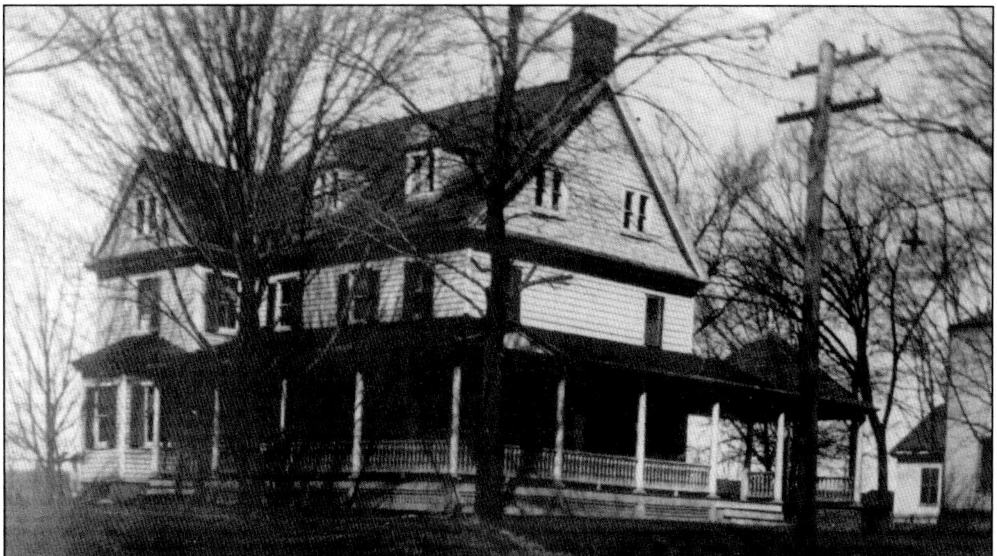

Dr. William J. Nelson's home, found at 470 New Market Road, has a number of Queen Anne–style modifications, but the main block may date from *c.* the 1860s. It is best known in local lore for a murder committed there in 1867. An employee of the family, Bridget Durgan, killed her mistress, the wife of Dr. William Oriell, perhaps motivated by an obsessive interest in him. She was convicted and executed in less than six months. The house is recognizable, despite a number of modifications, including removal of the porch and conversion to apartment use. (Collection of Cynthia Harris.)

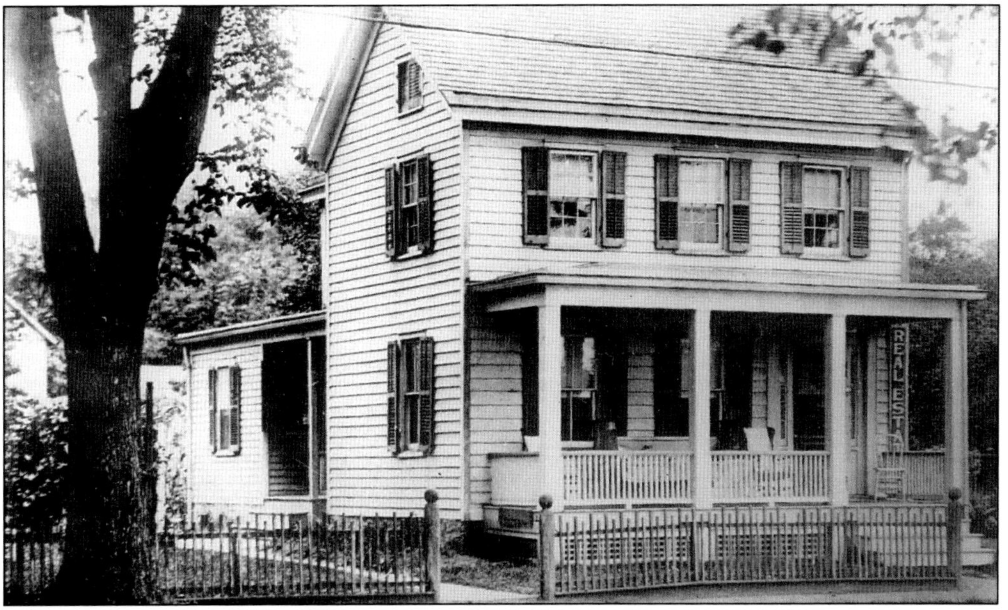

This *c.* 1905 photographic postcard provides a sharp image of a simple mid-19th-century traditional-style house. The rear is likely a later addition. The then-home of Stanley Day still stands at 426 New Market Road, at Vail Avenue, recognizable despite changes that include removal of two of the second-story windows, brick facing, and the addition of an exterior chimney at the left. (Collection of the Metlar House.)

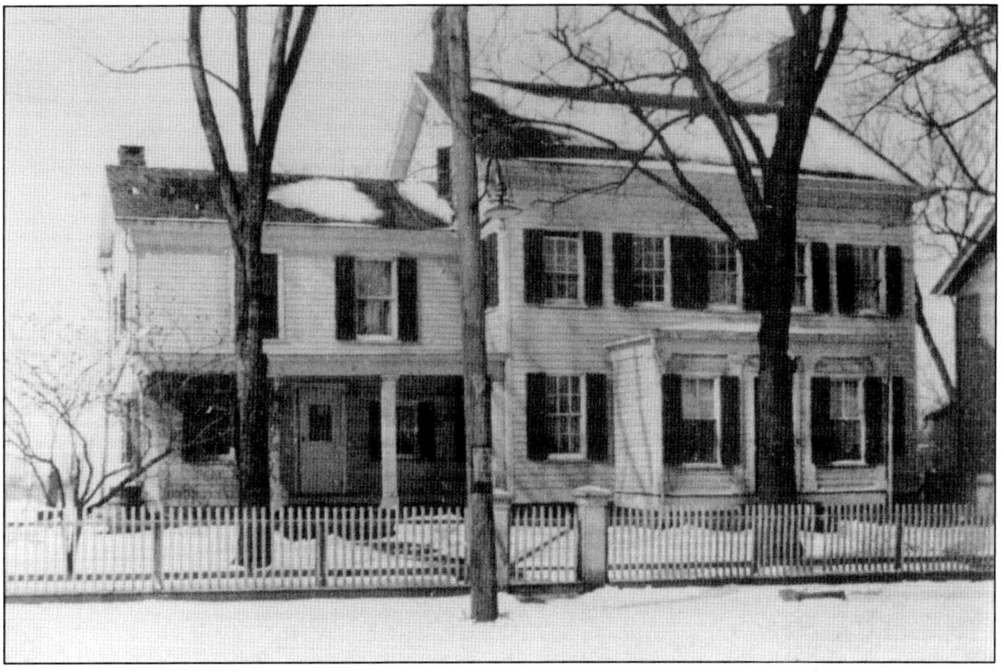

Charles Stanley Day emigrated from England in 1860, came to New Market in 1870, and bought this house at 10 Stelton Road, which is stylistically dated from *c.* the 1850s. He left the area for business pursuits but returned to this house about 10 years later. (Collection of the Metlar House.)

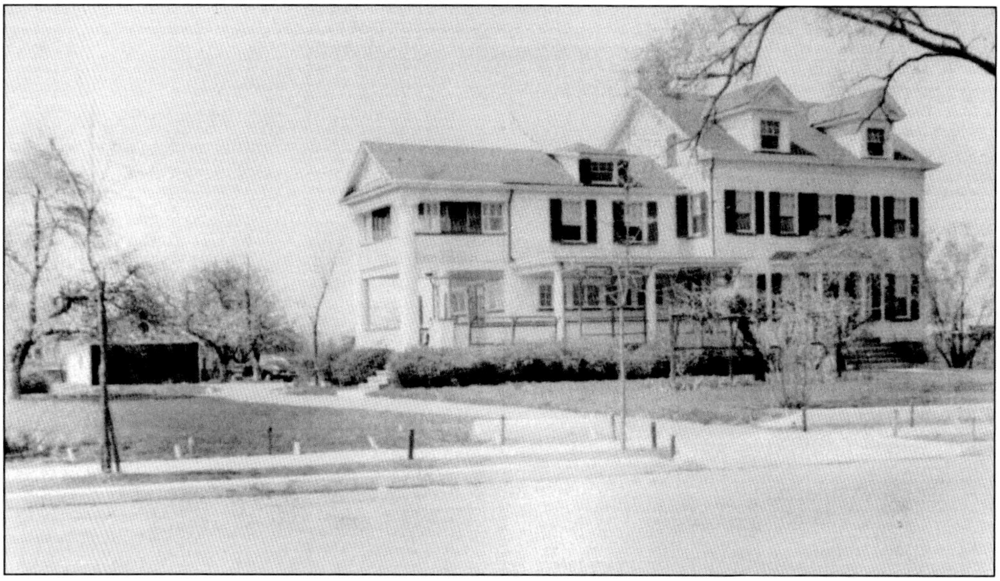

The most prominent change at 10 Stelton Road during the residency of Charles Kupper was the *c.* 1910 addition of a two-story porch wing on the south side of the building. He also added dormers and modified what was an entry vestibule or a small room on the main block to an open porch. The house was remodeled as offices and has been home to Brownworth Engineering Associates since the 1970s. The garage at the left is gone. (Collection of the Metlar House.)

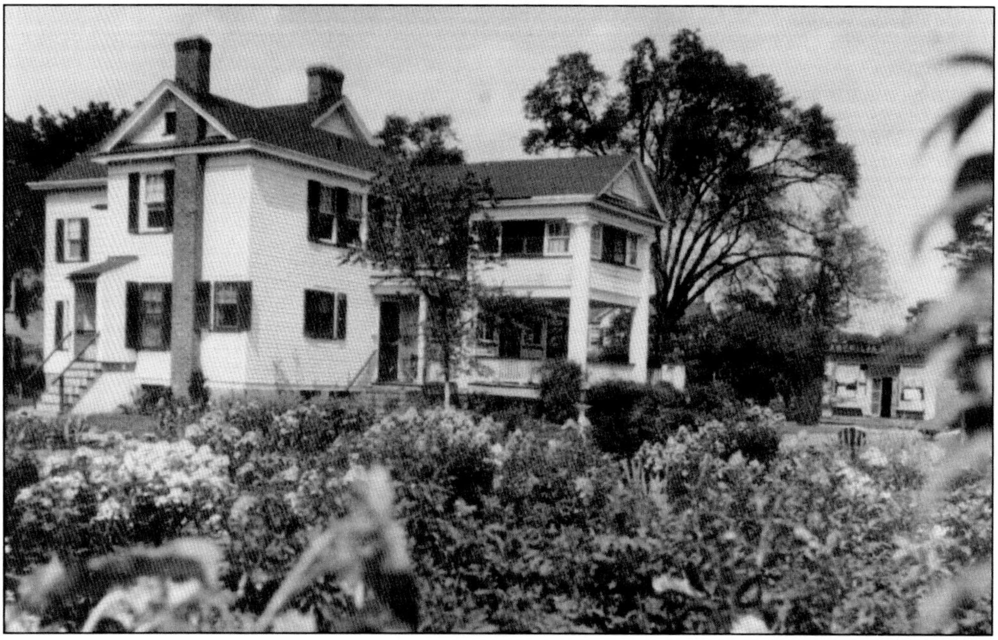

The rear of 10 Stelton Road shows an addition to the west facade, probably contemporary with the one on the south. Brownworth made two major renovations, including an early-1980s expansion on this facade. The porches were enclosed and some second-story main block windows were removed. A parking lot replaced the pictured flower garden. The firm maintains an ambiance of the old but still adapts the space to current office needs. (Collection of the Metlar House.)

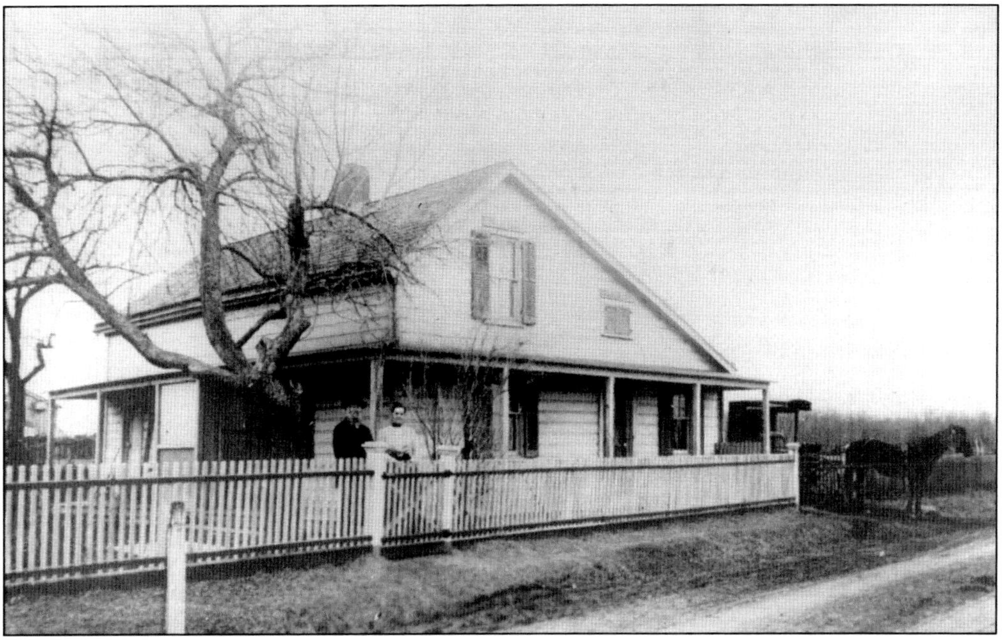

Included in this photographic postcard are an expanded early-19th-century house, its likely owners, a horse and wagon, and a bending, aging tree—all of which give it a powerful pictorial appeal. The picture is of Van Alstein's New Market bungalow, although the exact location is not known. (Collection of Cynthia Harris.)

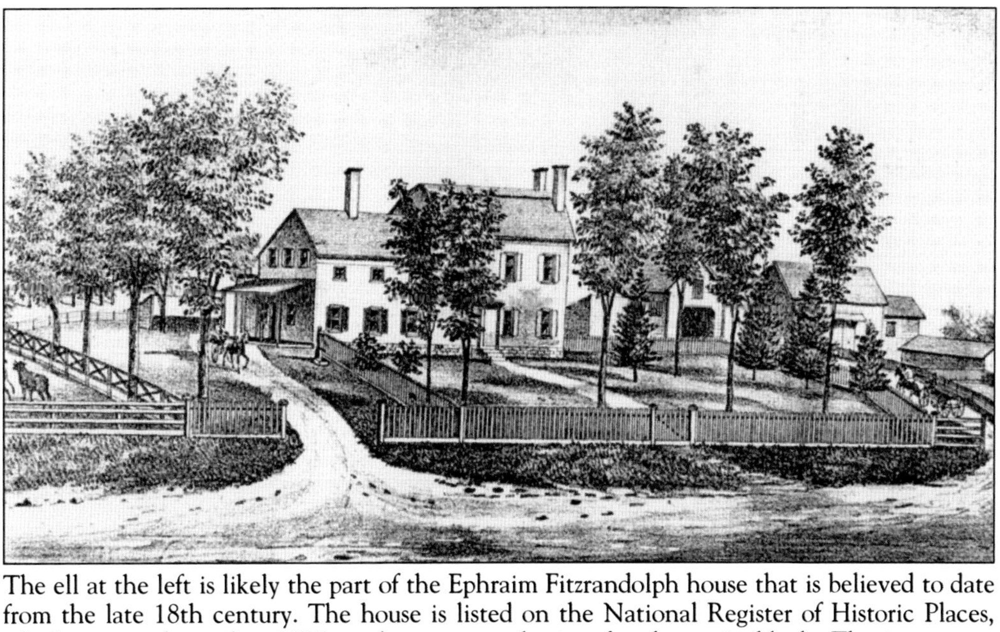

The ell at the left is likely the part of the Ephraim Fitzrandolph house that is believed to date from the late 18th century. The house is listed on the National Register of Historic Places, which uses a date of c. 1825, perhaps an attribution for the main block. The image was published in the 1876 Evarts and Stewart *Atlas of Middlesex County*.

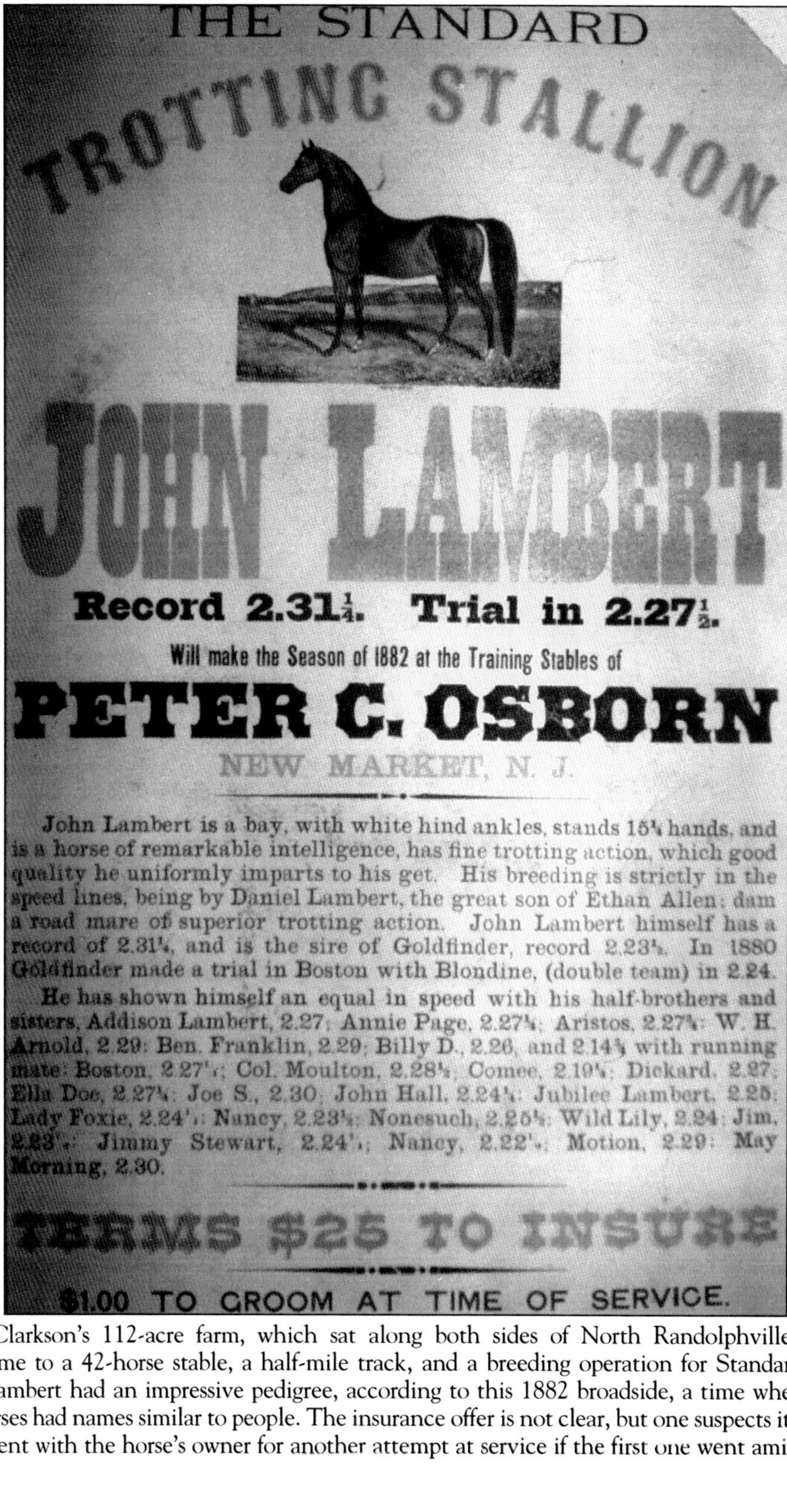

Peter Clarkson's 112-acre farm, which sat along both sides of North Randolphville Road, was home to a 42-horse stable, a half-mile track, and a breeding operation for Standardbreds. John Lambert had an impressive pedigree, according to this 1882 broadside, a time when most racehorses had names similar to people. The insurance offer is not clear, but one suspects it was an agreement with the horse's owner for another attempt at service if the first one went amiss.

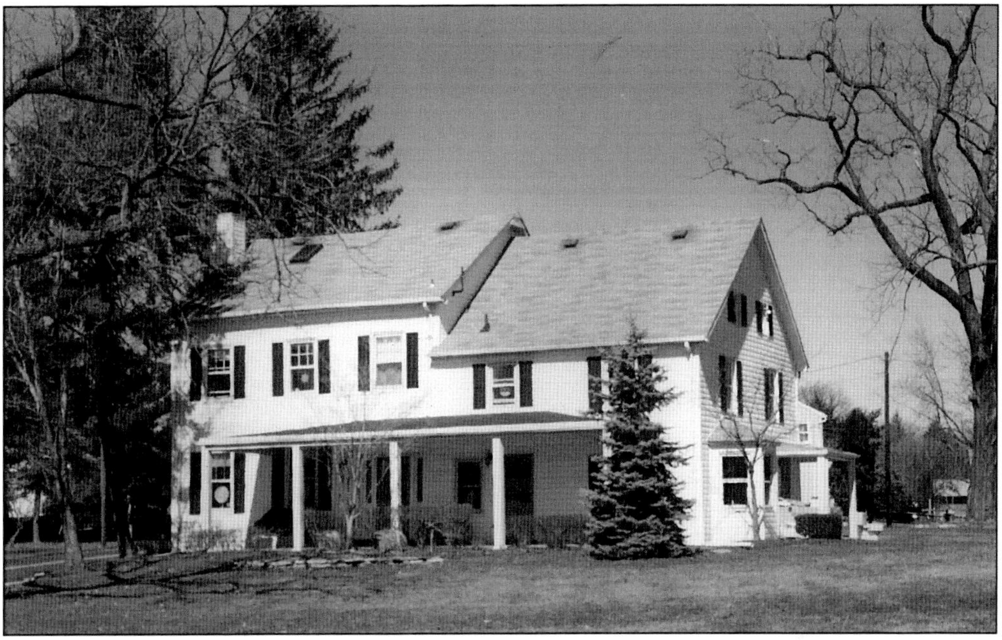

The original section (right) of the Peter Clarkson house is dated 1734 by virtue of that date carved on a beam. The taller section is attributed to the late 18th century. Clarkson and Osborn descendants farmed the place for more than 200 years, a rare distinction in New Jersey agricultural history. The house sits on a spacious lot at 125 North Randolphville Road, but the farm has been developed.

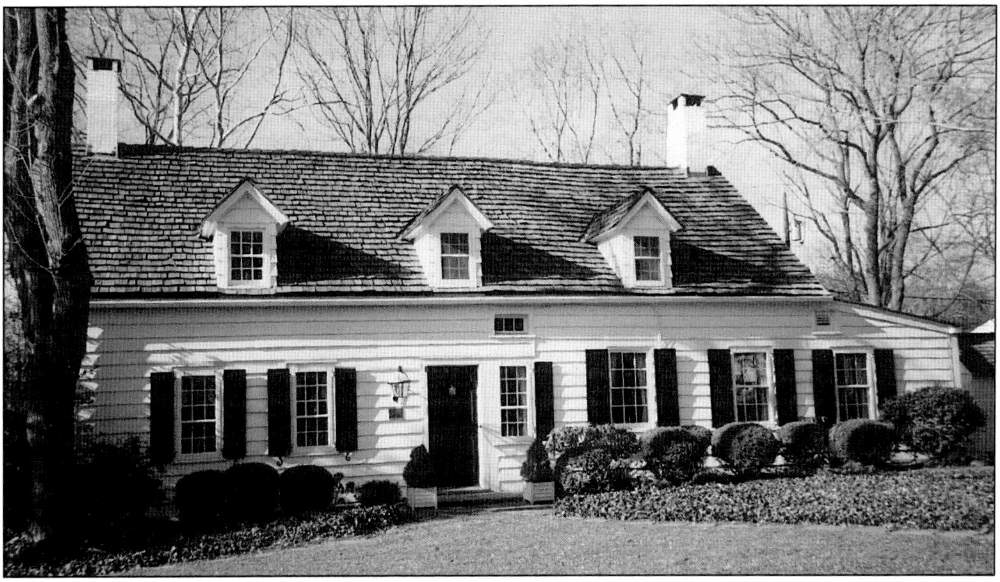

The Matthias Smock house at 851 River Road, the oldest one documented in Middlesex County, was built c. 1720 by a member of the New Utrecht militia who moved from that section of Brooklyn to Piscataway in 1718. The older section of the clapboard-clad, one-and-a-half-story, 53-by-27-foot house is on the left. The addition, by Smock's son John, dates from the middle of the 18th century. The house, owned by the Jennings family since 1962, is little altered; Jennings removed a small entry porch.

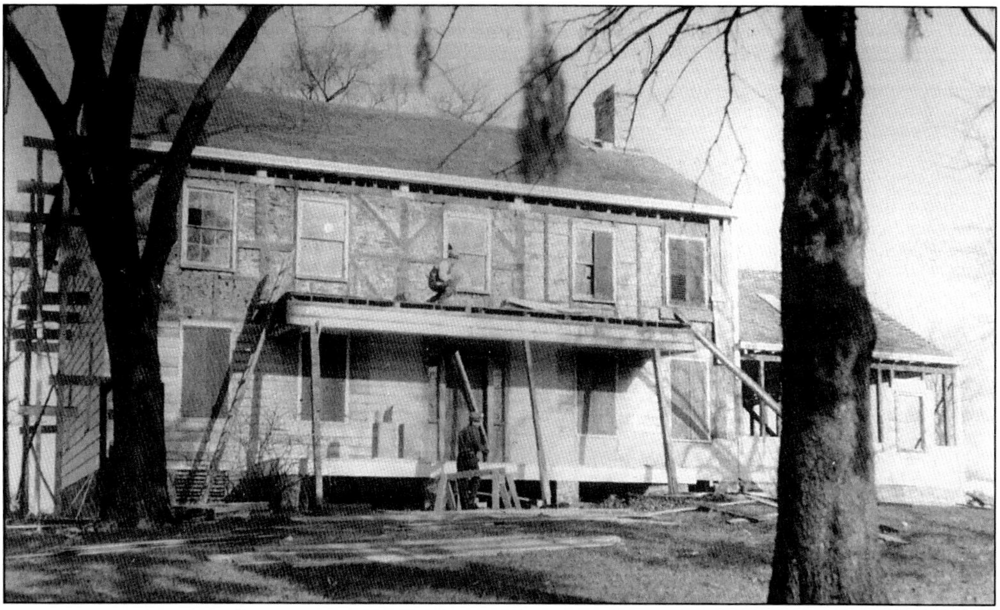

The Isaac Onderdonk house at 685 River Road is pictured around 1939, when Walter and Julia Meuly purchased the long-vacant and neglected place from Max Jelin and began a massive preservation and modernization project. The house, set well back from the road, faces south. The facade is visible in this image showing the repair of the porch and replacement of a kitchen wing on the east with a garage and a laundry room.

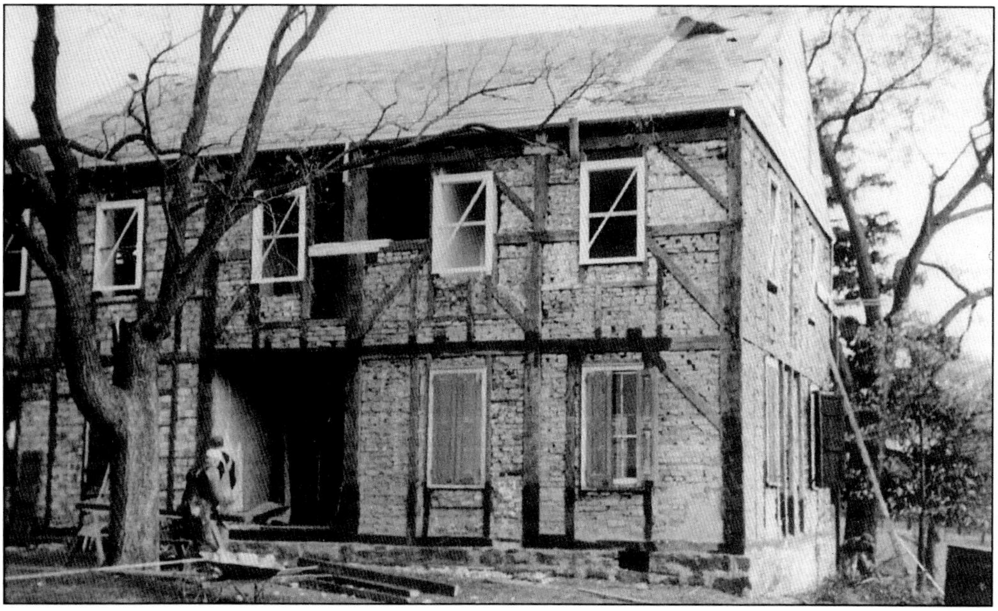

The house likely originated around the middle of the 18th century as a one-and-a-half-story structure about half its present size. The main block is now about 30 by 40 feet and is two rooms deep. Its wide clapboards were removed during the project, exposing the house's brick lining and mortise-and-tenon-joined framing. Onderdonks of the prominent Dutch van der Donk family first came to America in 1637, arriving at New Castle, Delaware. They later moved to Long Island, prior to Isaac's purchase of River Road land in 1745.

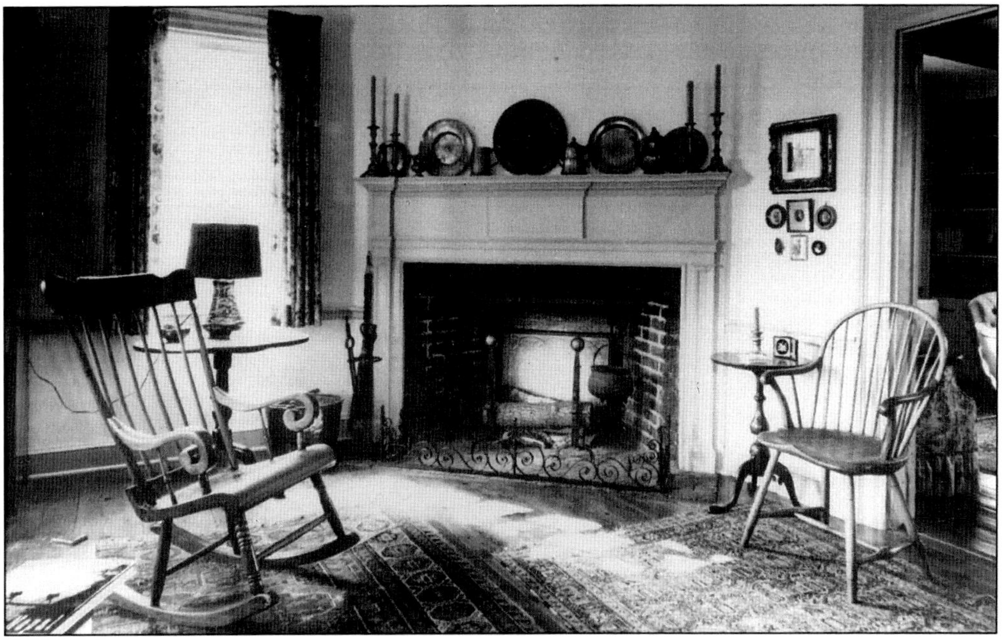

Walter Meuly (page 125) married Julia in 1932 and rented a house in Piscataway in 1935. They opted against the cost of new construction, purchasing this old place against the advice of knowing observers. The last Onderdonk sold 100 acres to a developer *c.* 1930. The Meulys purchased five acres with the house but accumulated more later. In 1963, they donated 25 acres of fields and woods to Middlesex County. The tract, known as Meuly Woods, became part of Johnson Park. (Collection of the Metlar House.)

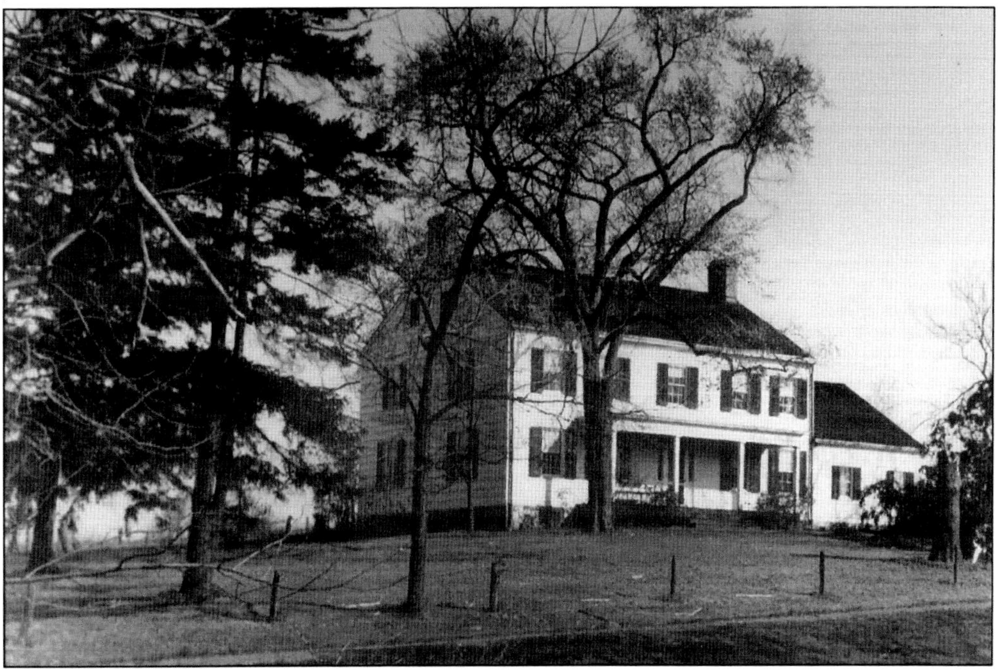

The restored house is pictured *c.* the 1960s, bearing an appearance maintained today. The house was listed on the National Register of Historic Places in 1973.

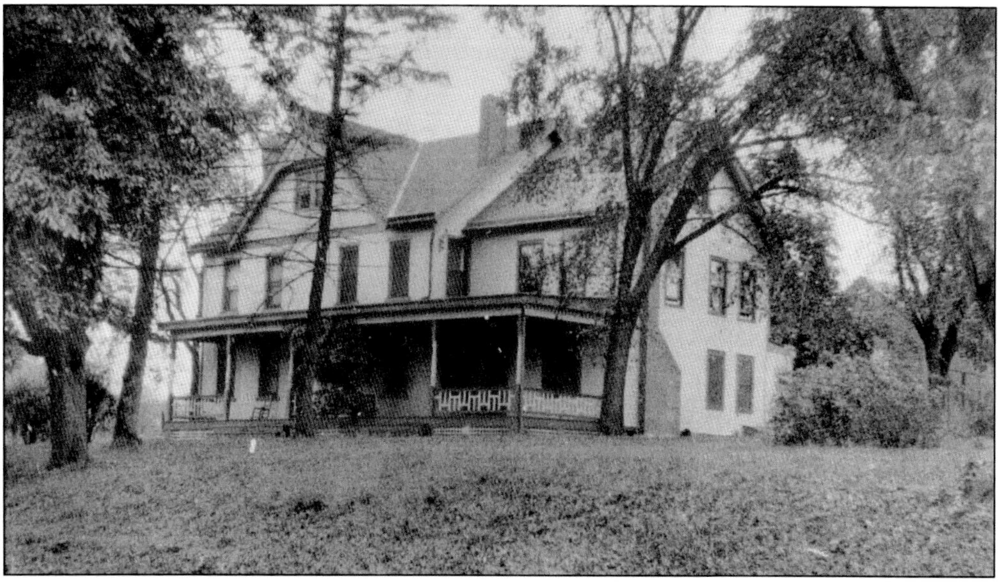

Lewis Onderdonk and his brother acquired the southern half of the Isaac Onderdonk Farm in 1854; Lewis later bought his brother's interest. The origin of the much altered house is attributed to the early 1840s, but one suspects the original structure is older, specifically the 15-by-35-foot living room behind the entrance pictured on the west facade. The cross gables date from the late 19th century; the wing on the south (right) was added in 1925. The house is still readily recognizable, despite the removal of the porch.

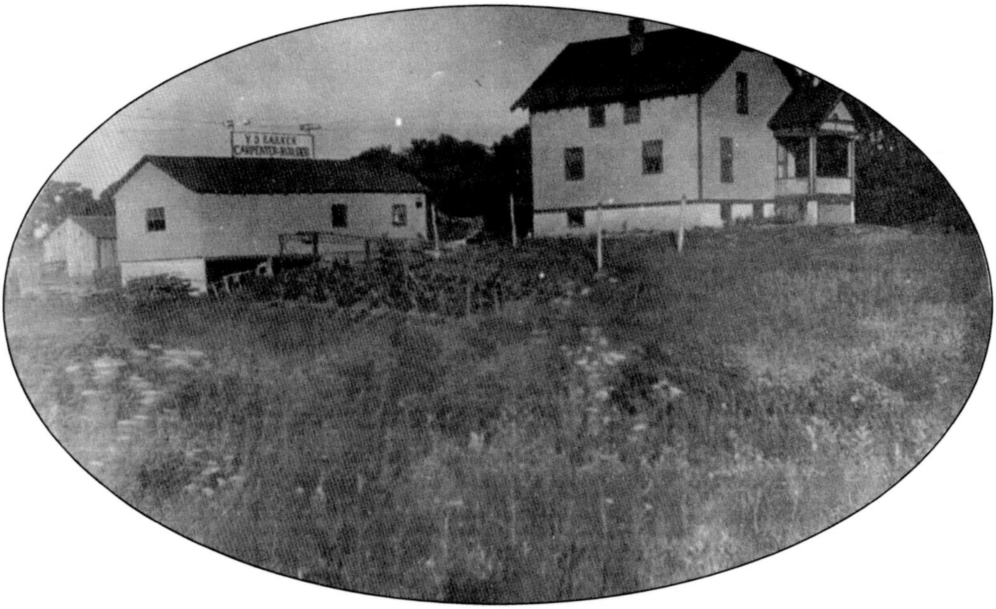

Bound Brook Heights' development by the Schwartz Land & Improvement Company of New York began in 1910. Yute D. Bakker, an immigrant from the Netherlands and a local builder, erected a house on Newark Avenue in 1911, becoming the first resident of a new neighborhood that remained sparsely settled for years. He built this house at 13 Plainfield Avenue for himself and his family in 1924. The house, pictured when new, is located next to Romano's Pizza and is still recognizable after changes.

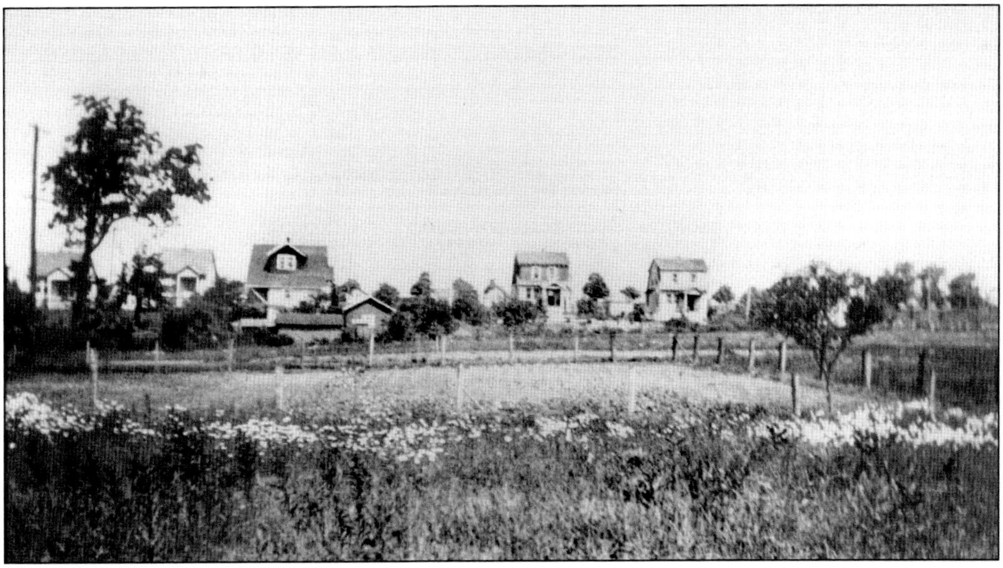

The north side of Netherwood Avenue is pictured *c.* 1920. The house in the center, located at 17 Netherwood Avenue, has changed little and is recognizable, but the house on the left was extensively altered. No. 15 was later built between them. No. 19, another little-changed house, is on the right. The south side of the street was developed later. The Bound Brook Heights Community Club, formed in the 1920s, was a force in convincing the township to take over the neighborhood's once private dirt roads.

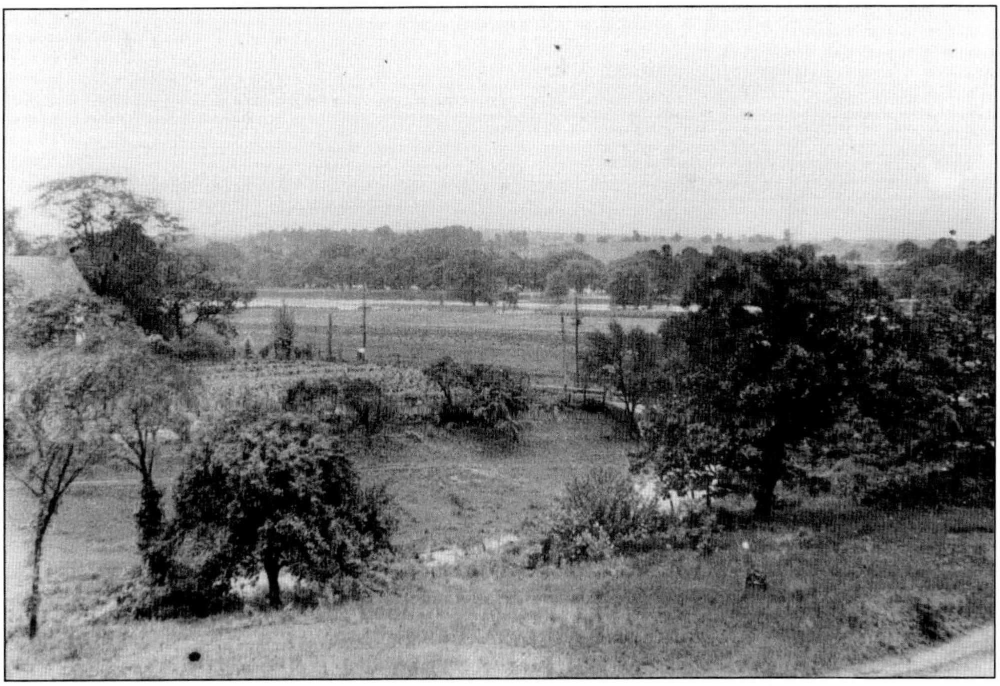

River Road in the Bound Brook Heights area is pictured with the overflowing Raritan River in the background. The flood, perhaps in the 1920s, probably prompted the photographer to capture this shot. Lush vegetation west of the road would make this image, taken from the Plainfield Avenue area, difficult to replicate in 2001.

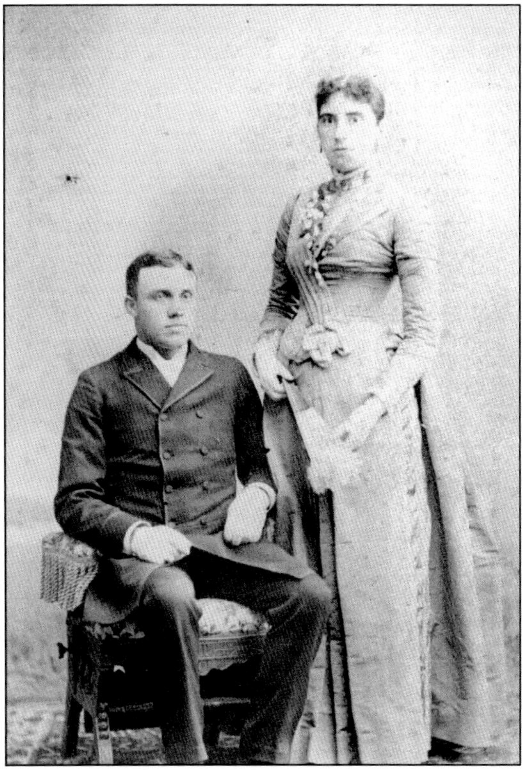

David J. Perrine of Cranbury married Emily Onderdonk in 1888. She was born at the famed Onderdonk Farm (pages 40 and 41). Although the original photograph is not dated or annotated, the formality of the attire suggests wedding clothes. David died in 1930 at age 64; Emily survived until 1958.

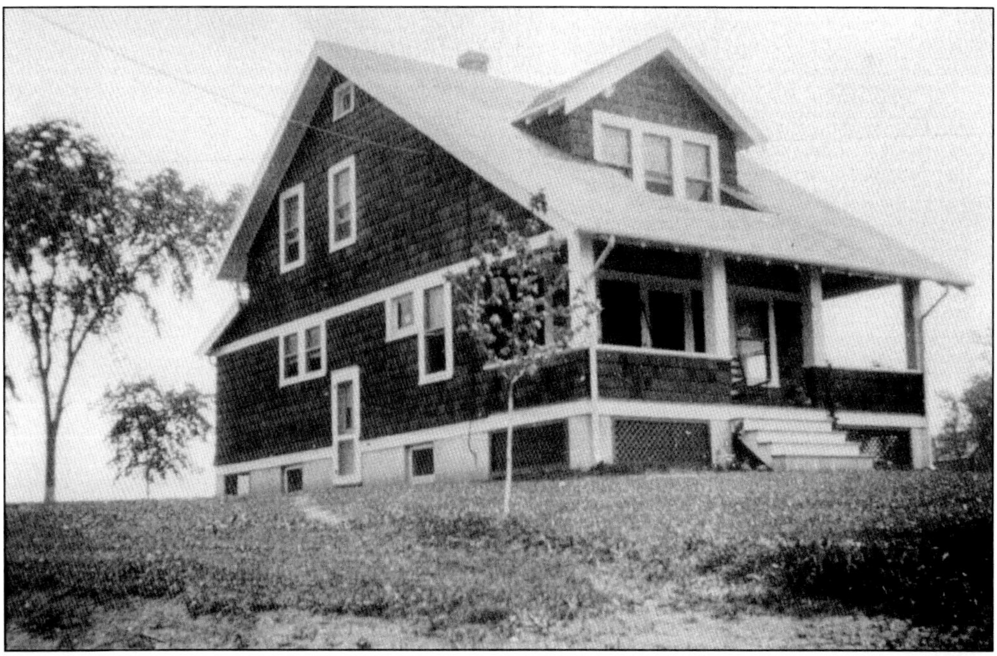

David and Emily Perrine built this house, erected by Y.D. Bakker, in 1925 at 635 River Road, the northeast corner of Runyon Avenue. They moved from the larger Field house at 625 River Road (page 32) after son Clarence married Lydia Tyler. The home is recognizable even though the porch was enclosed and two of the dormer windows were covered.

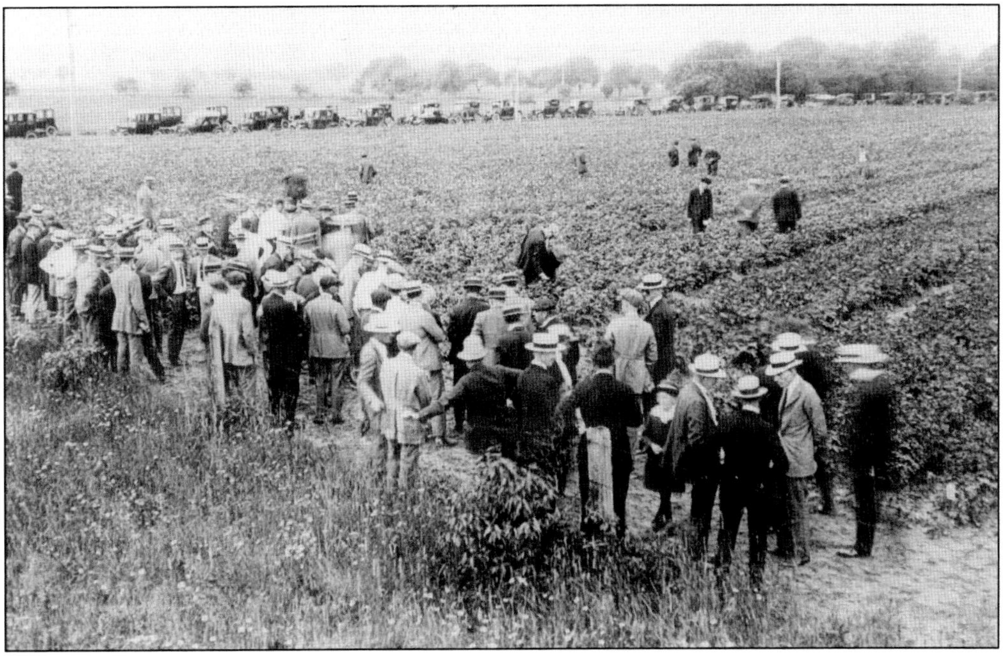

This local potato field is not identified, but the gathering suggests it may be an agricultural experimental planting. Rutgers' Cook College has been the center of New Jersey farm education for more than a century.

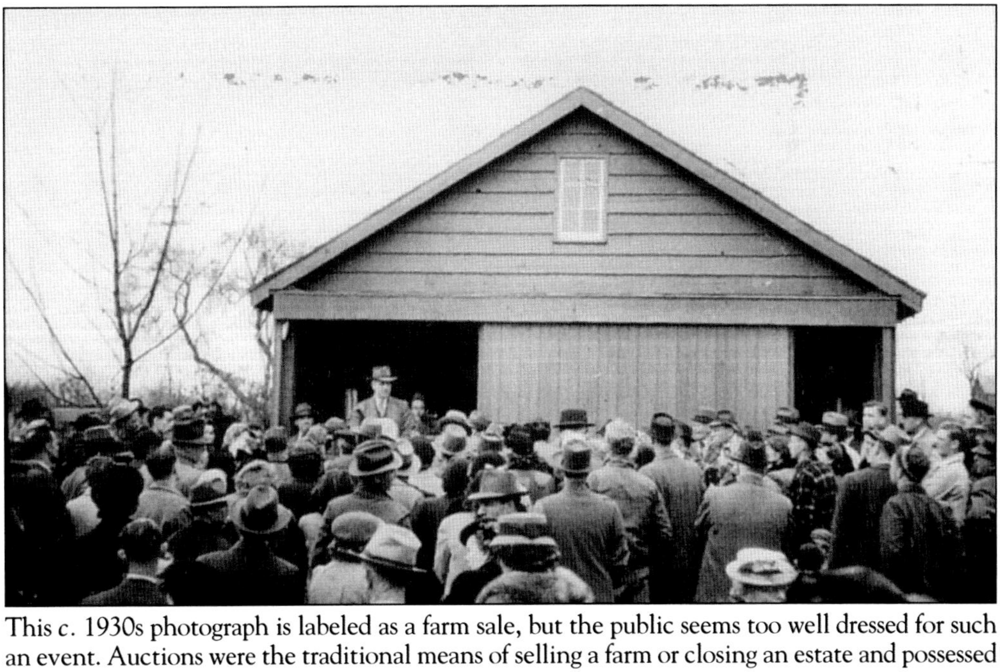

This *c.* 1930s photograph is labeled as a farm sale, but the public seems too well dressed for such an event. Auctions were the traditional means of selling a farm or closing an estate and possessed an important social element as well.

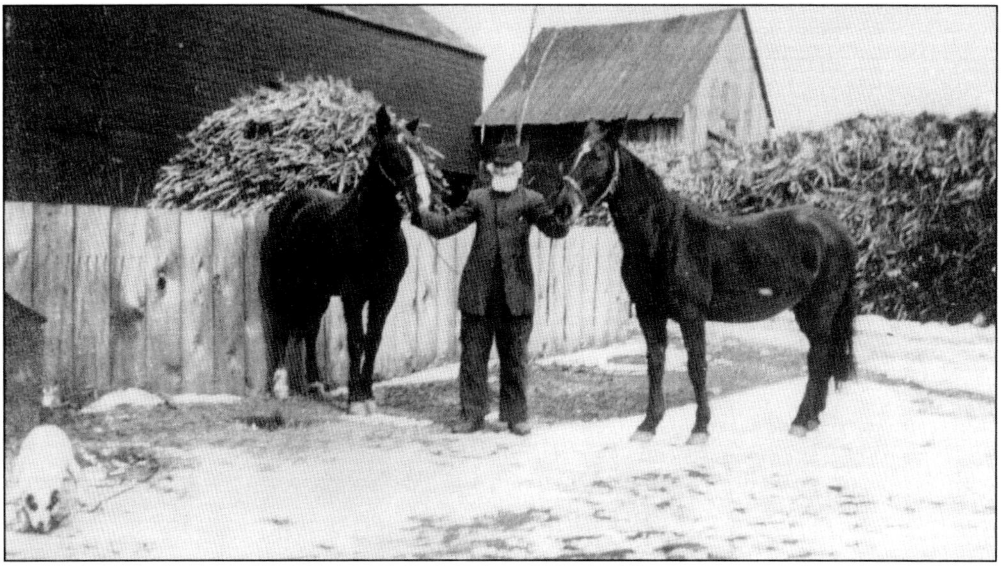

The elder David Perrine is pictured with two fine horses and one farm dog.

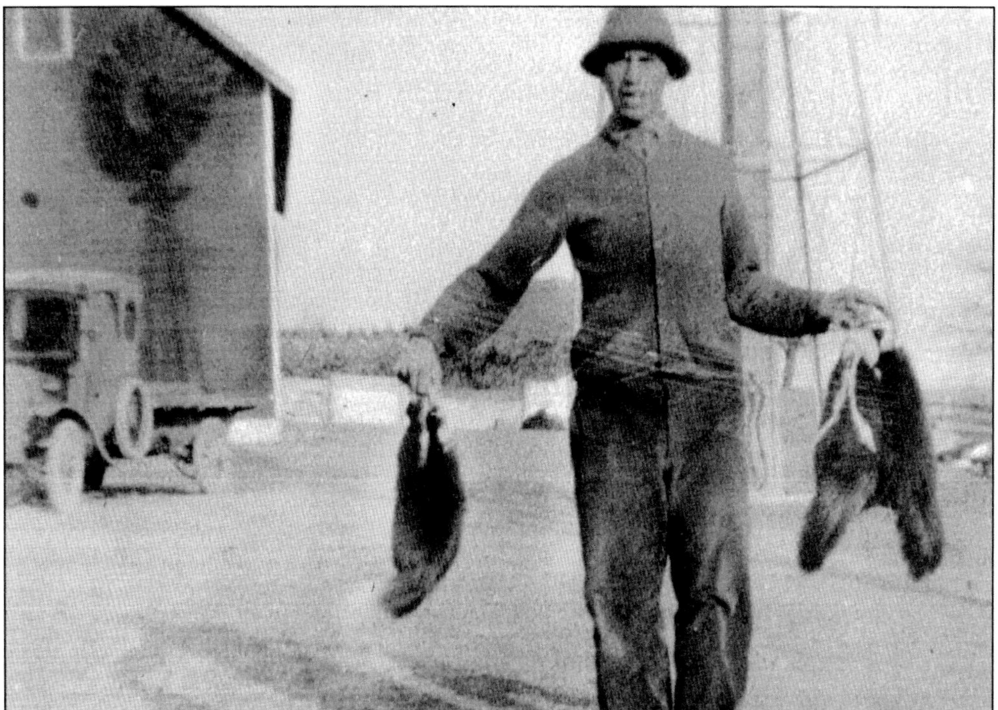

Clarence Perrine is pictured holding the pelts of three skunks, critters trapped for their cash value for fur. Wearing skunk seems inexplicable around three-quarters of a century later, but perhaps you had to ask the woman who owned one.

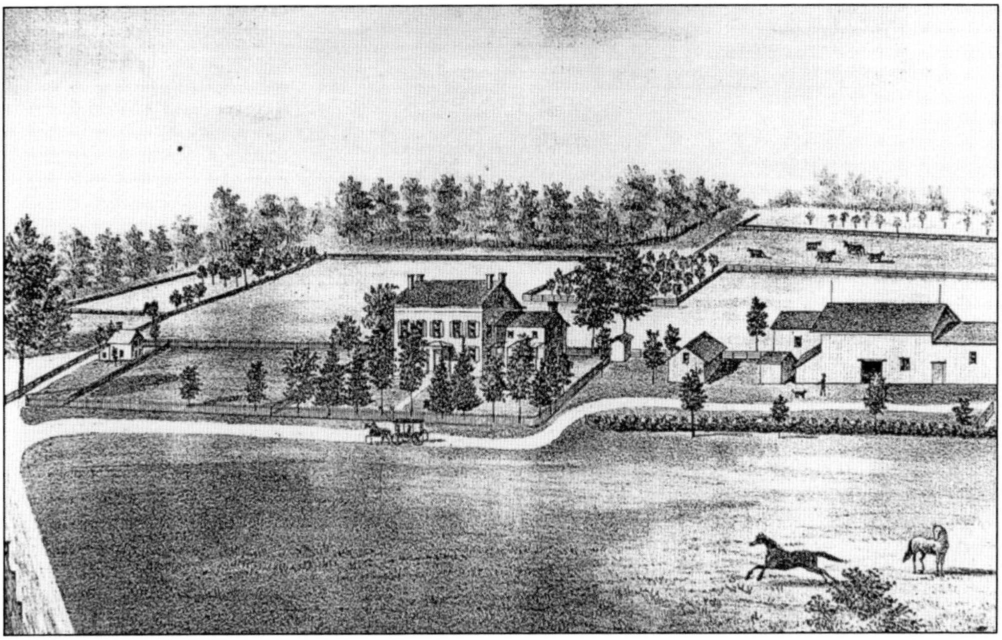

The Nelson Blackford house stands at 100 Doyle Street, now without the ell on the right. Although the house is traditionally attributed to the 18th century, one suspects there was a major 19th-century addition to an older house. The illustration was published in the 1876 Evarts and Stewart *Atlas of Middlesex County*.

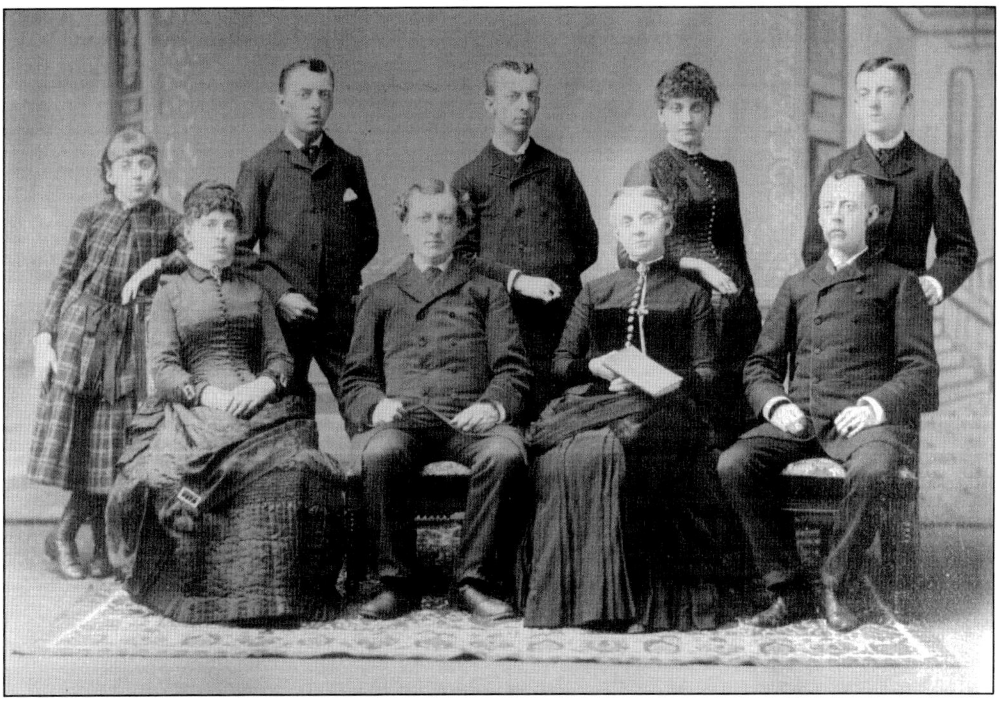

This dignified family left their visages at the Metlar House without leaving their names, but appealing late-19th-century garments merit their inclusion even without identification. (Collection of the Metlar House.)

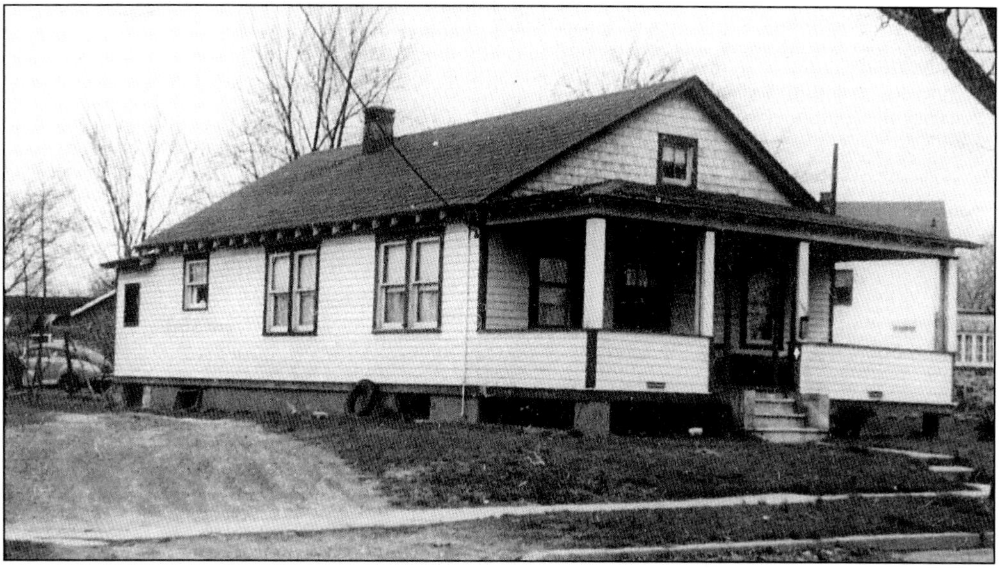

The Arbor neighborhood in the northeast section of the township was developed in the late 19th and early 20th centuries through the sale of small lots. Their location was within walking distance (according to standards of the day) of the Dunellen and Clinton Avenue, North Plainfield railroad stations. Early Arbor dwellings are readily distinguishable from the post–World War II examples, typically ranches, that filled-out the area. Many of the inexpensive early houses were the pattern book or kit variety. This one, at 1500 West 4th Street, appears to be a Sears model called the Hampton. It stands little changed today, clad with siding, although the section of porch on the right is enclosed.

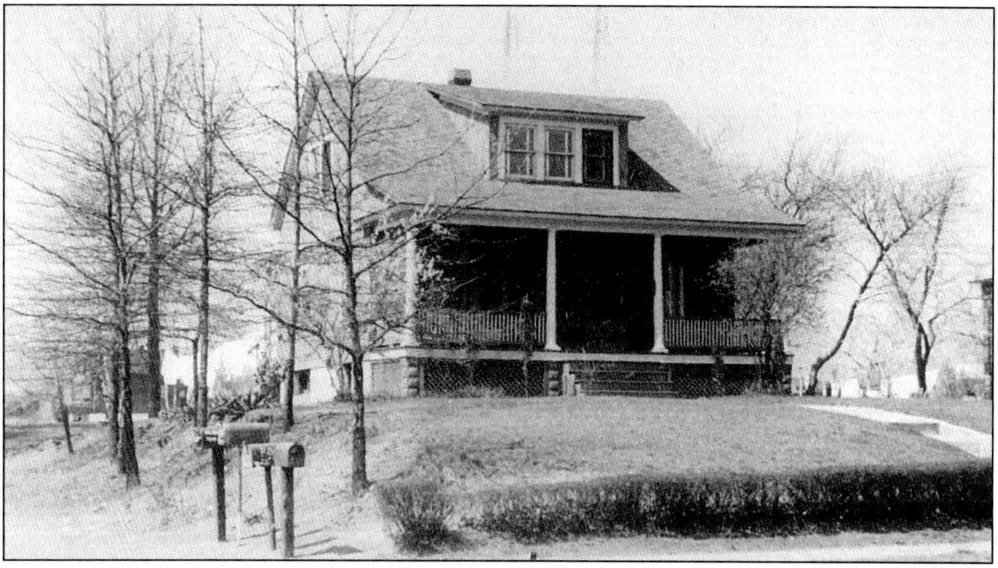

Changes at 1750 West 4th Street at the southwest corner of Hazelwood Place are virtually unnoticeable, although the porch columns are now bare four-by-fours. Many vendors sold pattern book house plans; this one also appears to be by Sears, whose house product was distinguished by its sale in a kit that contained all the materials needed to erect the house and instructions able to be followed by the handy homebuilder. Both houses on this page are pictured in 1947.

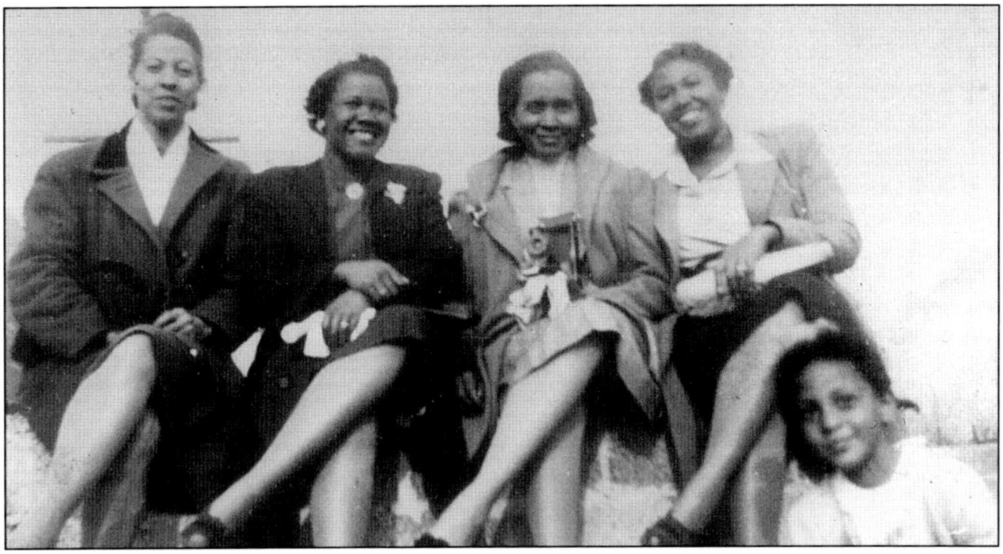

New Brunswick Highlands developed *c.* 1915 by the N.T. Hegeman Company as the township's first black area. Running east from River Road around Park Avenue, it has been described as being "one mile long and five blocks wide." Small lots and sparsely built streets characterized the neighborhood's early years, as is pictured below in 1944. Its residents called the area the Heights, or the Hill, but Margaret Kruse recalls that whites called it the Park Avenue section or the Holmes Marshall section, the latter for the school on page 78. Showing leg in April 1944 are, from left to right, Marie Woodson, Agnes Smith, Essie Jackson, and Claudia Smith. Rosemarie Woodson is in the lower right corner.

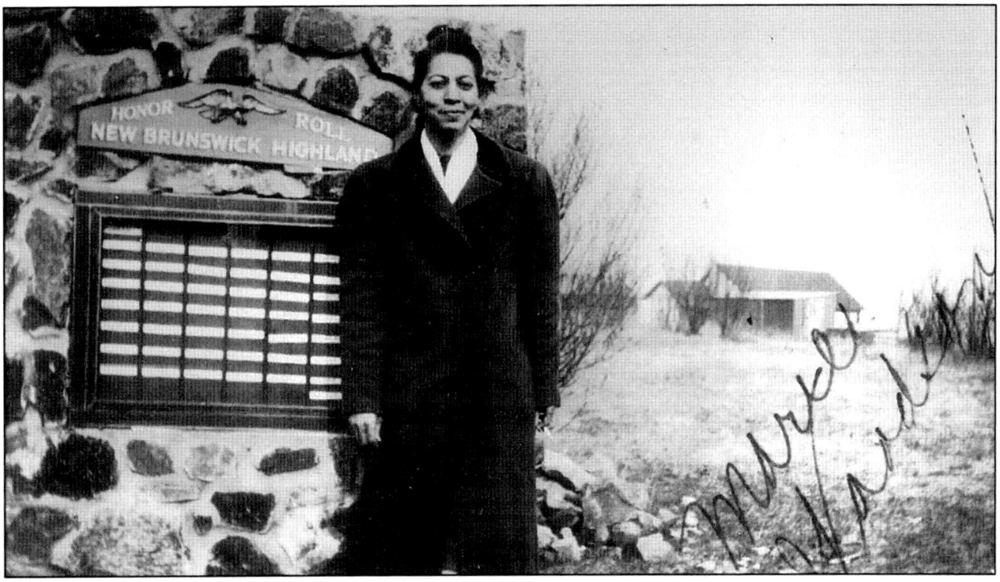

Heights residents paid for this stone World War II service memorial erected at the circle formerly at Park Avenue and Deborah Drive. Most towns had temporary wood memorials, but this one appears to have been able to endure longer than any postwar peace the author can remember. However, it was destroyed by workers removing the circle, a gesture that created more than a little unhappiness. A modest stone in front of the Holmes Marshall Firehouse represents a replacement. Marie Woodson poses in front of the memorial.

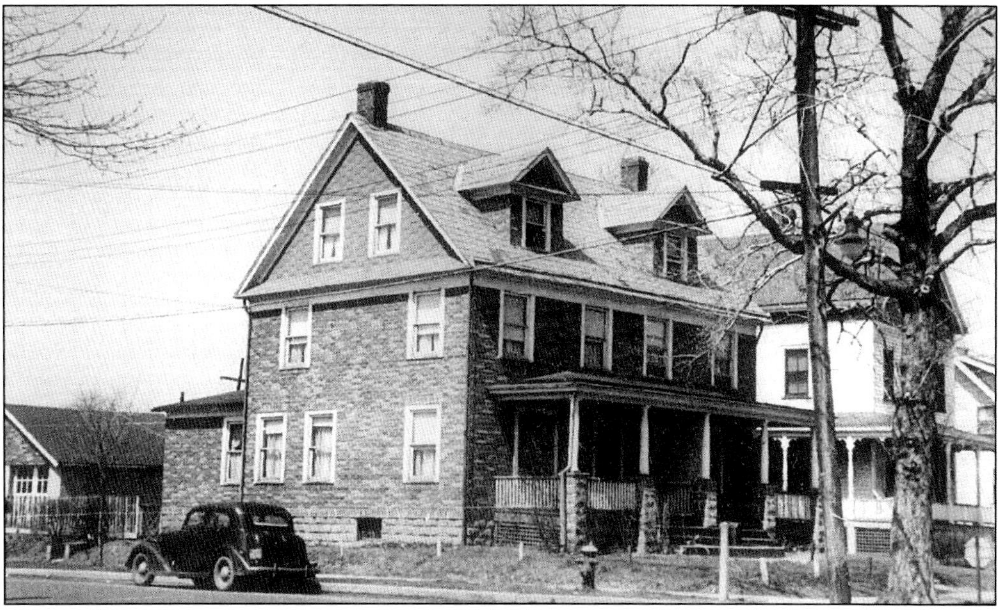

This traditional two-and-a-half-story, side-gabled house, in style basically Georgian, was likely one of the most substantial residences in Arbor when built around the early 20th century. It faces West 4th Street at its northwest corner with Rock Avenue. The extensively remodeled, siding-clad dwelling is now a two-family house. Its dormers and porch are removed, but the corner is recognizable by the house's foundation and garage and the glimpse of 1694 West 4th Street on the right.

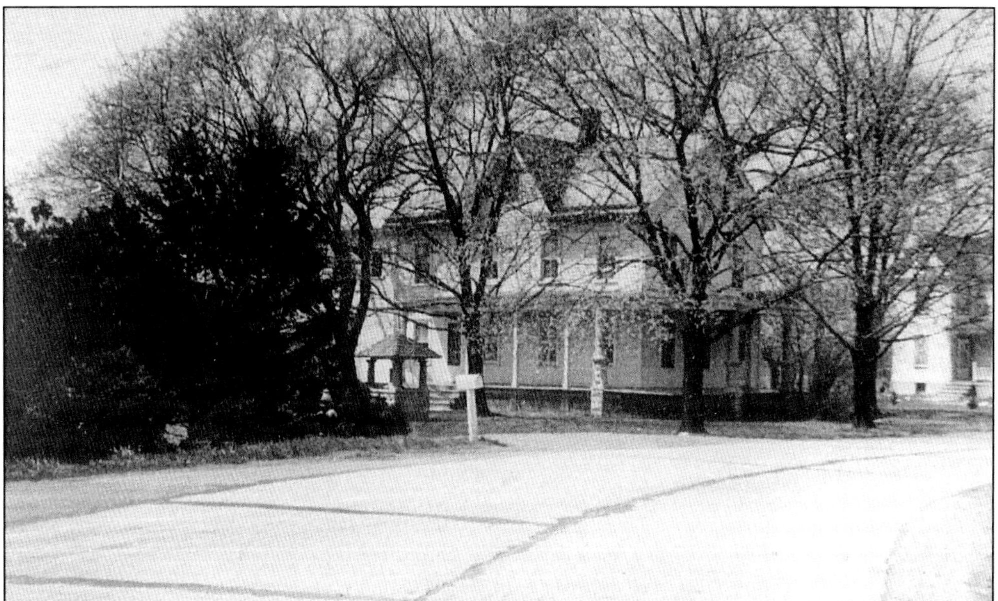

This *c.* mid-19th-century house, south of the Eisenhower School on Stelton Road, was razed in the late 1990s for the construction of the houses along Marissa Court, a process often repeated in the last half-century's paving-over of the township. That street was built through the house lot, pictured here *c.* 1947. A glimpse of 360 Stelton Road is visible on the right.

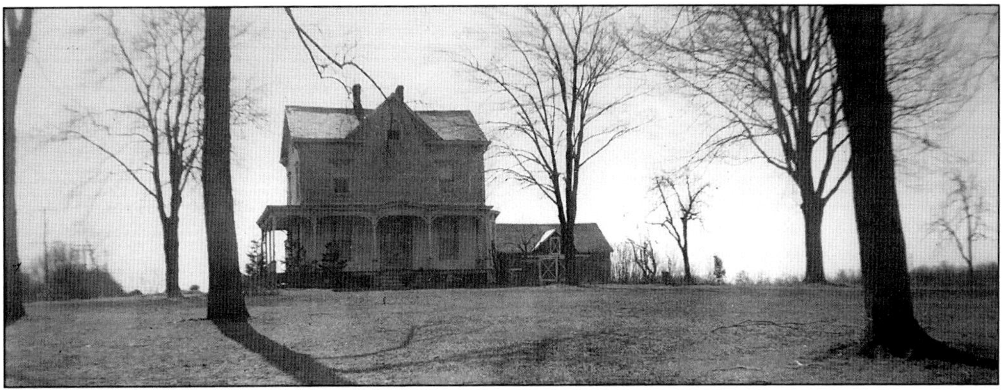

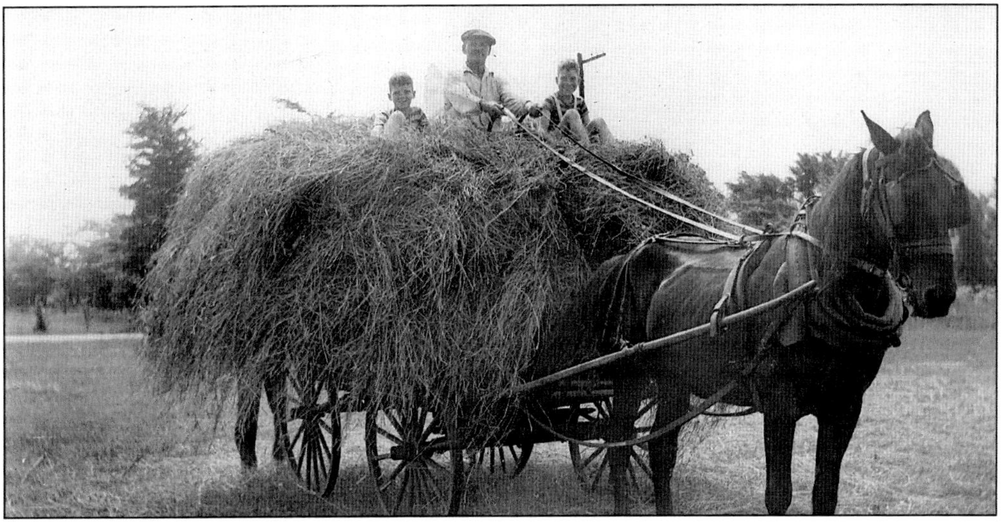

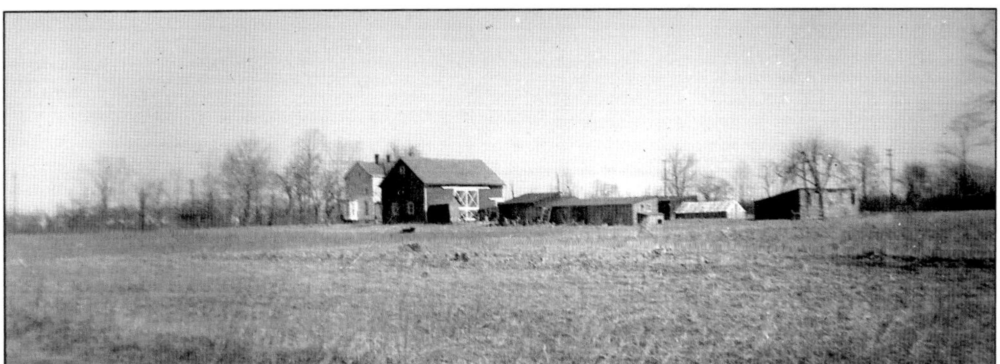

The La Costa family found themselves unexpected farmers after 1941, when builder Daniel Ernest purchased approximately 25 acres around William Street and Dupont Avenue. The family moved into the 8 Dupont Avenue house (top) that October, but Daniel's entry into the military caused a delay in his plans to develop the property. Sons Robert (left) and Dan flank farmhand Mr. Meches on the hay wagon in July 1942. The farm buildings facing William Street (bottom) are gone, but the house survives, although it is now surrounded by newer ones. After World War II, Daniel built about 14 houses there, selling the still-standing house pictured at top in 1965. Other builders added more.

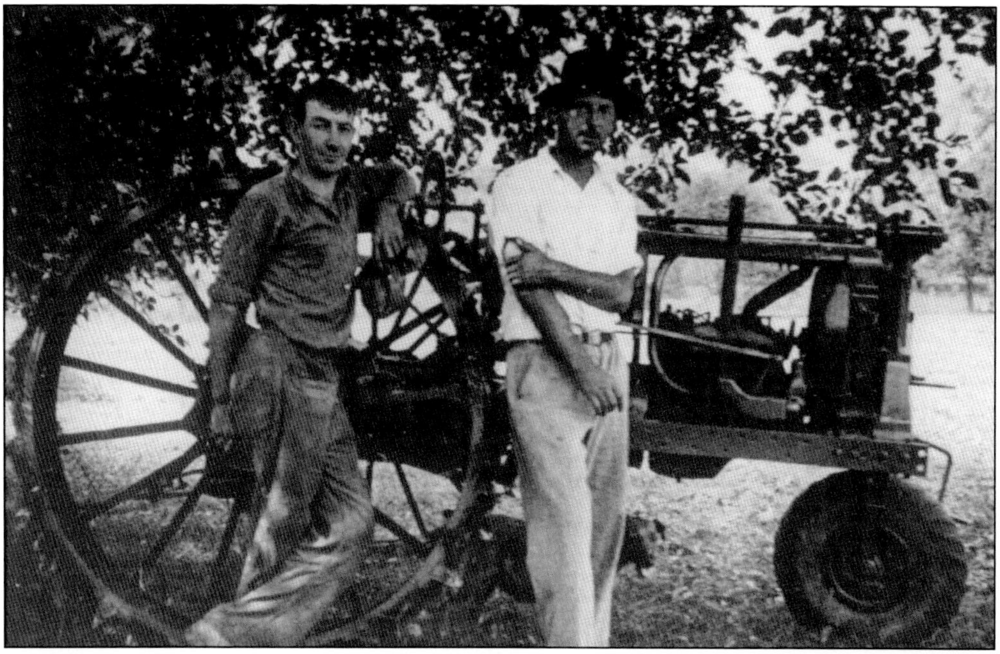

Bill Miller and a farmhand pose in front of a Farmall tractor in an undated photograph. The enormous rear wheels must have had a purpose, perhaps for stability on a vehicle type not known for that quality.

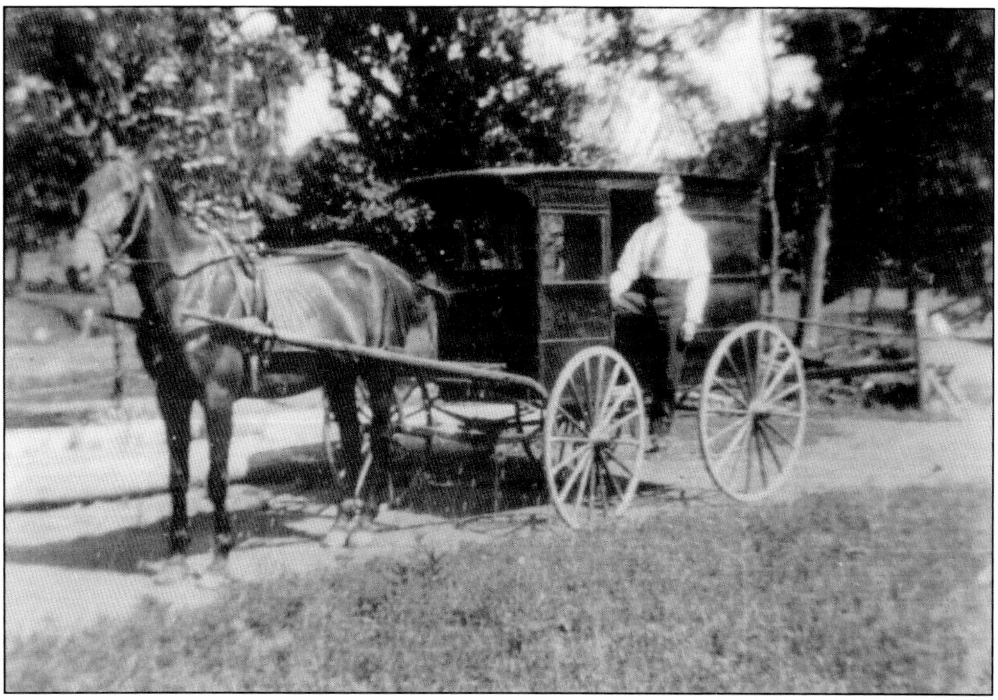

Horace and his milk wagon are pictured in an early-20th-century photograph. The horse would appear to benefit from a diet rich in calcium and butterfat.

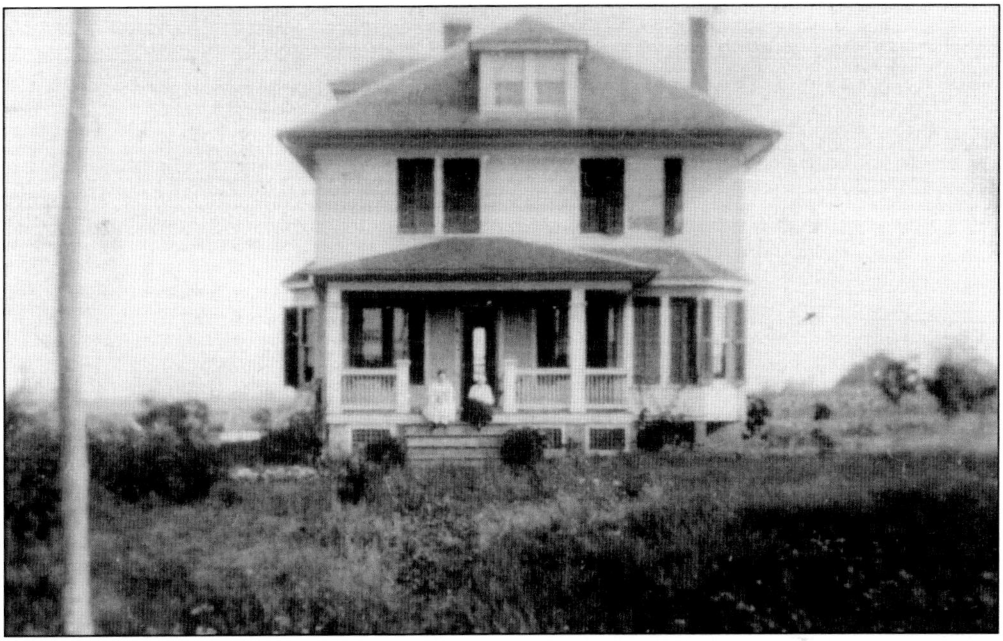

The Williams home at the corner of Sidney and Behmer Roads is similar to the four-square houses built in great numbers during the first two decades of the 20th century. However, it has a few decorative flourishes, including the bay window, one-story tower, and overhanging eaves. Sidney Road is said to have been named for Sidney Williams.

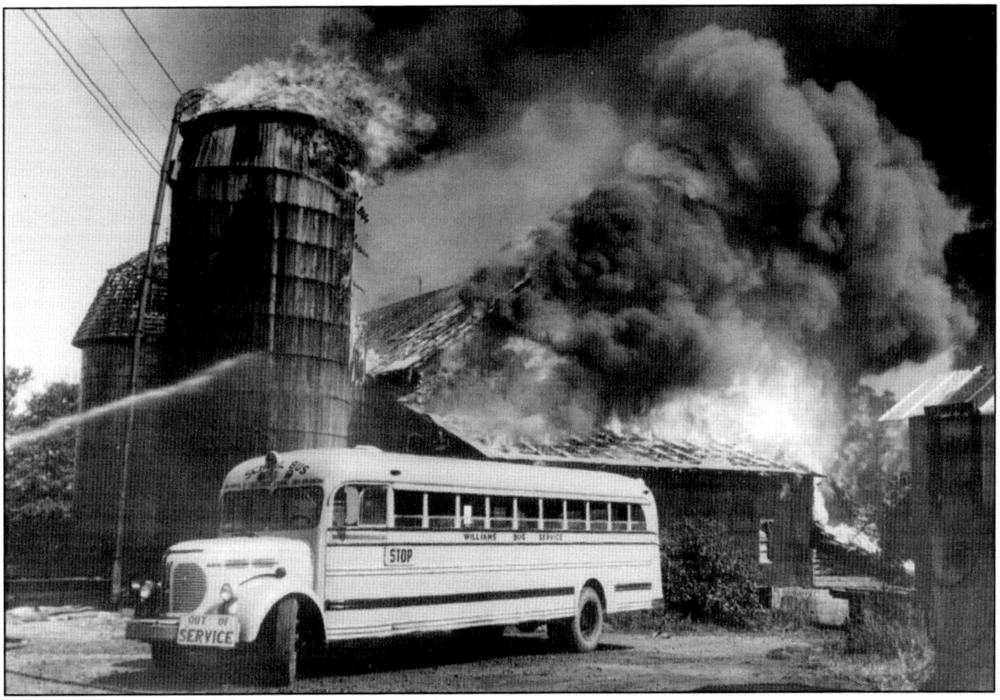

The bus was not all that was out of service when fire struck the Williams Brothers Dairy Farms on August 31, 1953. The fire resulted in an estimated $250,000 in damage (a major loss in those days), including destruction of this barn.

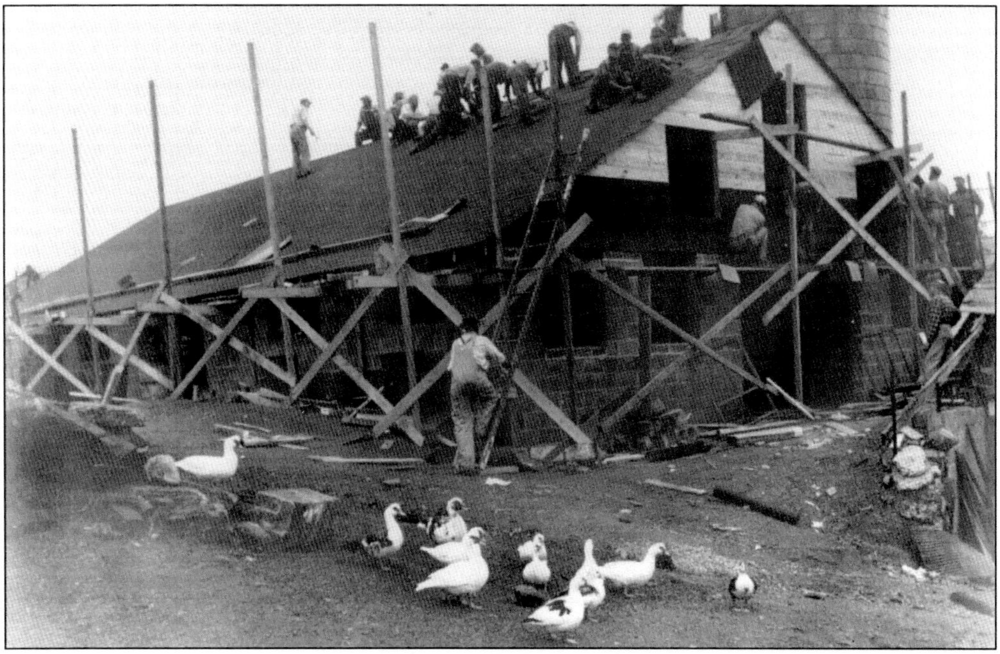

About 60 friends and neighbors of Wilbur and Robert Williams gathered on October 24, 1953, to help rebuild the barn. Their efforts were facilitated by precut roof rafters and cinder-block walls that had been constructed earlier. Work is pictured late in the afternoon when long-awaited rain (which actually should have come the day of the fire) halted work but pleased the ducks in the foreground.

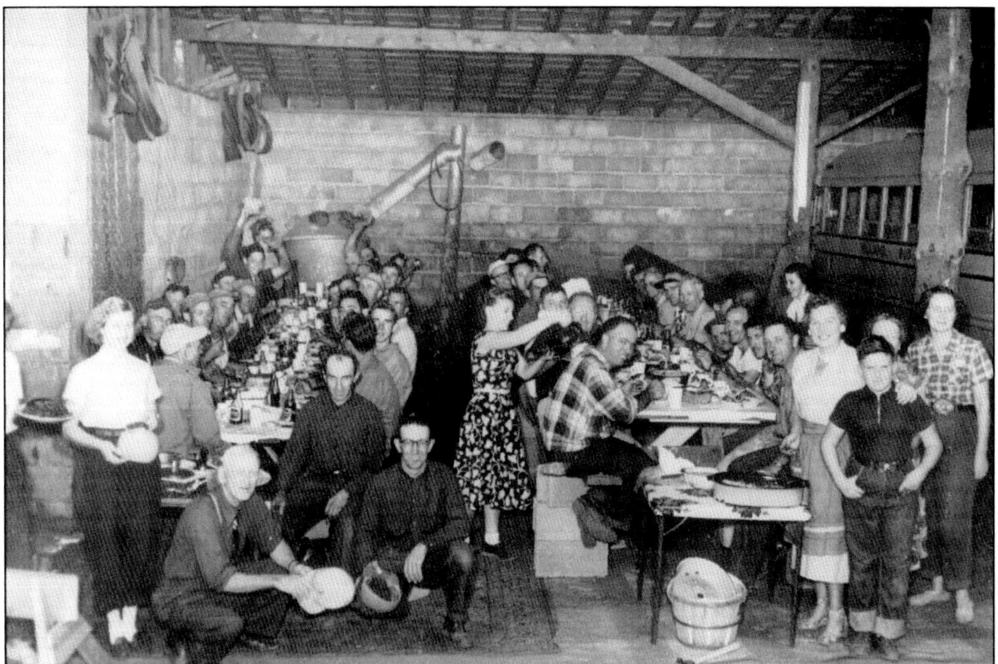

The barn workers raised their bottles (amber, no dairy, please) after raising the roof at the Williams Brothers Dairy Farm and were served a hearty dinner.

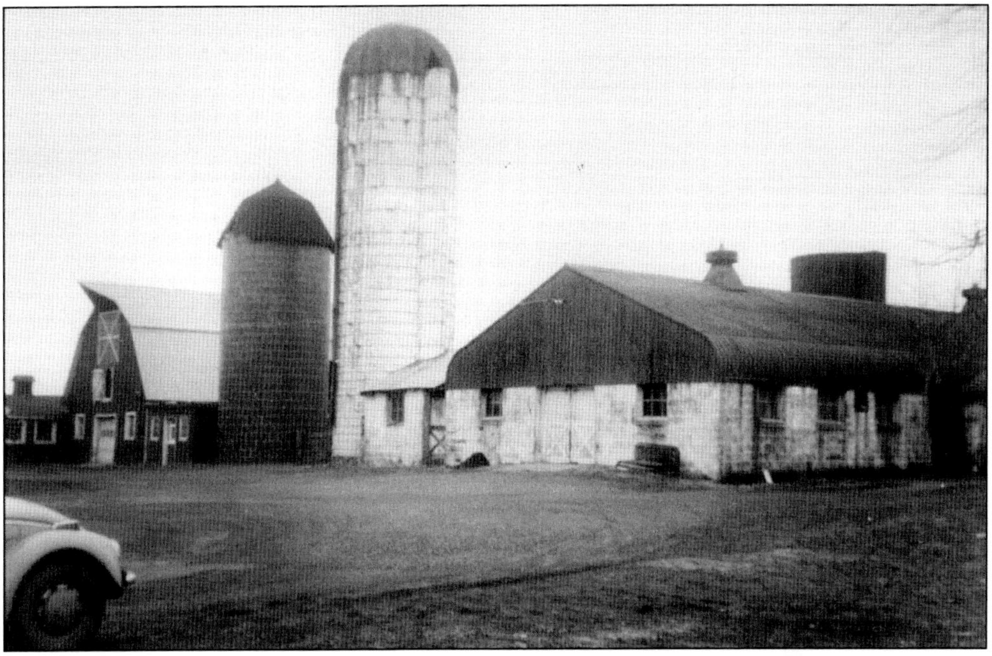

Louis and Thomas Sudzin bought part of the Field holdings in 1920 and started a dairy operation, Maplehurst Farm. (The house is on page 23.) The herd was gone by *c.* 1970, but the place maintained a retail operation for a time. A housing development is on the site now.

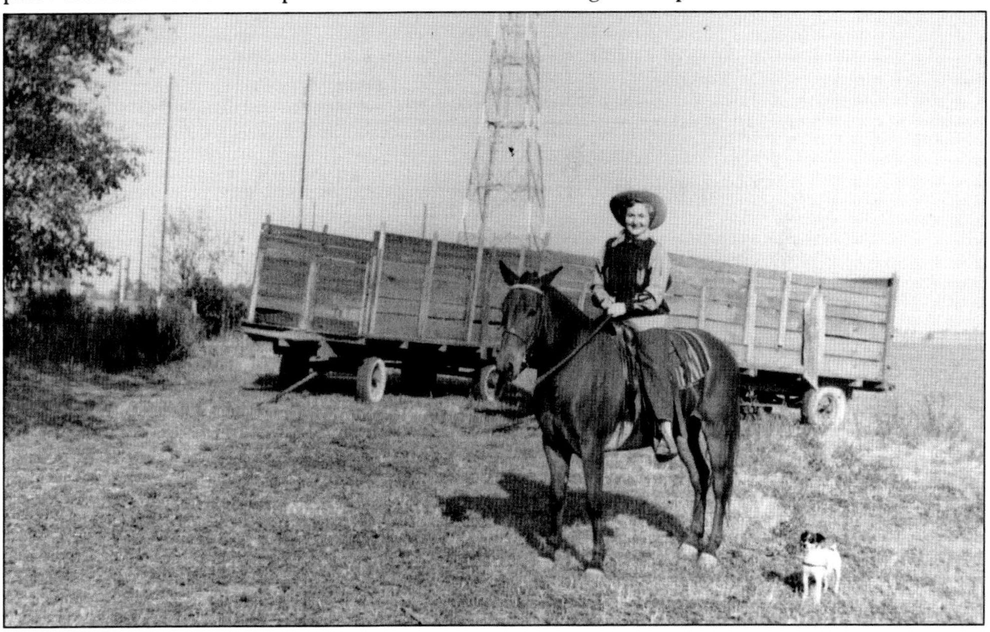

Commercial radio station WJZ established early broadcasting in western Piscataway. It was converted to Voice of America use around the early 1940s, but a stronger signal was required. The federal government condemned land on Maplehurst Farm during World War II and erected a tower that was used for a number of years. The government, however, was reluctant to remove it when operations concluded. Goldie Sudzin is pictured on her horse in the mid-1940s in front of that tower.

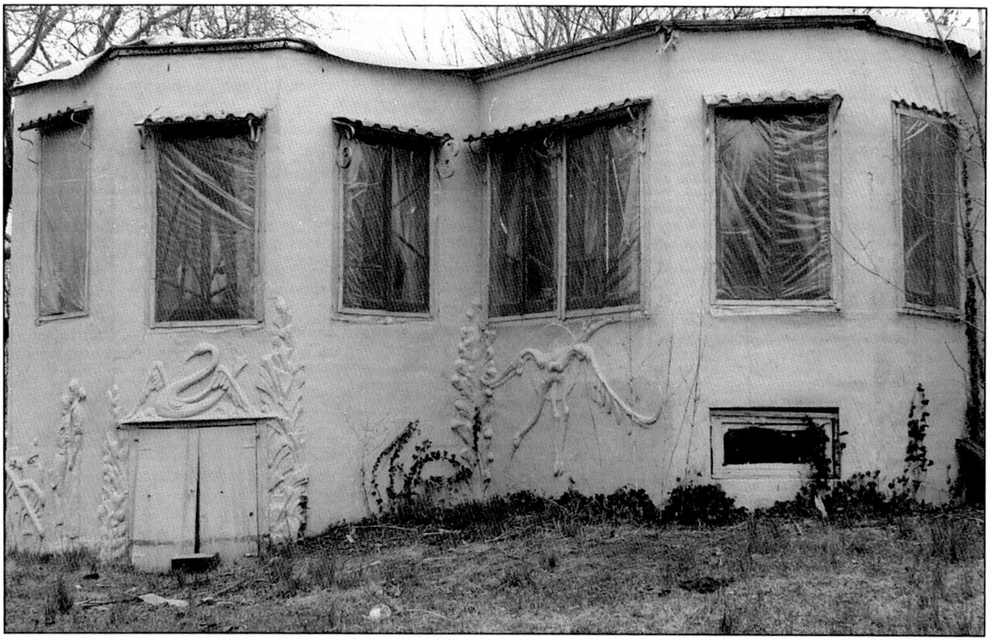

Sculptor Samuel Goldman built his Fellowship Farm house at 141 School Street with his own hands. It was an eclectic series of assembled cubes. Goldman, born in 1882 in Russia, lived to the age of 90, attaining the longest residency at the colony. His house was well known for its series of bas-reliefs. Time and the elements have taken a toll, but many survive.

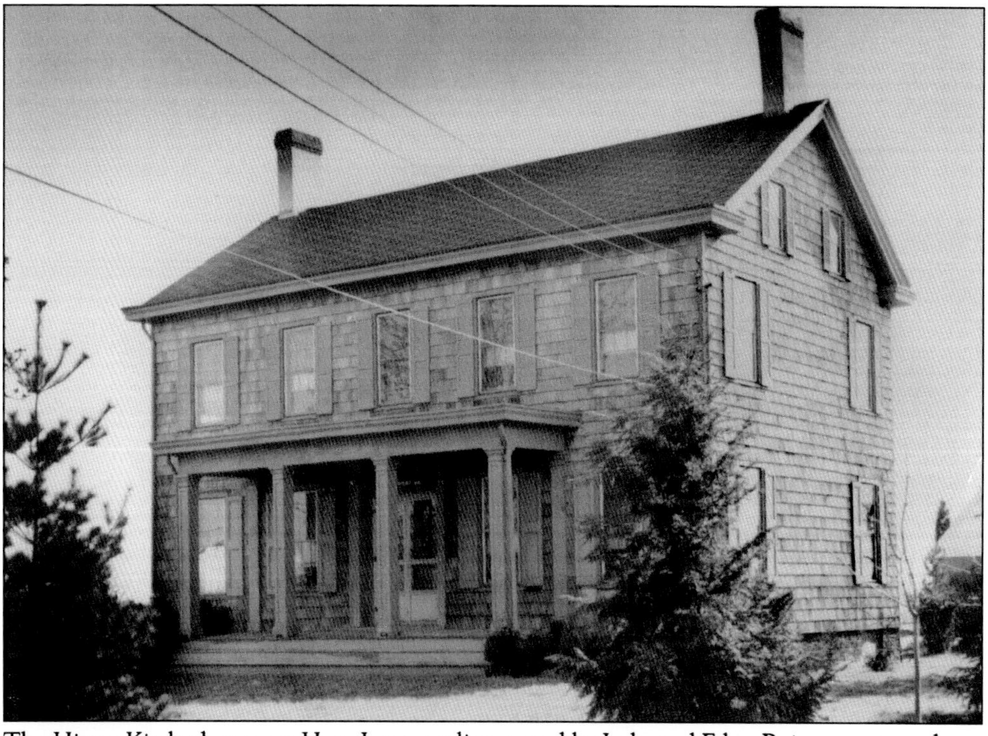

The Hiram Kistler house on Hoes Lane, earlier owned by Lulu and Edna Boice, was torn down for construction of the AT & T facility pictured on page 74.

Selman Abraham Waksman, born in 1888 in the Ukraine, immigrated to America in 1910, settled with a New Jersey relative, and received a B.S. and M.S. in agricultural biology at Rutgers. He earned a Ph.D. at the University of California, Berkeley, and worked for Cutter Laboratories in the World War I effort. Waksman returned to Rutgers in late 1918 as a lecturer in soil microbiology. He remained there for the rest of his professional life, rising to the directorship of the Rutgers Institute of Microbiology, since renamed for Waksman. He spent much time studying the effects of humus and exploring antibodies in microbes—studies that led to the discovery of streptomycin, which brought him the 1952 Nobel Prize for medicine or physiology. Waksman coined the term antibiotic. He married Bertha Deborah Mitnik in 1910, and the couple had one child. Waksman died on August 16, 1973. (Collection of the Metlar House.)

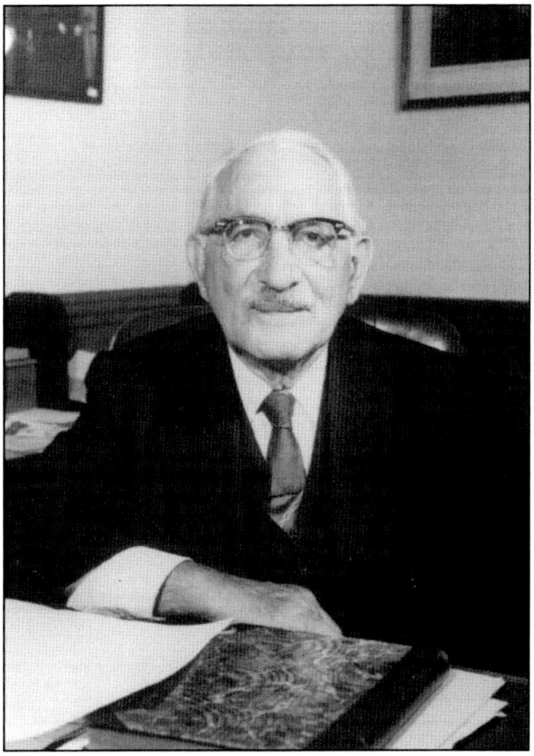

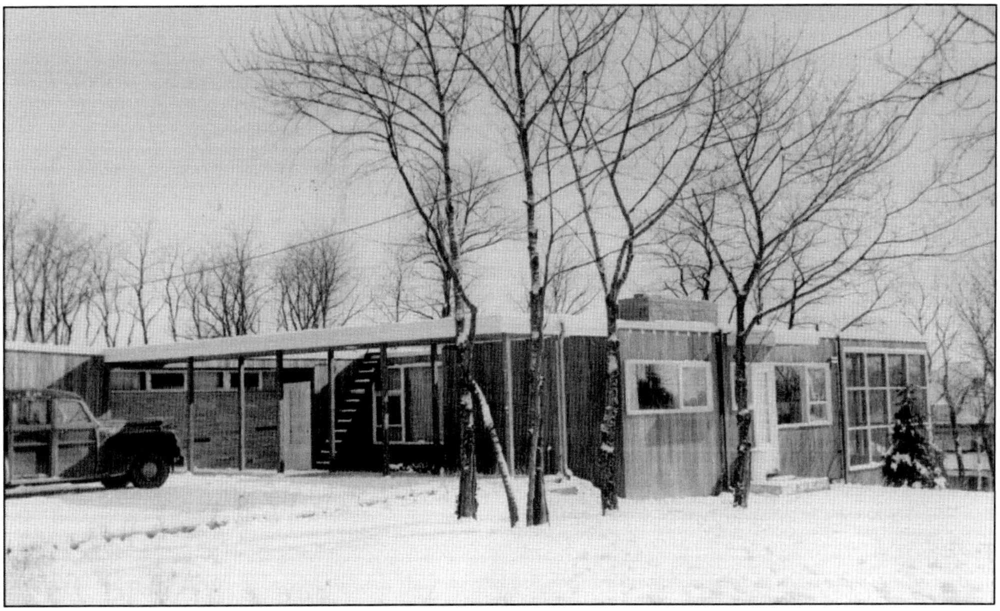

Selman Waksman built this Contemporary-style house at 16 Logan Lane c. 1950; it was designed by architect Henry Kibol. The house was at the 50-year benchmark for National Register of Historic Places listing and was eminently eligible for landmark status by association with Waksman, a figure with demigod stature in the Rutgers and Piscataway communities. While preservation efforts were being organized, the house was demolished by its owner in early 2001. An enormous house was under construction in the spring of 2001.

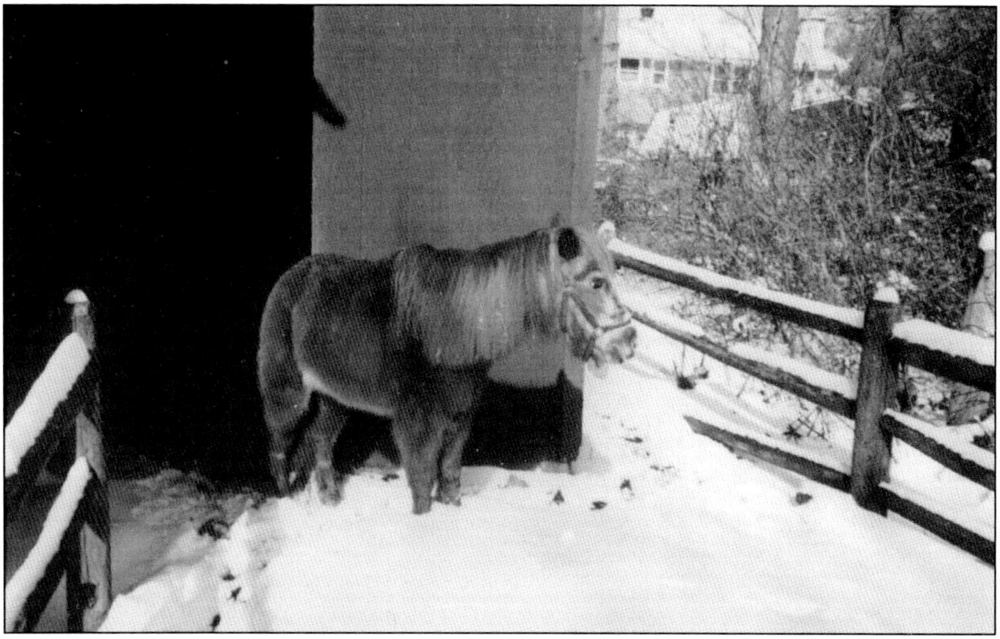

The horse Sugar symbolizes the transformation of a rural township into a developed one. Available for rides, she had been the neighborhood pet for 30 years. Sugar even merited an exemption when horses were banned in the developing areas. Owned by Bob and Sue Lachenmayer, Sugar was widely mourned when she died in 1996 at age 35.

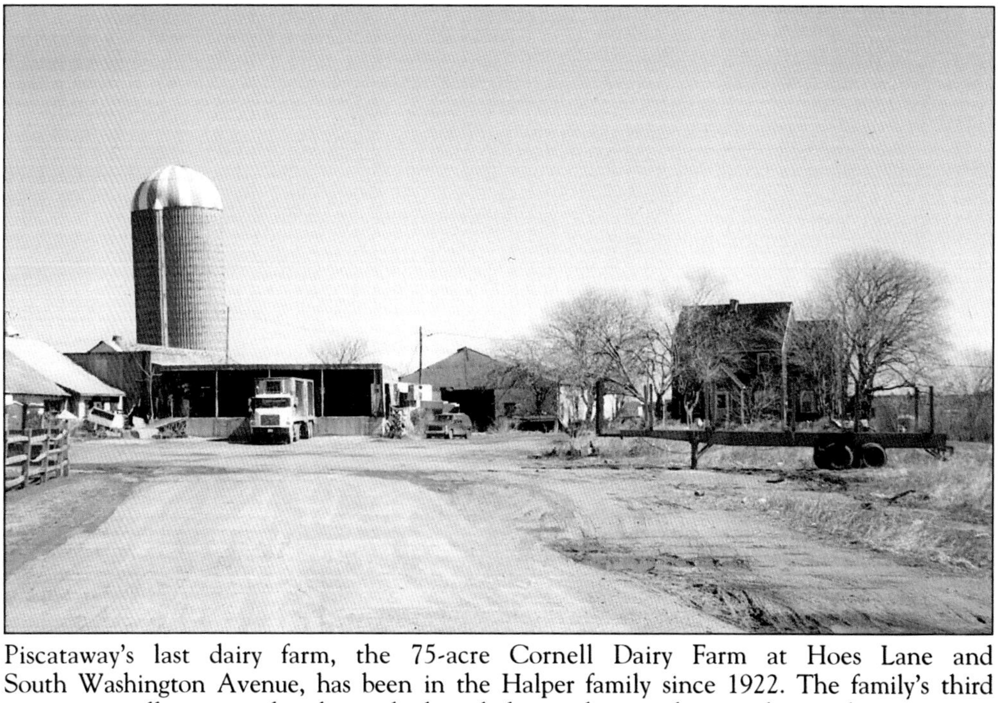

Piscataway's last dairy farm, the 75-acre Cornell Dairy Farm at Hoes Lane and South Washington Avenue, has been in the Halper family since 1922. The family's third generation still operates the place, which includes a riding academy and a retail operation in the building on the left. According to news accounts, the township desires the farm for a park and has threatened an eminent domain acquisition as the owners aim to continue farming.

Three

Business

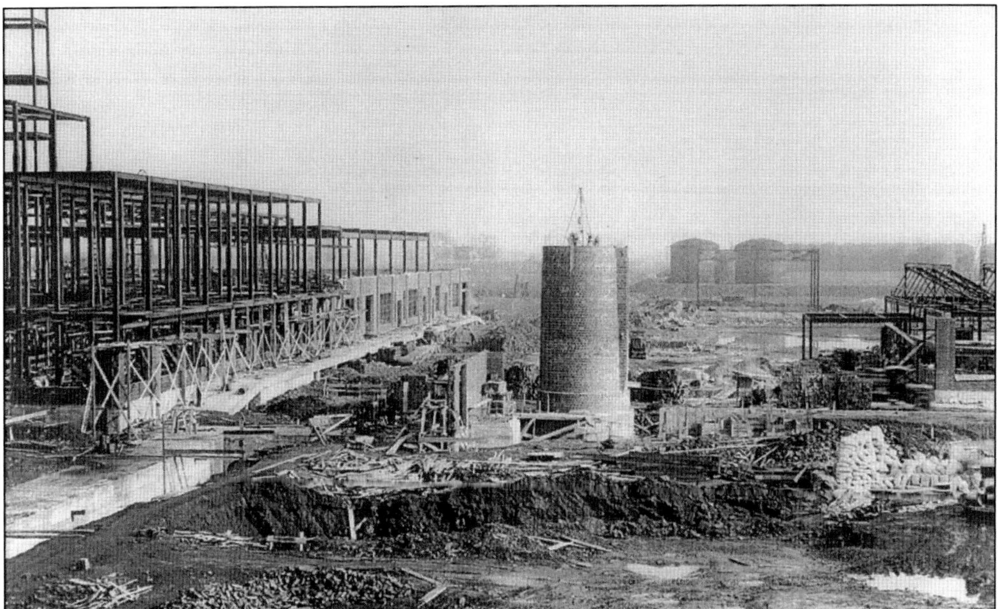

The Bakelite Corporation (pages 68 and 69), having outgrown its original Perth Amboy and other factories in the 1920s, acquired property on the northern stem of River Road in 1929 and began construction of a massive plant that became the township's major employer. The factory was designed by Francisco & Jacobus, New York engineers and architects, and was built by the Karno Smith Company of Trenton, New Jersey. This construction scene is dated November 1930. The image centers on the massive chimney that became a major local landmark. The facility, completed in 1932, became known as the Bound Brook plant for the better-known postal town nearby. (Courtesy of Union Carbide Corporation.)

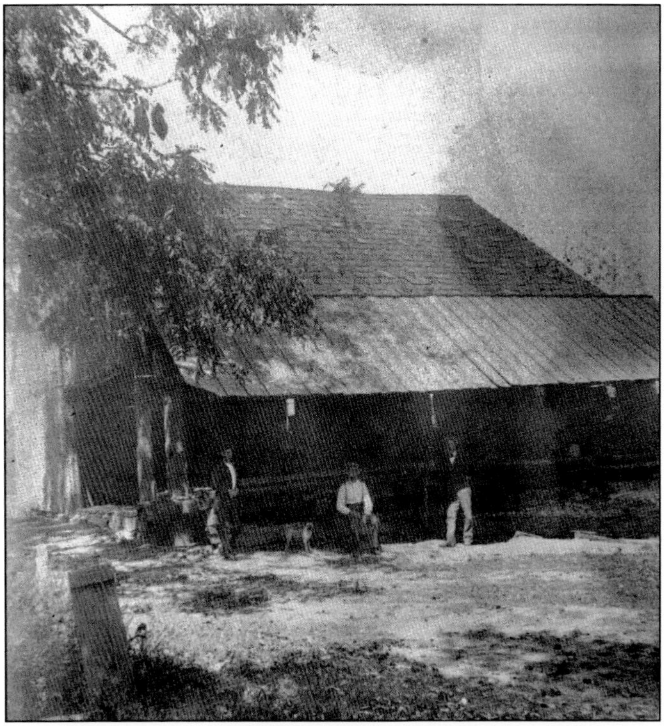

This late-19th-century photograph of Martin's Distillery is in a Piscataway collection, but the place appears to have been located in Piscatawaytown, now in Edison Township. The pressing of apples for cider and the distilling of much of it was an operation local to the growing areas, by necessity in view of the cost and difficulty of inland transportation. If New Jersey had a state beverage, the leading candidate would be apple jack, the proverbial Jersey Lightnin'. The industry became centralized in time and few producers survived the Prohibition era. (Rutgers Special Collections and University Archives.)

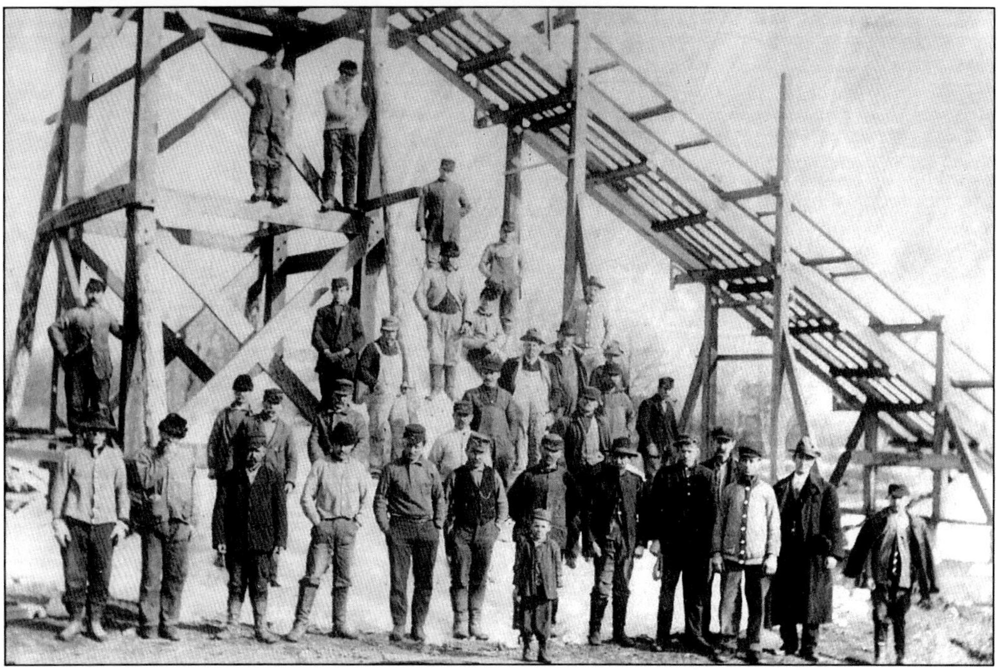

The Raritan Ridge Clay Company was likely located in Edison Township on the Lehigh Valley Railroad, which ran a branch from New Market, through Edison and Metuchen, to Perth Amboy. The seasonal ice-cutting crew reflected only a fraction of the activity of this major firm, one that employed a reported 130 people a few years after this c. 1912 photograph was taken. (Collection of the Piscataway Public Library.)

The ice on this unidentified pond was often 10 to 20 inches thick. It was typically cut in 22-by-32-inch blocks. The principal products of the Raritan Ridge Clay Company, however, were terra-cotta and fire clay ceramics. Secession activists attempting to organize Raritan Township in 1870 sought to rid themselves of the claybank clique. The connection with the image is tenuous, but the suggestion of political power by the interests of clay and its related industries is real. (Collection of the Piscataway Public Library.)

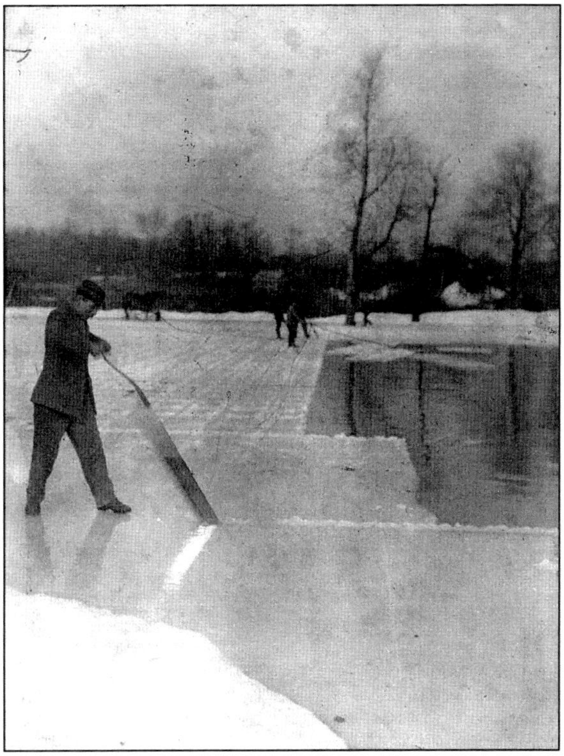

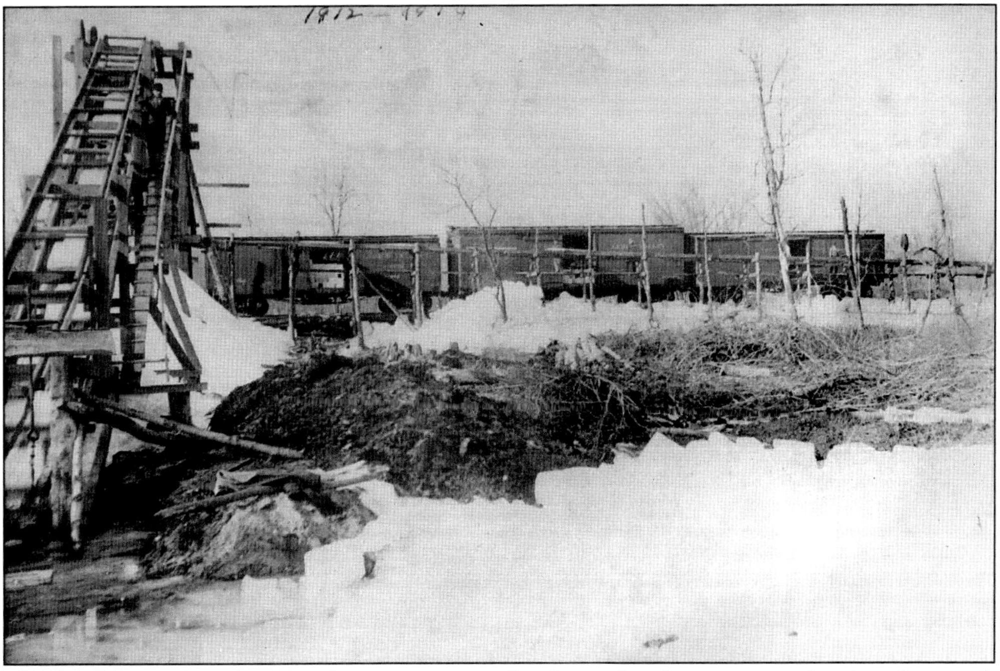

The loading operation pictured opposite is made clearer by this image embracing the pond, conveyor, and the Lehigh Valley boxcars. Obviously, the railroad was close to the pond. An annotation on the original c. 1912 photograph indicates the wholesale price was then 35¢ per ton. The loading schedule totaled 15 cars per day. (Collection of the Piscataway Public Library.)

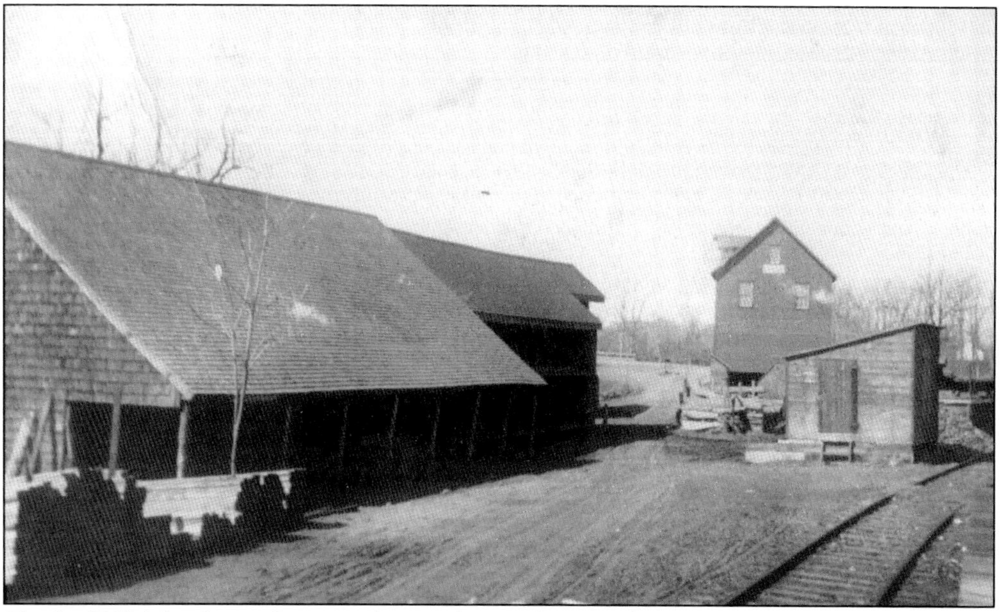

Charles Kelly's lumberyard, pictured *c.* 1905 on a photographic postcard, was located along the Prospect Avenue stem between the railroad and William Street. The rail siding was a virtual necessity for bringing in heavy building material supplies. The locale of the long-gone business is likely indicated by the siding tracks that now disappear into a vacant lot on the east side of Prospect Avenue. (Collection of Cynthia Harris.)

The Bound Brook is dammed at New Market Road, forming New Market Pond, a site identified in early documents as the King George Grant. A milling operation had existed there since Colonial times. The dam was wrecked by ice in December 1910 and was rebuilt the next year. The postcard image dates from that period, although it is not ascertained if this is the new or old dam. The building on the far right, once the site of the fire bell tower seen on page 88, no longer stands; its lot is the site of Columbus Park. The buildings to its left, now facing Lakeview Avenue, survive, but an old photograph indicates they were once perpendicular to the street. The small building in the rear is a former icehouse. (Collection of Cynthia Harris.)

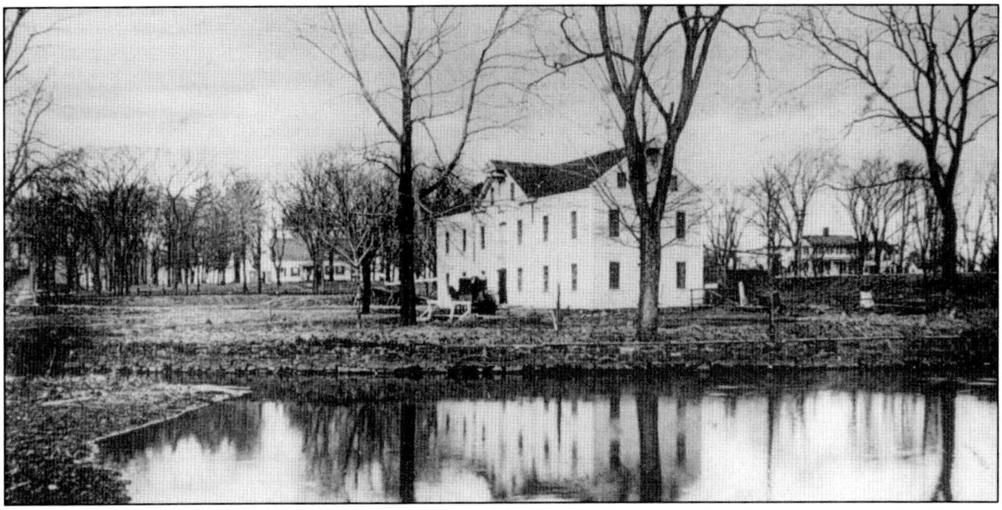

The New Market Roller Mills were on the north shore of the pond, a location near the former Lehigh Valley Railroad tracks. The mill occupied a *c.* 1860 building that was originally an oakum factory, a plant that treated hemp or jute for use in ship caulking. This *c.* 1910 postcard also shows the old, still-standing Vail cottage at 576 Sherwood Drive, left of the mill, and the no-longer-standing Mahlon Vail house right of it. The mill building was later expanded, as is visible below. (Collection of Cynthia Harris.)

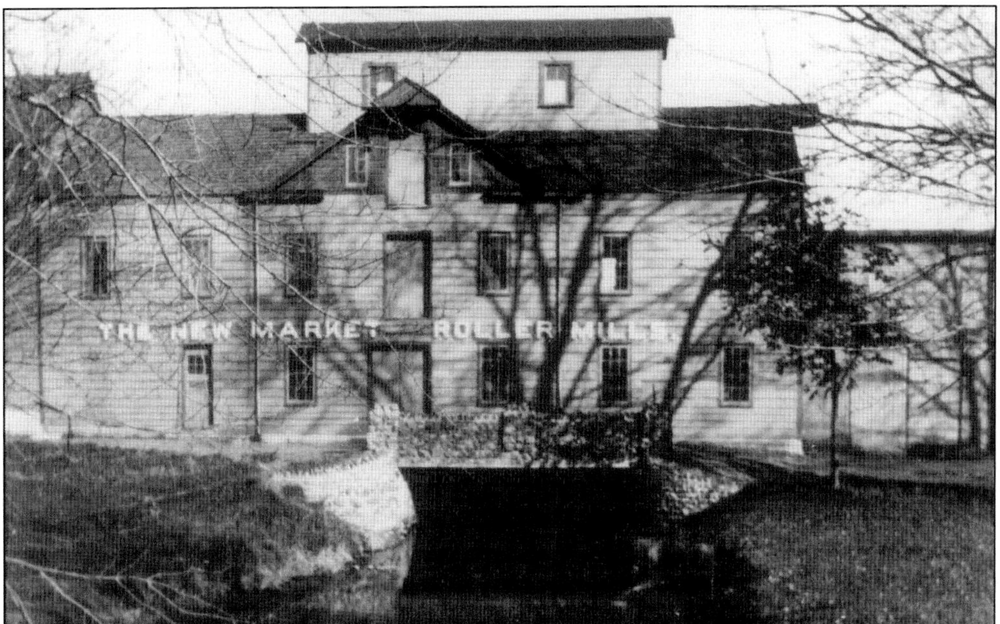

The mill passed through various owners prior to its 1919 acquisition by George T. Van Boskerck & Son and partners. They expanded the building to four stories and operated the business under the name Middlesex Milling Company. The mill and considerable finished product were lost in a spectacular blaze on the night of February 14, 1924. The mill was not rebuilt, but smaller structures on the site were used by a number of businesses. The place was known in the recent past as Baird's Farm Supply, a business started by brothers Clifford and Walter Baird in 1948 and sold by the former's widow, Eleanor, in 1980. (Collection of the Metlar House.)

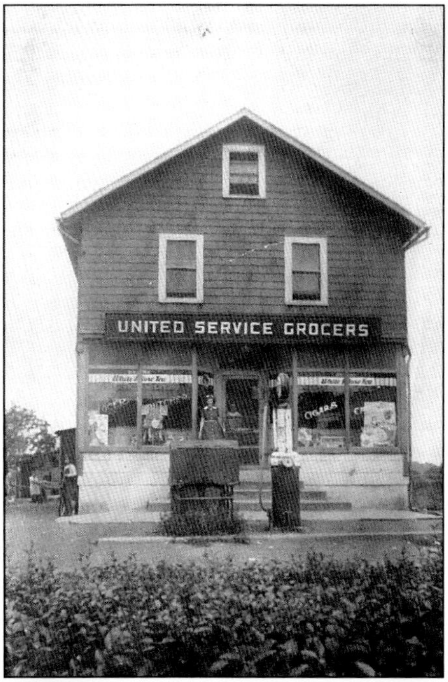

Hanko's United Service Grocers store at 415 Plainfield Avenue is pictured in 1937, reminiscent of a time when many small neighborhood grocers accounted for a fair share of the retail food trade. Hanko also owned a bus that he operated for school service. The building is entirely residential now, its contours, stairs, and above-grade windows instantly recognizable. The storefront windows were rebuilt to a dwelling type; the mid-block gas pump is long gone. (Collection of the Piscataway Public Library.)

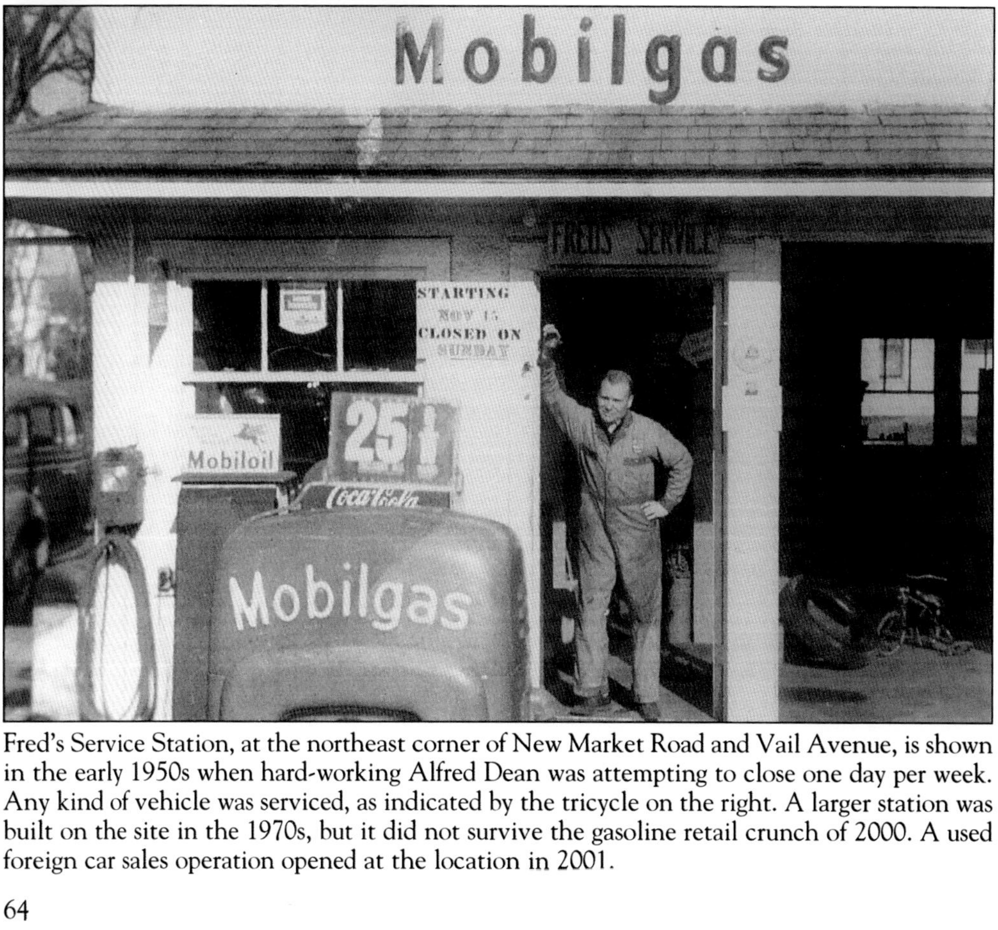

Fred's Service Station, at the northeast corner of New Market Road and Vail Avenue, is shown in the early 1950s when hard-working Alfred Dean was attempting to close one day per week. Any kind of vehicle was serviced, as indicated by the tricycle on the right. A larger station was built on the site in the 1970s, but it did not survive the gasoline retail crunch of 2000. A used foreign car sales operation opened at the location in 2001.

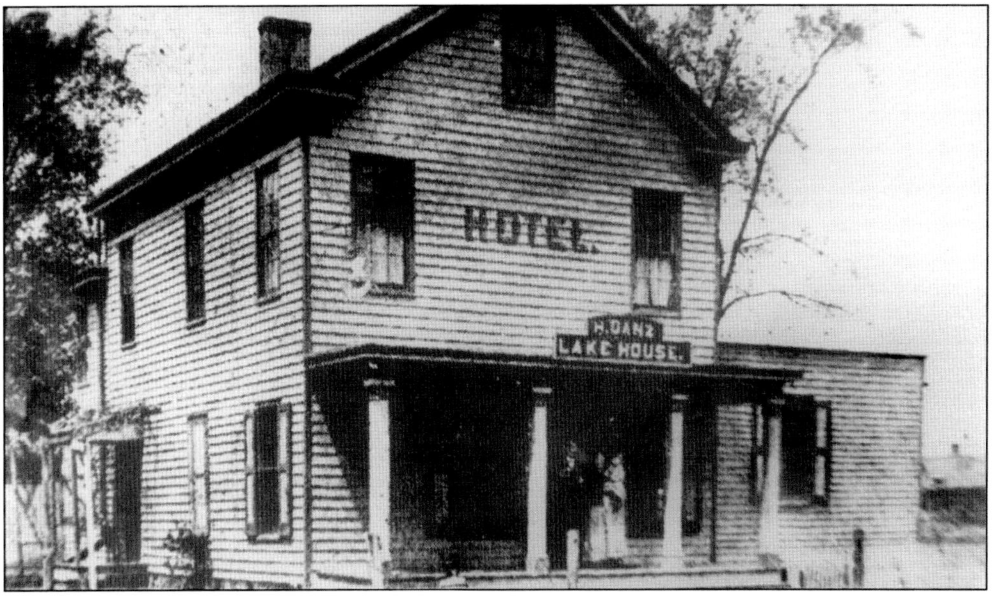

The Lake House, located at the northwest corner of William Street and New Market Road opposite the dam (page 62), appears to date from about the mid-19th century. Pictured around the 1890s, the hotel had various names and many owners. It received its greatest notoriety in August 1895, when William Darling shot and killed Harry Dunham (also known by his birth name, Harry Hardy) apparently over an insignificant argument. Darling was never apprehended and was believed to have died in a Pennsylvania penitentiary two years after the New Market crime. The hotel, destroyed by fire on March 21, 1952, was replaced by the present structure, which has been occupied by various establishments, including the Bull in 2001.

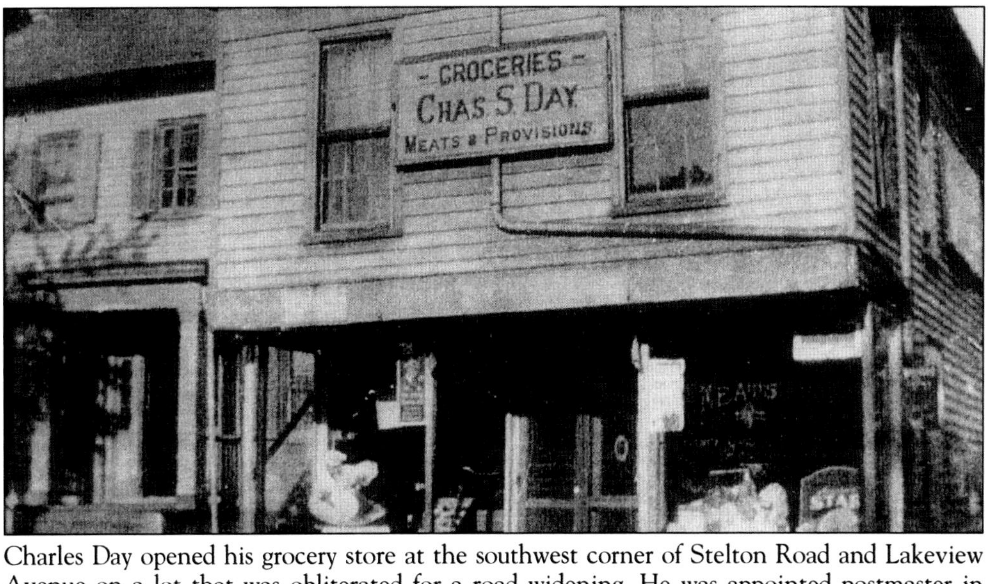

Charles Day opened his grocery store at the southwest corner of Stelton Road and Lakeview Avenue on a lot that was obliterated for a road widening. He was appointed postmaster in 1898, keeping the post office in the store, which effectively became a town center. Day's career in Piscataway was notable not only for the respect he commanded and the positions he held but also for becoming the first person not from an ancient township family to have earned this degree of esteem.

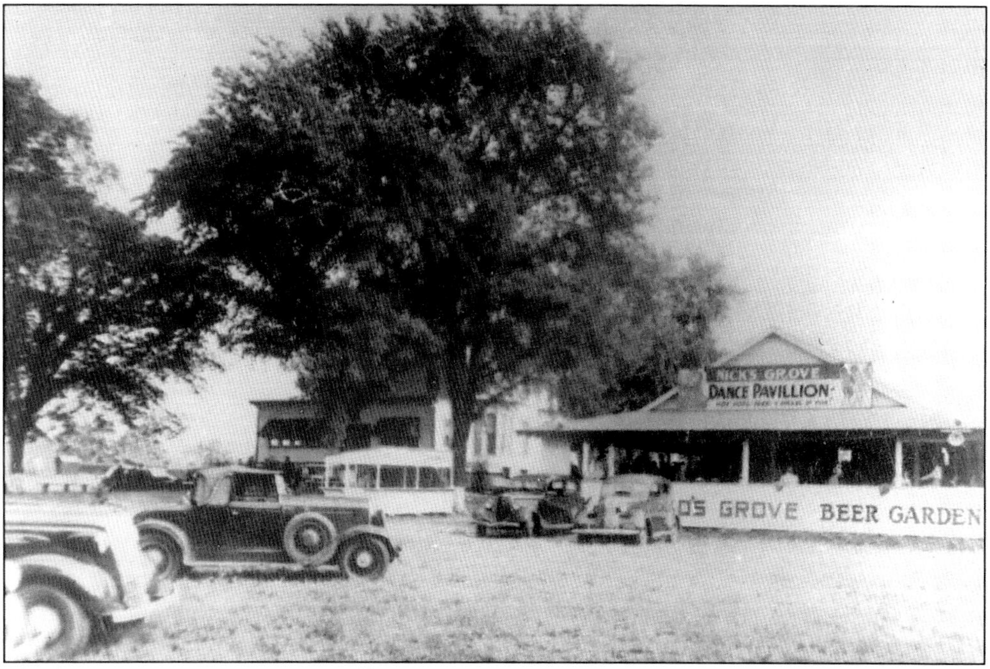

The former Roma Farm at 318 William Street was converted to a restaurant-bar. This pavilion was built behind the large house on the left, identified on the 1876 Evarts and Stewart *Atlas of Middlesex County* as owned by C.B. Heydon, a real estate developer.

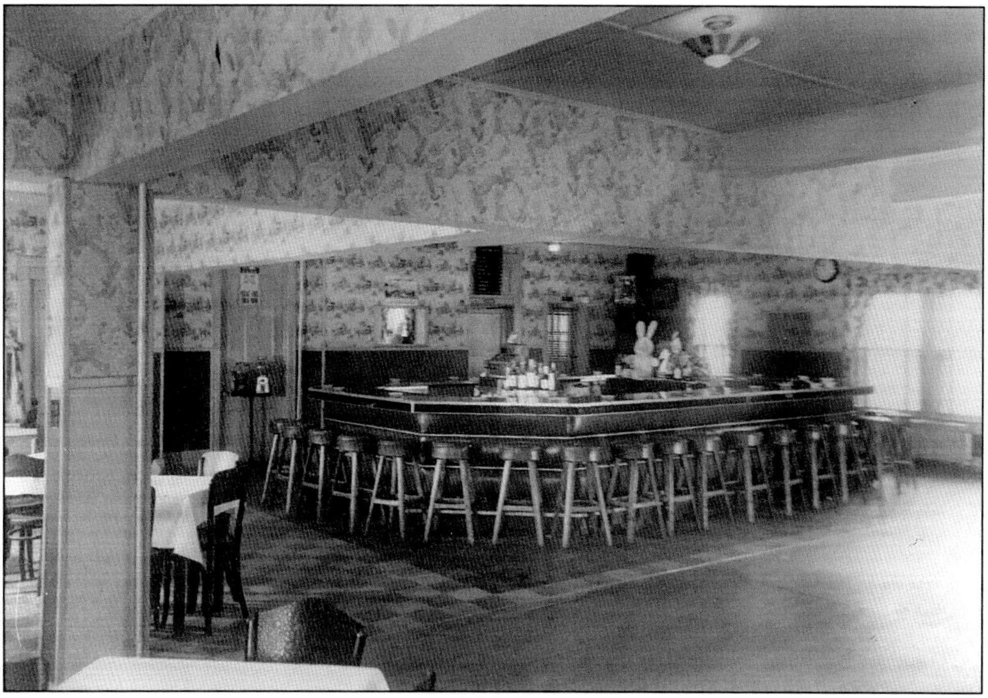

The bar, inside the house, underwent minor modifications over the years. The place endured through 2000, well-known as Bobby and Mary's, but plans for housing are currently in an advanced state.

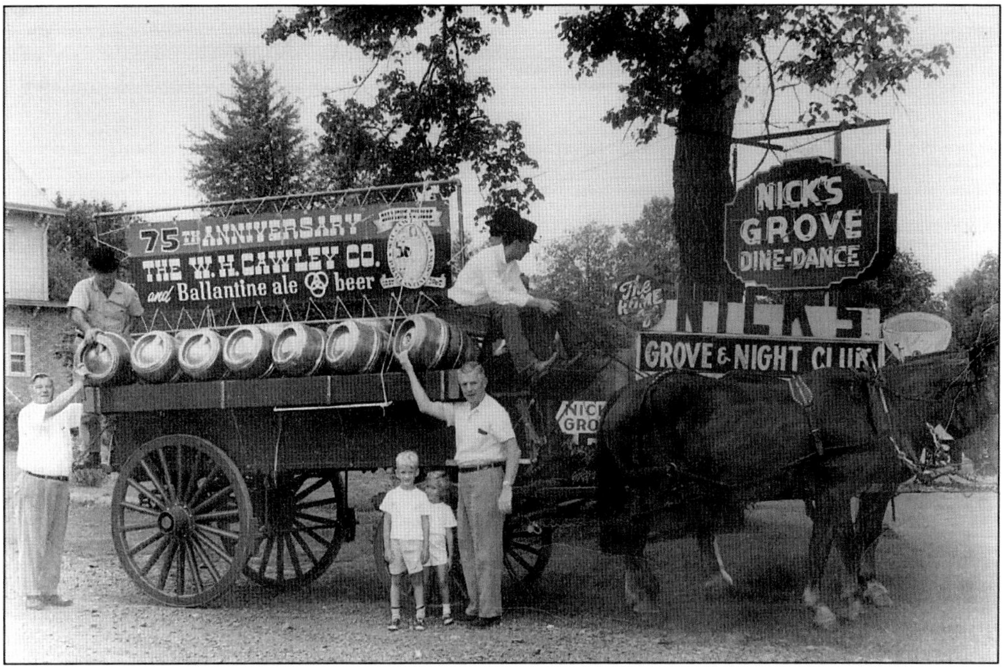

Nick Firdirko owned Nick's Grove from 1932 to 1988, at first leasing out the premises until he secured an early repeal liquor license. A local distributor uses a historical guise to celebrate his diamond anniversary. The Grove also had playing fields, including a baseball diamond; it attracted an active patronage from Camp Kilmer.

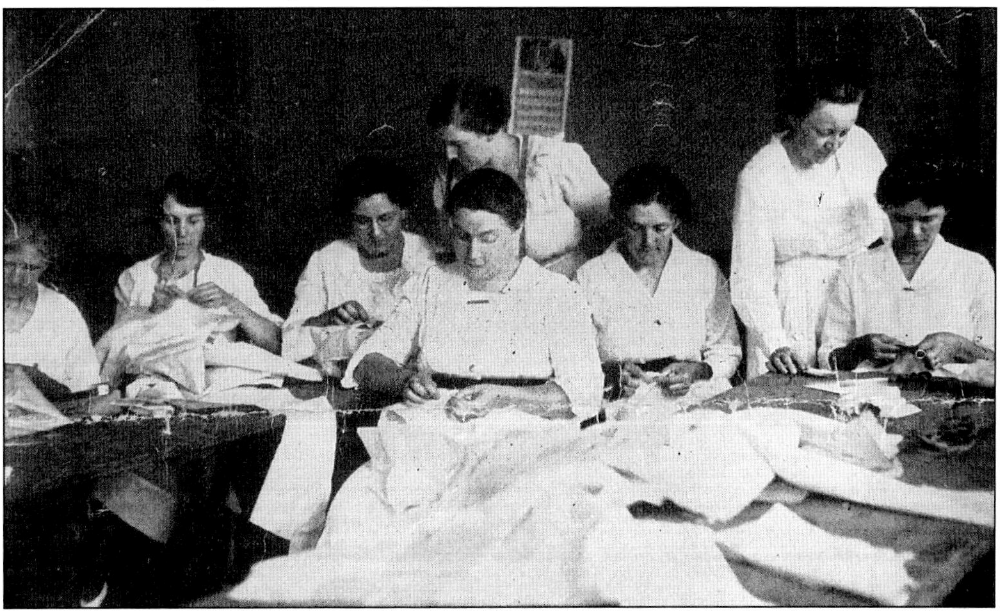

This rare, previously printed image may have been a promotional picture for a small, local business. The caption on the original says, "Permanent patterns for Randolphville," a Piscataway locality name in use by the third quarter of the 19th century. The women are, from left to right, as follows: ? Mitchell, Anna Fitzrandolph, Marjorie Witter, Marta Fitzrandolph (foreground), Edith Hadley (standing), ? Hunt, ? Wheeler, and ? Randolph.

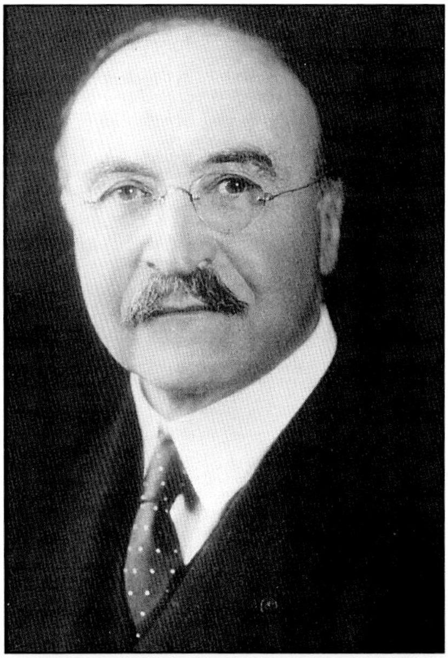

Dr. Leo H. Baekeland, born in 1863 in Belgium and a professor at the University of Ghent, immigrated to the United States in 1889, the year he married Celine Swarts. An early Baekeland discovery was Velox photographic paper, which revolutionized the industry. His sale of his work to the Eastman Kodak Company made him financially independent, permitting extended research activities. He began research of phenol-aldehyde reactions in Yonkers, New York, in 1905 and developed commercial uses for a new resinoid. In 1909, he announced his findings in controlling the phenol-formaldehyde process. Baekeland began commercial plastic manufacturing operations, forming the General Bakelite Company in a leased plant in Perth Amboy, New Jersey. The company was reorganized after a 1922 merger into the Bakelite Corporation. Baekeland was an inventive genius, holding some 400 patents. He died at age 80 in 1944. (Courtesy of Union Carbide Corporation.)

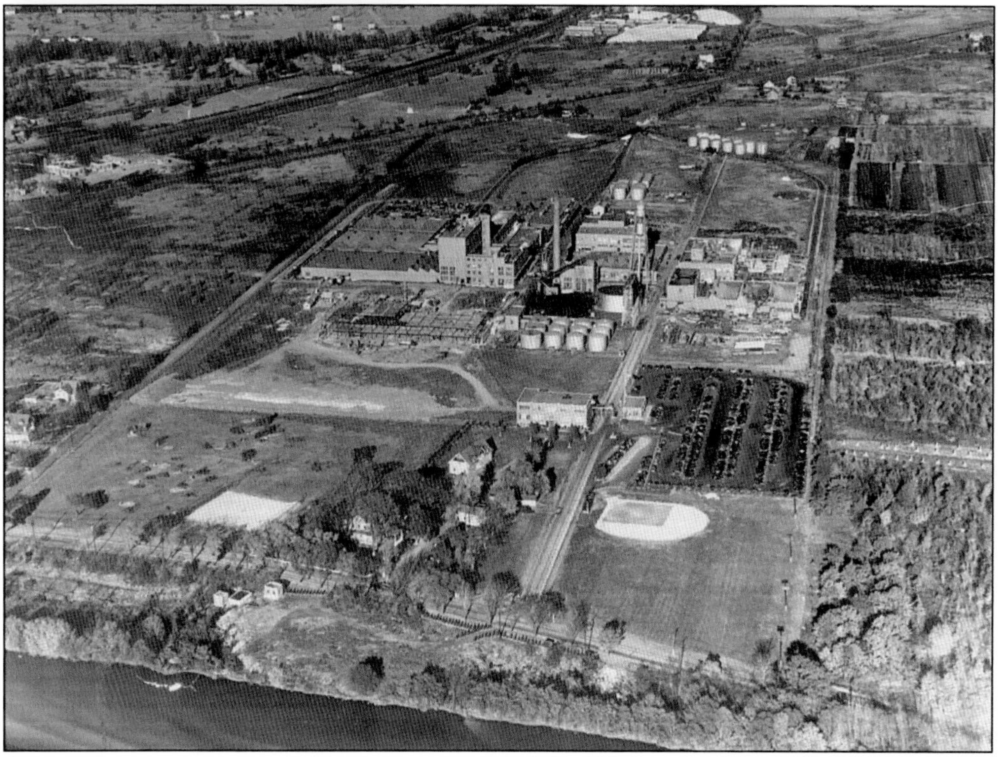

Union Carbide acquired the Bakelite Corporation in 1939 for 187,500 shares of stock. Bakelite complemented their plastics lines and provided an outlet for Union Carbide's resins. Each structure in the page 59 construction scene is visible in the growing plant pictured in this 1940 aerial, which also shows the plant's proximity to the river and railroad. That is a key year for dating Bakelite pictures, since construction was begun on a second stack and a new building to house urea molding material. (Courtesy of Union Carbide Corporation.)

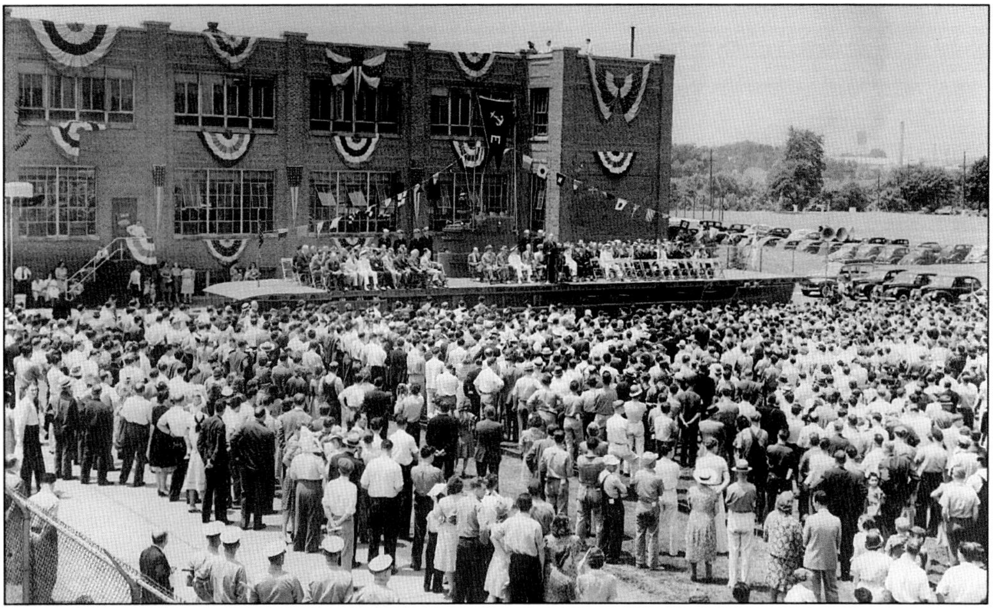

The U.S. Navy Department awarded Bakelite their coveted E Award (given for excellence in service and productivity), entitling them to fly the E pennant, seen hanging over the second story of Building 71 during an E Day celebration on June 19, 1942. Notice the extraordinary temporary stage, a 94-foot-long, one-eighth scale model of the aircraft carrier *Yorktown*. It was made of plywood, a product using phenolic resins, and painted gray. The Piscataway plant received its sixth E Award in 1945. (Courtesy of Union Carbide Corporation.)

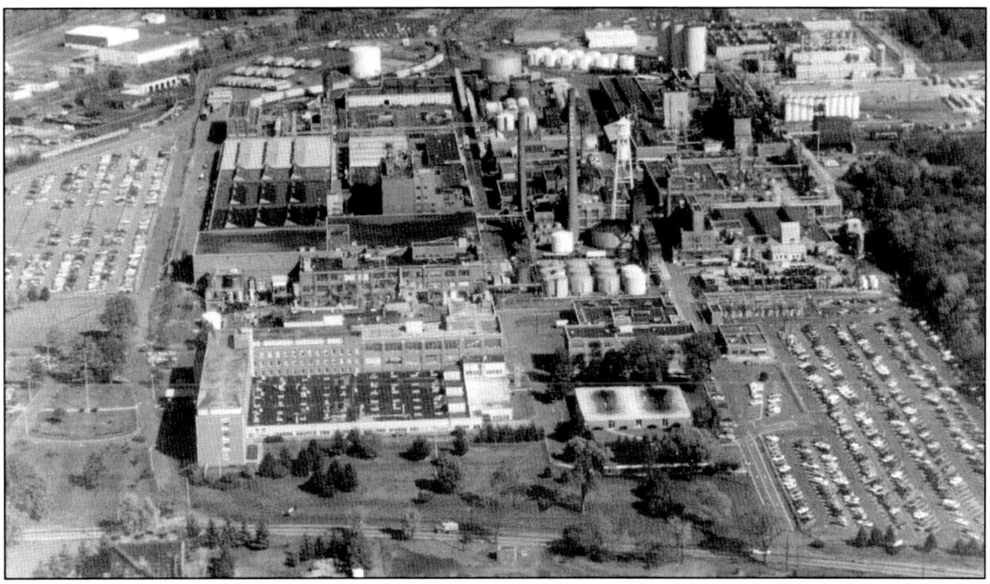

The plant has been expanded many times, evidenced by comparing this photograph from the recent past with the one opposite. A major research center was begun in 1955, and a data center was added in 1963. As product mix changed, new manufacturing buildings were erected. The Swayze farmhouse, visible opposite in the foreground, was demolished in 1951. Demolition of the 225-foot-tall chimney is scheduled in 2001. Union Carbide merged with Dow Chemical in 2000. (Courtesy of Union Carbide Corporation.)

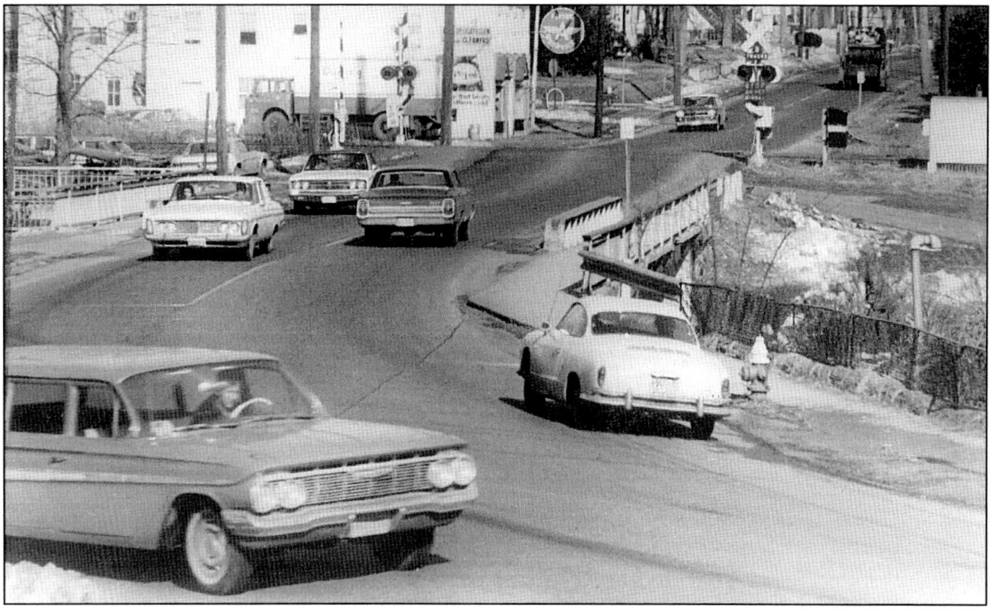

The bridge over the Bound Brook is pictured in this early-1960s image looking north on New Market Road. The plate girder span built in 1921 has been replaced. The shops on the left between the railroad and Union Avenue are contained in a structure that may date from the 19th century. The gas pumps are gone, but a garage is still in the rear, on the Union Avenue side. Above it is a partial view of 478 New Market Road. (Rutgers Special Collections and University Archives.)

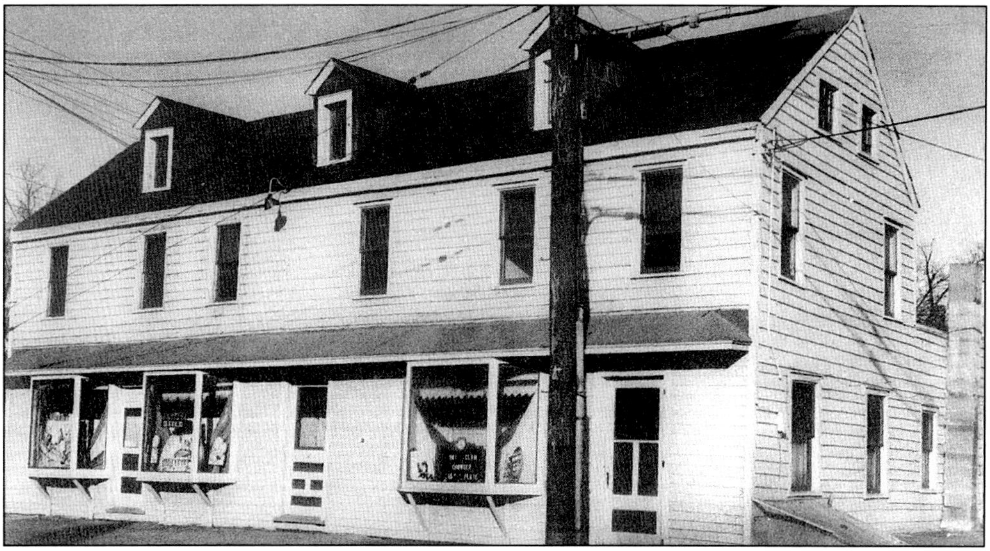

The tavern-hotel at 1 Stelton Road may have dated from Revolutionary times. It served as a town center when New Market was known as Quibbletown and as a stagecoach stop at other times. By the time of James Cawley's *c.* 1940 photograph, which appeared earlier in *Historic New Jersey in Pictures*, the building was altered to belie hints of its origins. It was known as the Hotel Nelson in the memory of present old-timers and as the Village Barn in the years prior to its 1960 demolition. It was replaced by a service station, the present occupancy of the lot at the southeast corner of Lakeview Avenue.

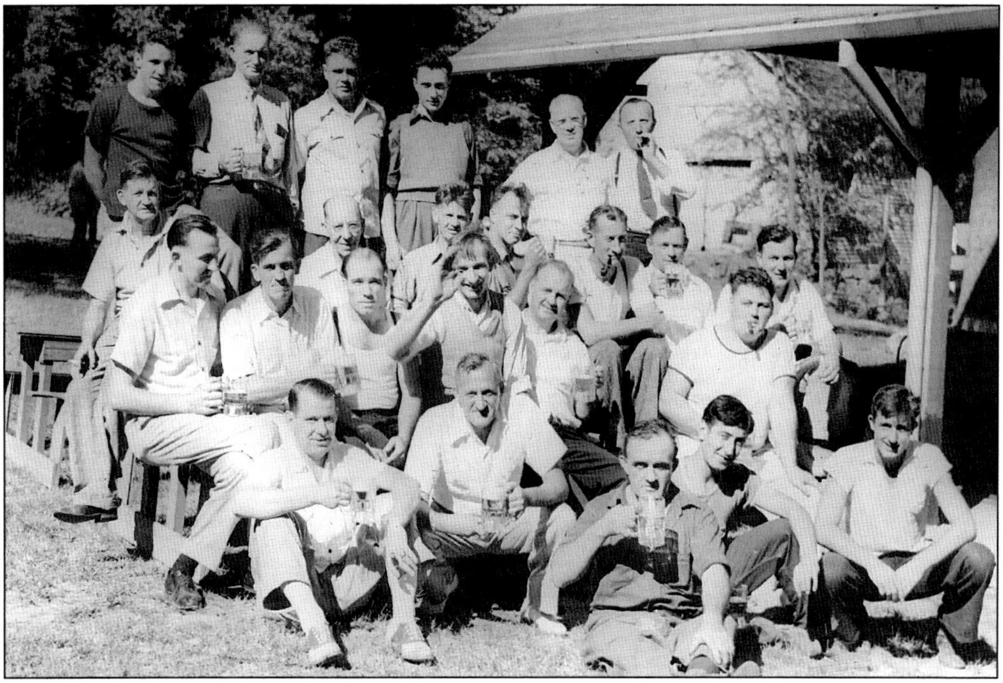

Arch C. Moore (first row, second from left) founded Moore's Trucking Company in 1918. He headed it until his death in 1942, when his widow, Lillian, took the reins for 22 years. From modest beginnings in Plainfield, the firm became a major regional carrier covering six mid-Atlantic states. The men are shown at a company picnic, perhaps *c.* 1940. When was the last time anyone wore a tie to such an event?

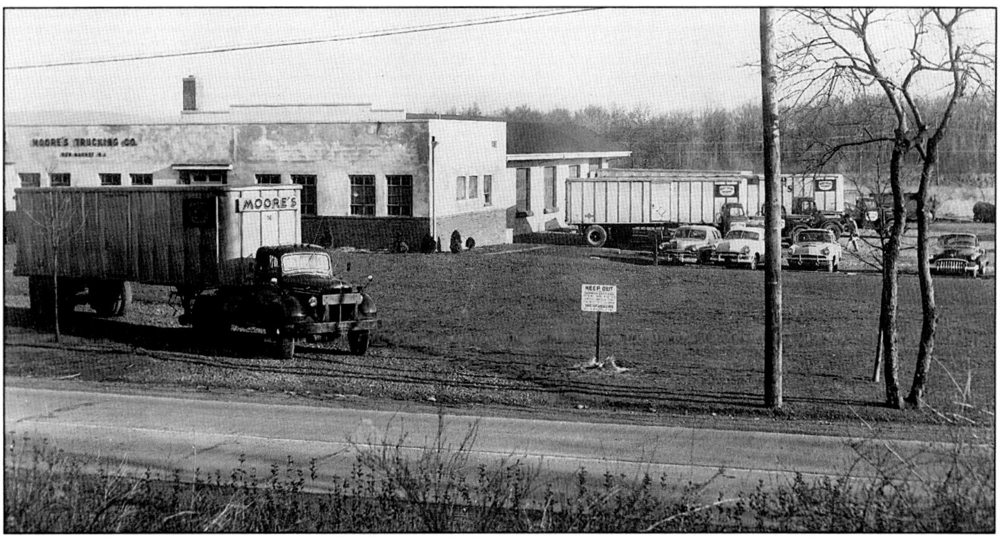

The company built this terminal in 1951 at 585 Stelton Road on the northeast corner of New Brunswick Road. A Camden location was opened in 1969. Four Moore sons later ran the growing business, but growth and profitability were marred by industry deregulation and high, fixed labor costs. Trucking operations closed in the mid-1990s; the property was sold in 1996 and the building demolished soon thereafter. A strip shopping center anchored by a large supermarket is now on the site.

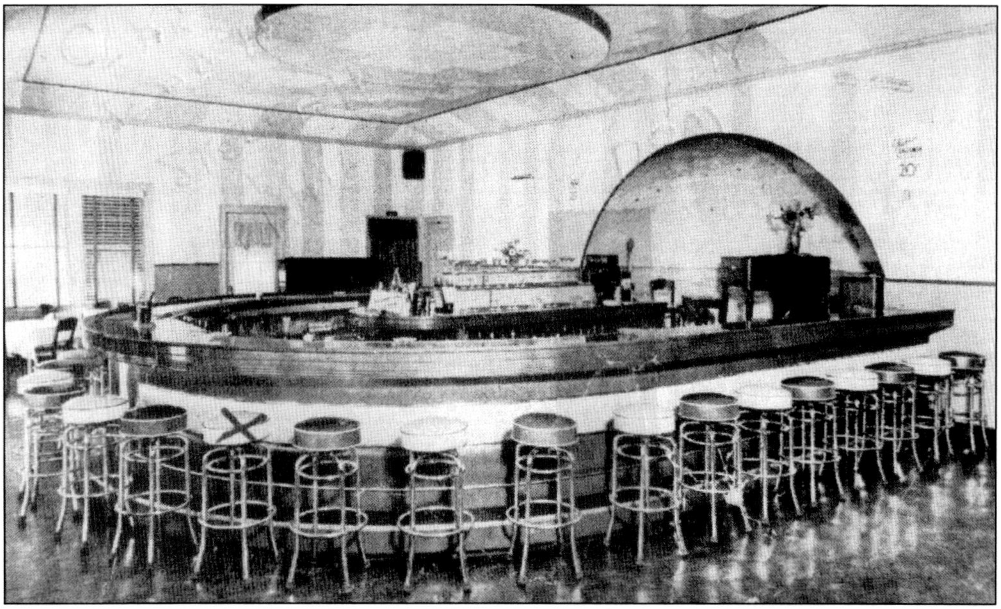

Louis Malang, who lost his Pilot Inn to fire in 1935, bought the Lake Nelson Community Club clubhouse that year. He moved the building to South Washington Avenue at the lake and opened the 9 O'Clock Club. Pictured on a 1930s postcard, the establishment (later the Carousel Lounge) was demolished perhaps *c.* 1990. The New Market area had an active role during Prohibition. One old-timer, Frederick Touzeau, claimed that "there were more stills in the New Market area than on any square mile in the world." However, a number of places would dispute that claim. (Collection of Cynthia Harris.)

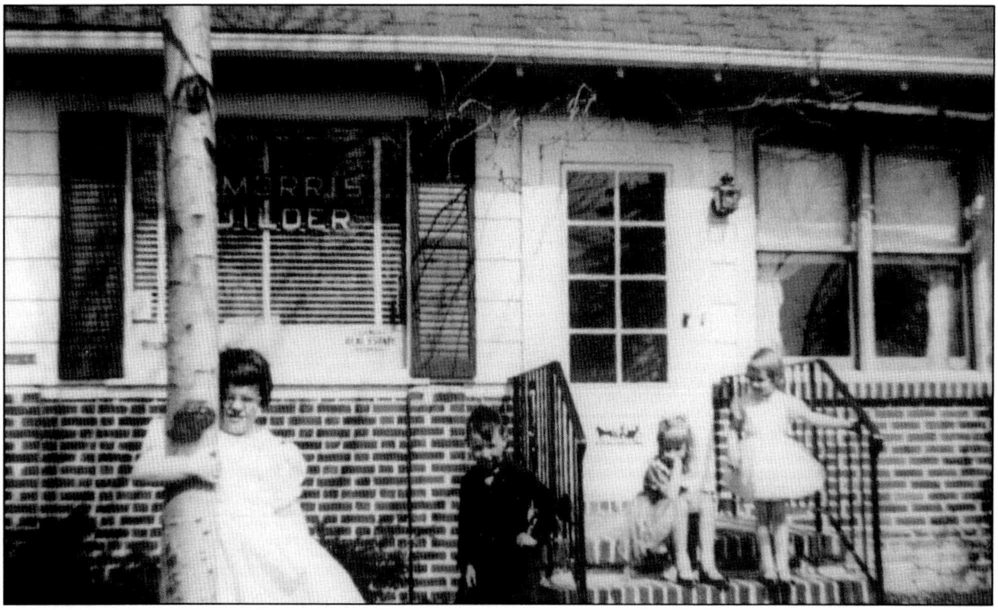

August Morris was a builder of note, maintaining an office and residence on Hoes Lane. The building was demolished in 1996, and the site is now a recreation area for the IEEE Building. Hanging out in 1950 are Barbara Mazuk, Jimmy Eberle, Betsy Williams, and Linda Williams. The three girls are Morris granddaughters.

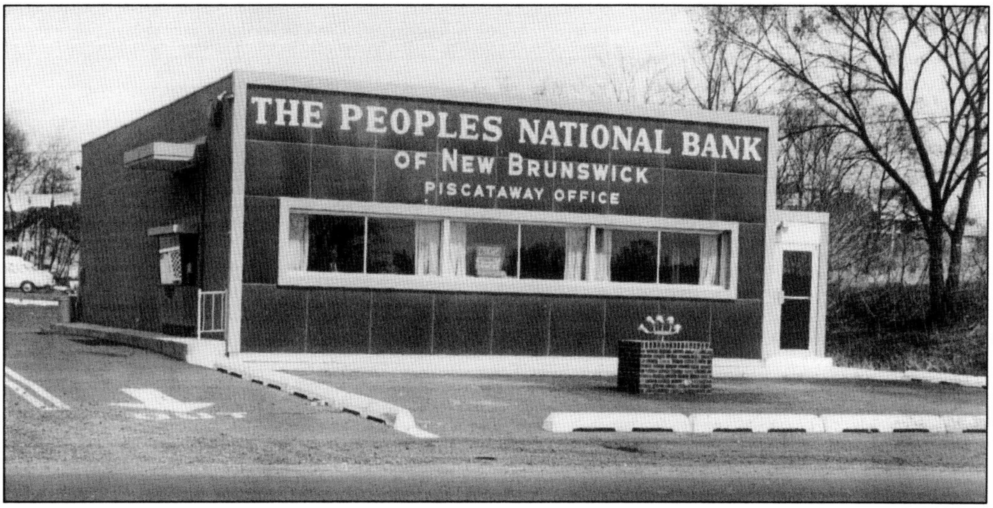

The practice of opening suburban branches by banks established in old towns and cities has characterized the business for at least four decades. The Peoples National Bank, which was founded in New Brunswick in 1887, opened this branch at 603 River Road in 1961. The building now houses a nail salon. However, the handsome facade, apparently of Carrara glass, has been covered with vinyl. (Rutgers Special Collections and University Archives.)

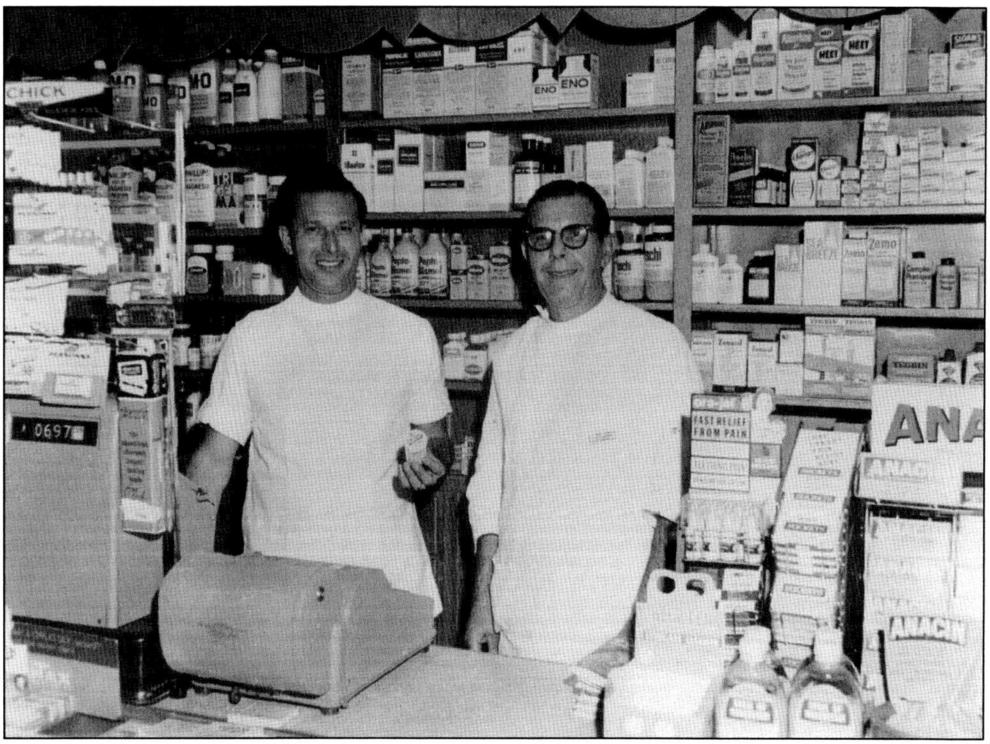

Bud Coopeman (left) and Pat Capone operated Piscataway's first and foremost pharmacy, Thrifty Drugs, at the corner of 7th Street and South Washington Avenue. They are pictured in 1965 in front of the indigestion remedy stock. One wonders if its placement in front of the cash register was coincidence or indicative of the times' critical health challenge. The shop is still a pharmacy, now part of the Eckerd chain. (Rutgers Special Collections and University Archives.)

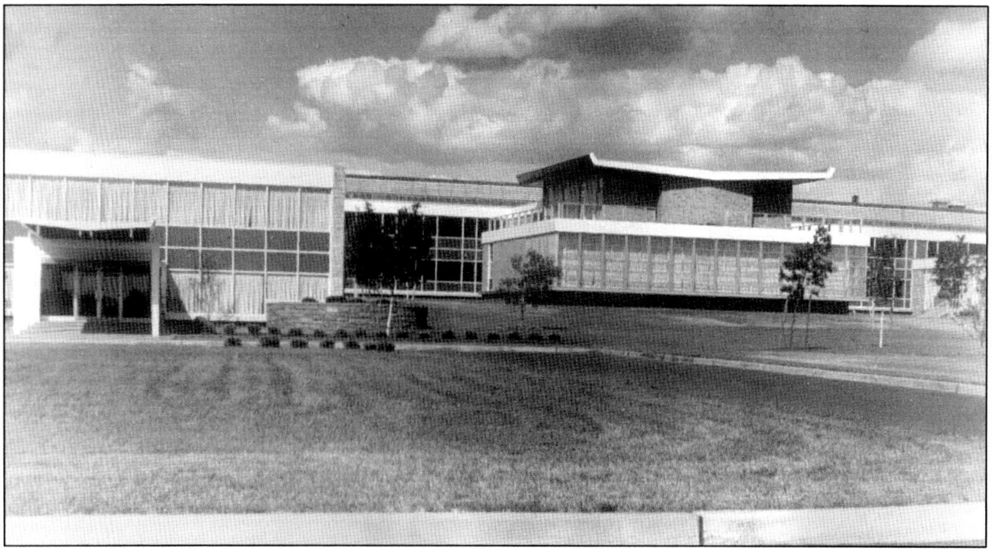

The Colgate-Palmolive Research Center, located at 909 River Road, opened in September 1962 for "fundamental chemical and biological investigations," or a research laboratory for many purposes. The building housed a unit of the Rutgers Medical School's Department of Microbiology for a period in the 1960s. This view of the new facility was altered by the construction of a major addition in front, on the right of the photograph. In addition, the entrance on the left was removed and the facade rebuilt.

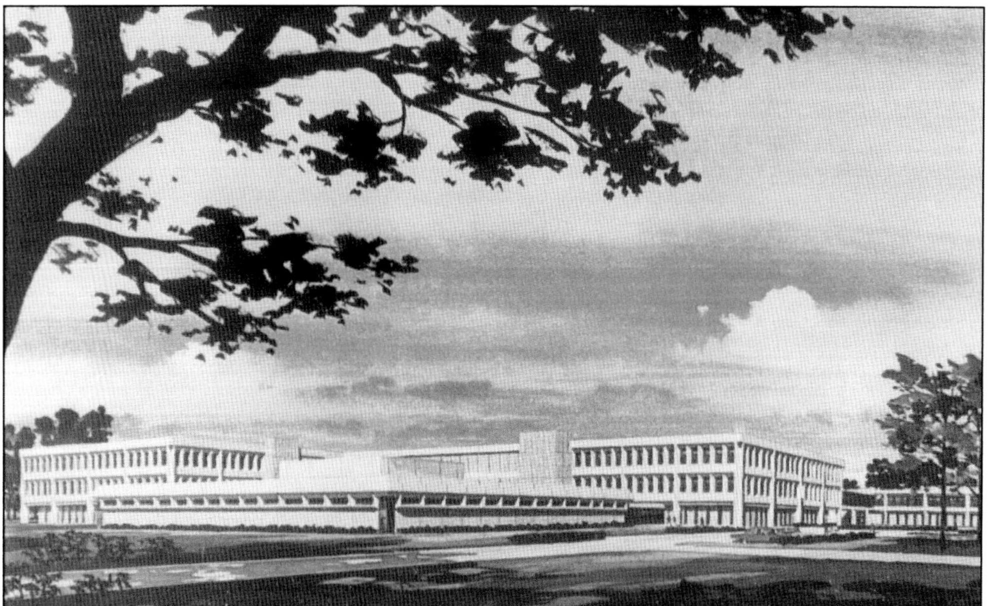

AT & T built this Raritan River Center complex at 444 Hoes Lane *c.* 1970 reportedly to house a stock recording operation. The site, pictured in an architect's rendering, has changed occupants and expanded. Telcordia, the successor to Bellcore, a spin-off of the breakup of AT & T, is the present occupant. A 12-story tower now stands on the site and a second tower is under construction. (Collection of Cynthia Harris.)

Four

Mind and Spirit

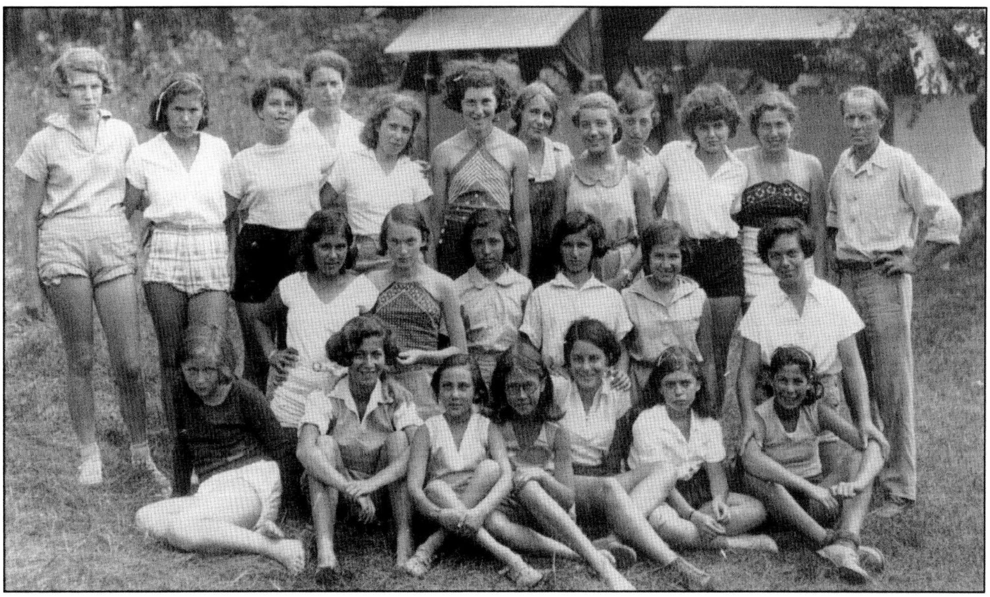

Spanish anarchist Francisco Ferrer's education theories gave rise to the modern school movement, the cause spurred by his execution in Barcelona in 1909. The Ferrer Modern School, founded in 1911 in New York City, moved its day school to School Street in the easternmost part of the township in 1915. The area was known as Stelton, named for the rail station in adjoining Edison (then Raritan) Township. The school's ethic embraced an appreciation of nature and the outdoors. These happy camper girls were part of their Pioneer Youth Camp; they are pictured *c.* 1930 with cofounder Alexis Ferm (right). (Rutgers Special Collections and University Archives.)

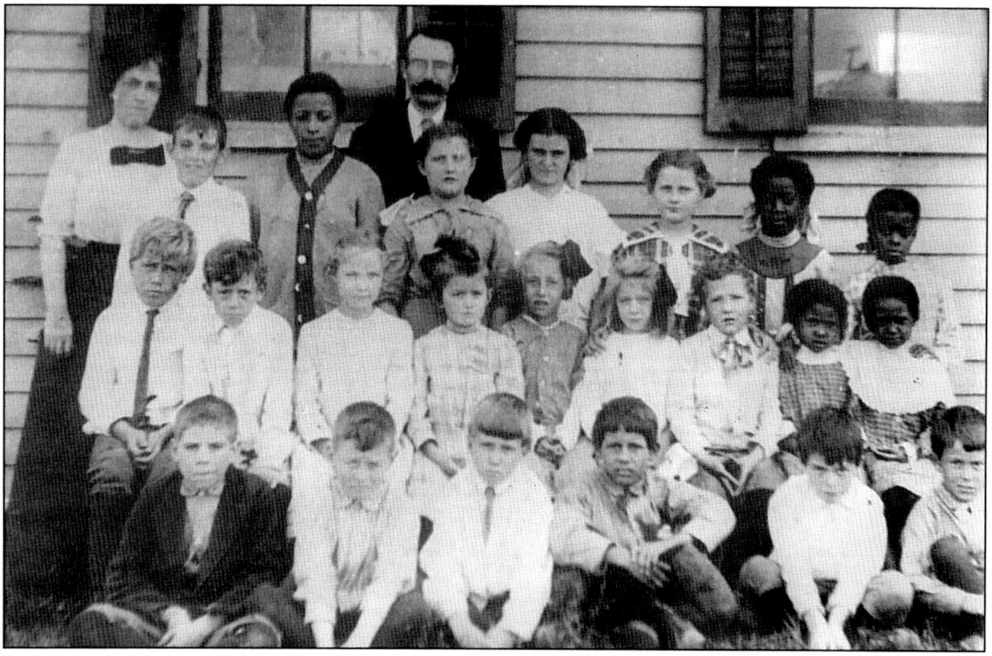

Union School, on Stelton Road near the future South Plainfield border, is pictured *c.* 1900 with an unidentified student body and principal W.F. Mets in the background. What was teacher Miss Blackford like? Ernie Day had her in the sixth grade and instantly recalled her as "a sassy bugger who would cut you short." She must have been good, as he admitted that later in life he appreciated her. The legend that students exhorted the principal to take them on outings by chanting, "Let's go Mets" is untrue. (Collection of the Piscataway Public Library.)

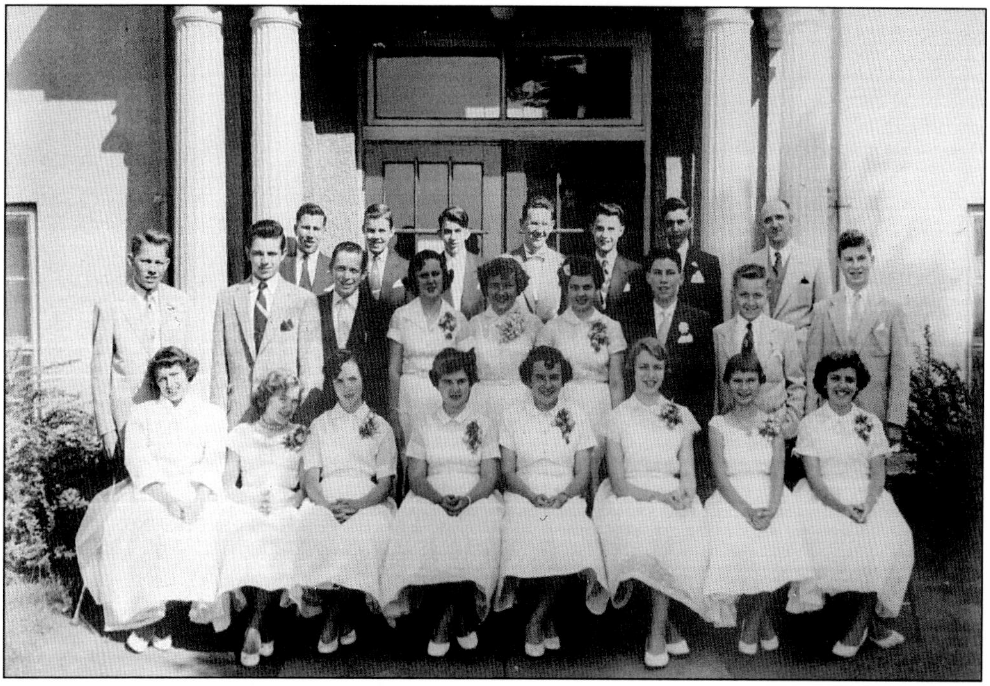

Arbor School in the mid-1950s produced a class of clean-cut, well-coifed graduates.

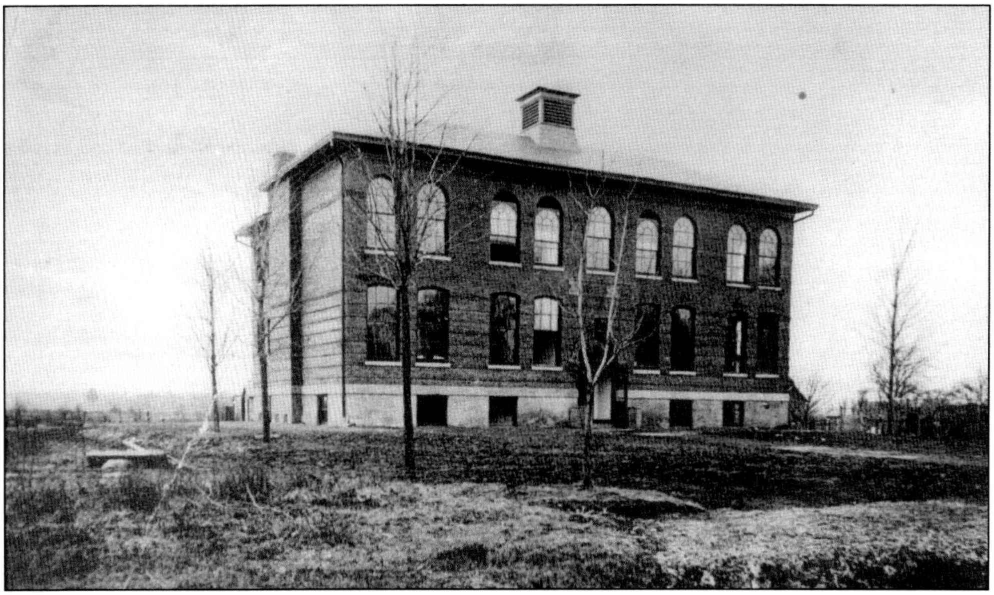

The third New Market School was built at 44 Stelton Road in 1905, replacing a structure destroyed by fire in 1903. It was, when constructed, a brick, two-story building containing six classrooms, an assembly room, and a board room. A four-room expansion was added in 1917. Pictured on a *c.* 1907 postcard, this school was destroyed by fire on January 29, 1929. Inadequate insurance and a pressing need to continue instruction challenged the township, but education was maintained by sending students to a number of nearby locations. (Collection of the Metlar House.)

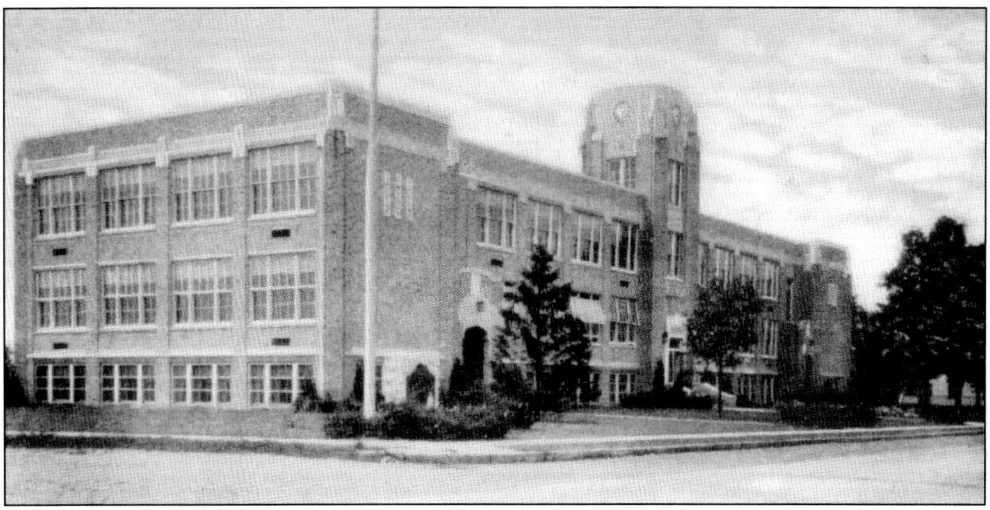

John Noble Pierson & Son, one of New Jersey's leading scholastic architects, designed this replacement school in the Collegiate Gothic style. Completed in 1930 on the same site, the building was dedicated on the evening of Friday, October 3, during which architect Aylin Pierson addressed a standing-room-only crowd. A parade on Saturday continued the festivities. Following the end of educational use around the 1970s, the building, pictured on a 1930s postcard, was remodeled to offices. Changes do not mar its recognition today; they include removal of the tower, replacement of windows, and the opening of a postal station in the southeast corner (behind the World War I monument). (Collection of Cynthia Harris.)

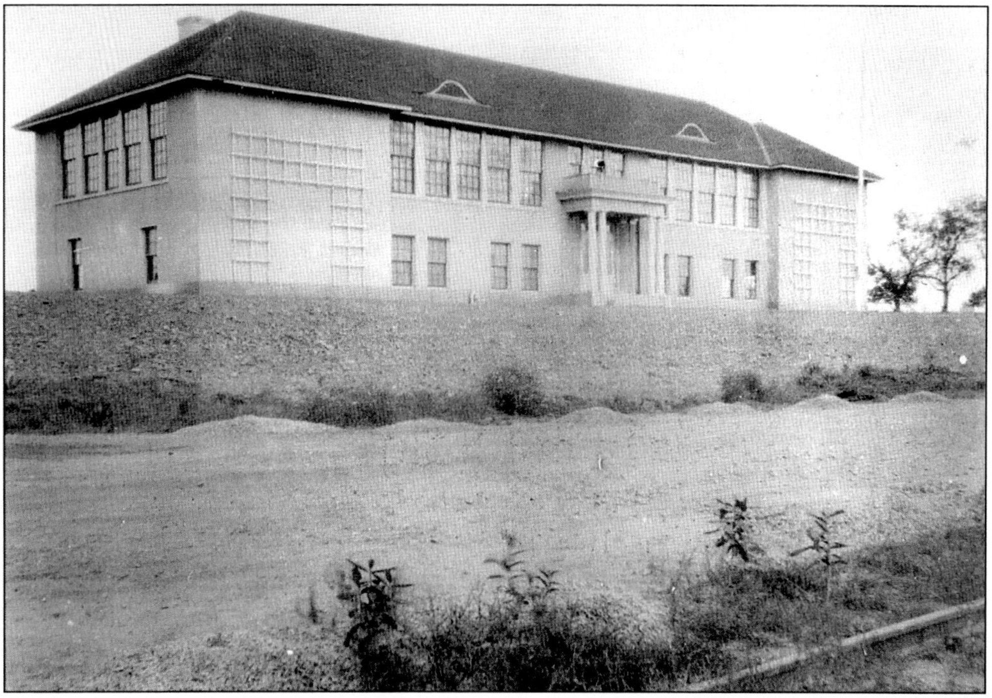

The Holmes Marshall School opened in 1923 at River Road and Park Avenue. The school—initially four rooms but later expanded—was named for a local man who was killed in France during World War I. Notice the River Road trolley tracks in the foreground. The stucco-clad building is now occupied as the Bright Beginners Learning Center. The trellises are gone, but the porch and eyebrow dormers remain.

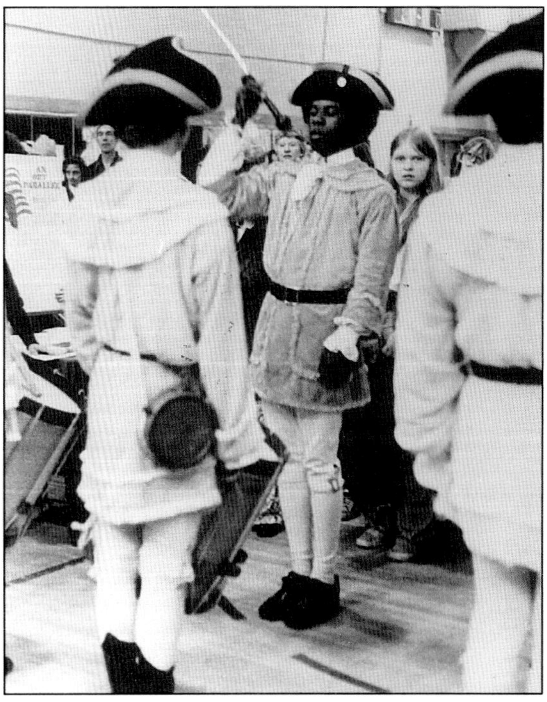

Drum major Michael Carr is pictured *c.* 1976 leading the Militia Fife and Drum Corps of the Piscataway High School Superchief Band. The award-winning group projected Colonial authenticity by their uniforms, instruments, and wood canteens. (Collection of the Piscataway Public Library.)

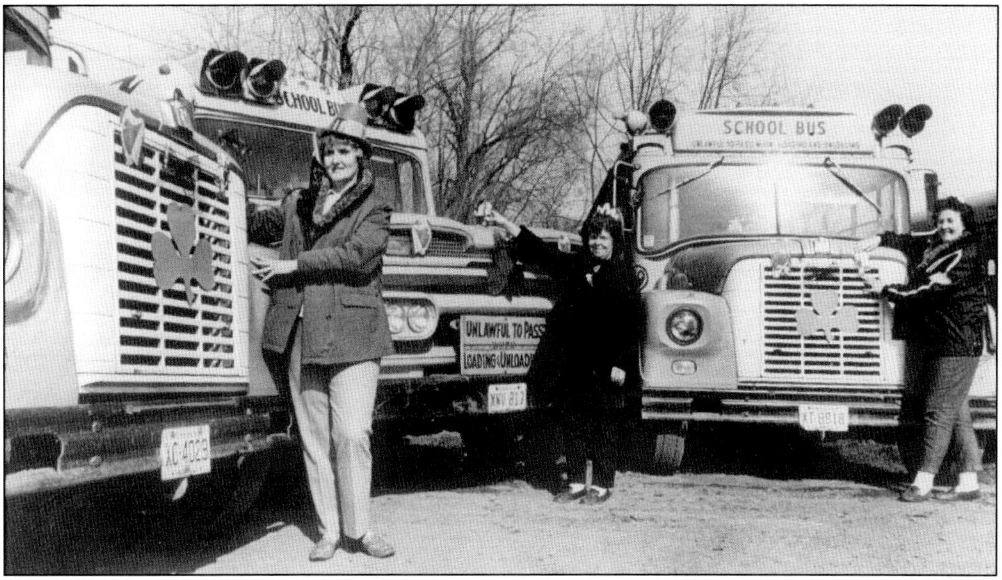

Three drivers for the Williams Bus Company pose before their decorated vehicles, obviously in the month of March, perhaps *c.* 1968. Williams started the business in 1917 with a horse and wagon equipped with bench seats. The firm peaked in the 1960s, running as many as 21 buses and terminated with the 1973 death of Wilbur Williams. Jeanette Fitzrandolph Duryea (right) preserved the image. She is pictured in front of her International, as is Connie Grabowski (left). Virginia Lowe poses with her Ford.

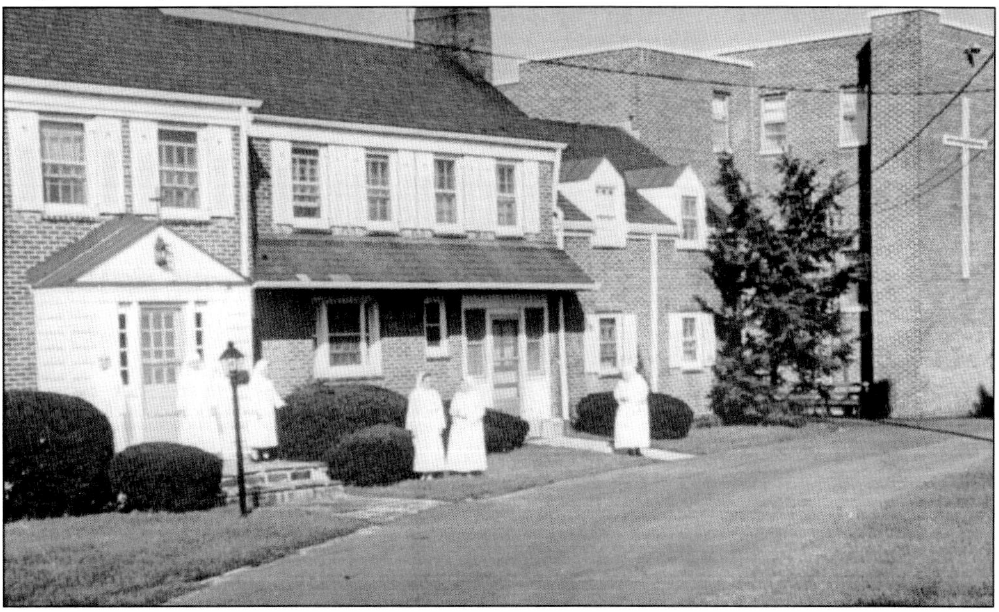

The American Province of the Sisters of Our Lady of Africa was headquartered at 999 River Road. The group ran about 145 missions in Africa, conducting nursing, religious education, and social work activities. They also published *Africa*. The building, vacated by the sisters around the early 1970s, was recently operated as River House. This building, now vacant, has changed changed little from this *c.* 1960s postcard image. The cross endures, its white brick composition discouraging easy removal. (Collection of Cynthia Harris.)

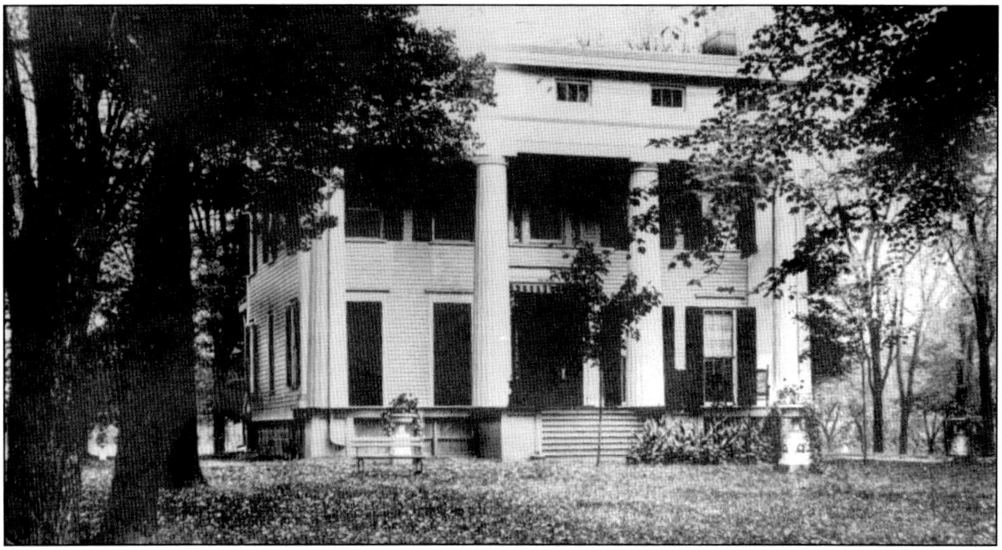

In the late 1840s, prosperous New Market businessman William Vail built Valmere, his fine Greek Revival house at 501 New Market Road. A new Roman Catholic parish, Our Lady of Fatima, was established in June 1948, on what had been the southern section of St. John's. It first celebrated Mass in the New Market Firehouse on July 4, 1948, but moved to the New Market School on July 25. The church bought the Edward J. VanWinkle property, including Valmere, later that summer and still uses the house for its rectory. (Collection of Cynthia Harris.)

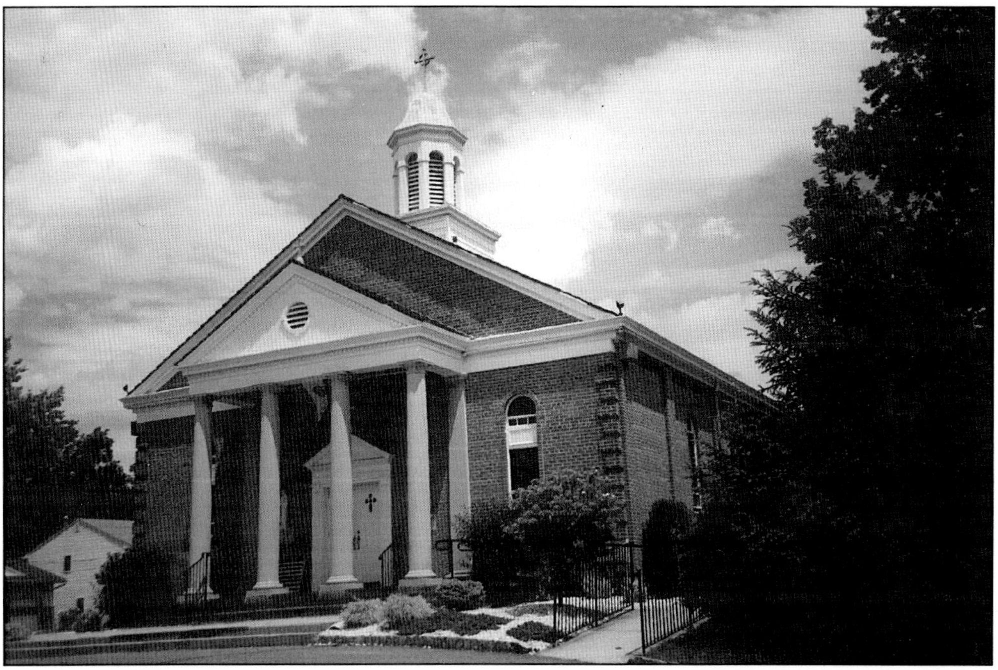

Our Lady of Fatima incorporated in 1949 and conducted its initial First Holy Communion and Confirmations that year. Ricker & Axt of Plainfield was hired to design this church, which was dedicated by Bishop George W. Ahron on May 27, 1951. A shrine to Our Lady of Fatima on the rectory lawn was completed in 1959. In 1961, ground was broken for an auditorium-gym. Classrooms were added to that building in 1964.

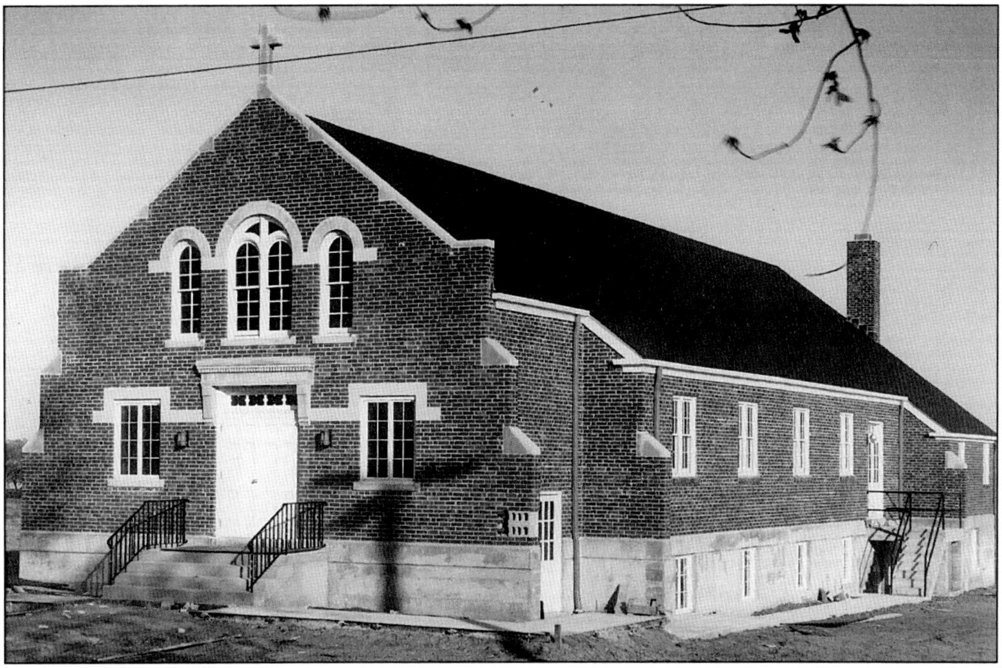

The first celebrated Mass of St. Francis Cabrini Church, established in 1946 as a mission of St. Joseph's of Bound Brook, was at the former River Road firehouse. Ground was broken for this edifice at 208 Bound Brook Avenue in October 1952. Bishop George W. Ahron of the Trenton Diocese dedicated the church on May 10, 1953. The picture was taken prior to the cornerstone laying, as indicated by the exposed cinder blocks on the right at the gabled end. (Archives, Regional Community, Sisters of Mercy of New Jersey.)

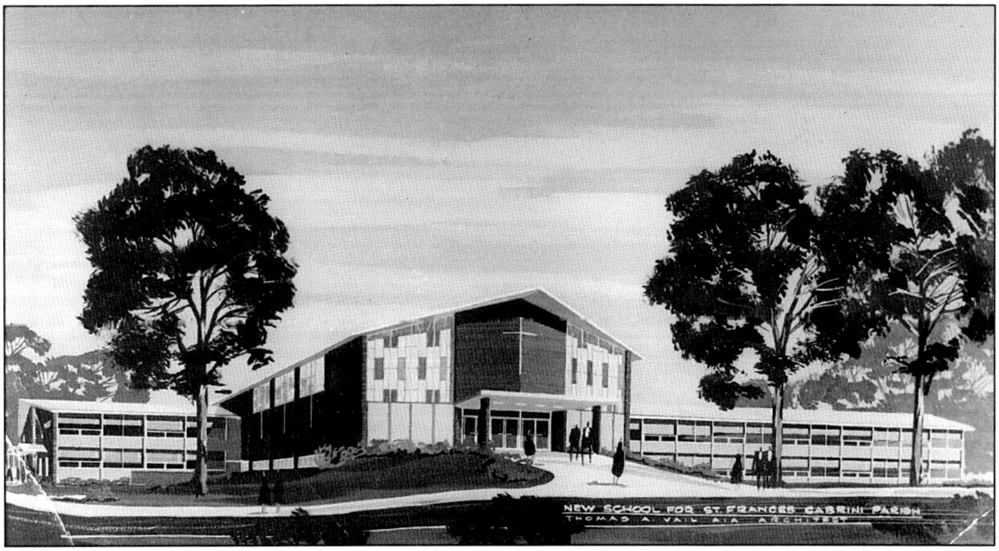

Beginning with an initial community of 75 families, St. Francis grew steadily, achieved parish status in 1961, and made plans for educating its children. Construction began in October 1965 for this school, pictured in an architect's rendering by Thomas A. Vail. The school opened in September 1966 and was staffed by the Sisters of Mercy of New Jersey, with Sr. Mary Faith Moore serving as first principal.

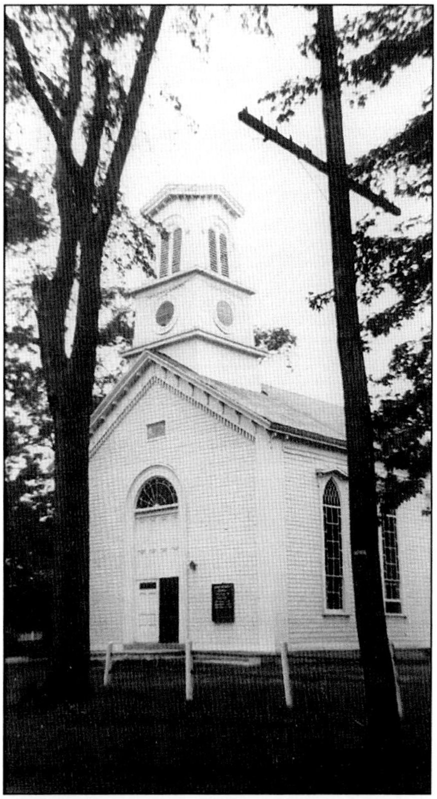

The Seventh Day Baptist Church of Piscataway was organized in 1705, initially meeting in private homes. They erected their first church in 1736, a second in 1802, and the pictured edifice in 1836. Located at Stelton and Old New Brunswick Roads, it measures 38 by 51 feet, cost $3,600, and was dedicated in February 1837. When active, the church was the oldest of its denomination in America and second oldest in the world, predated only by the Mill Yard Church in London.

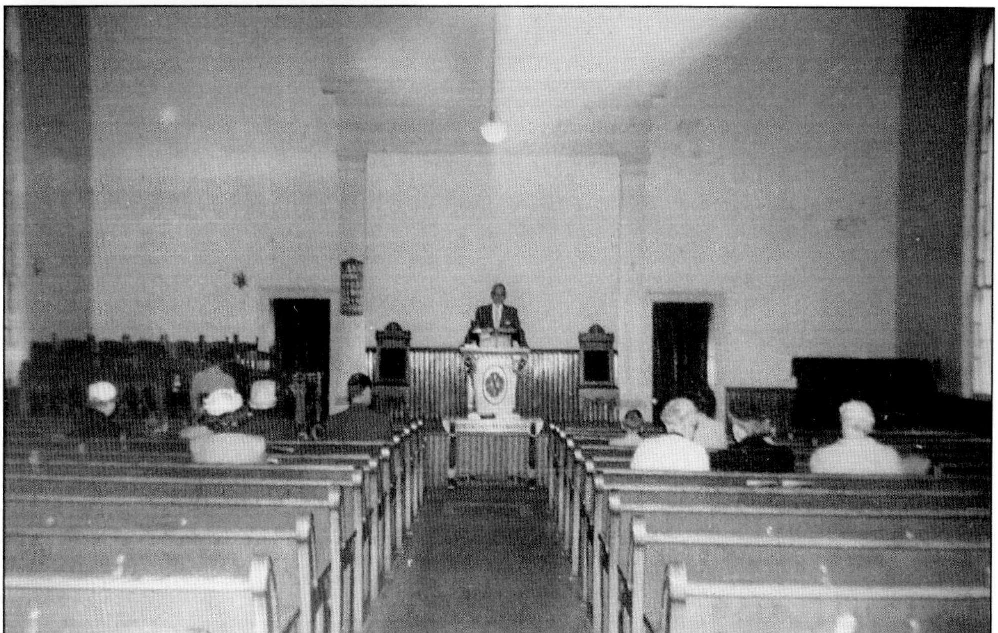

Pastor Frank R. Kellogg is pictured preaching in the early 1950s inside a church that was remodeled in 1895, a project that installed new seats, windows, and furniture. A shrinking congregation caused the church to close.

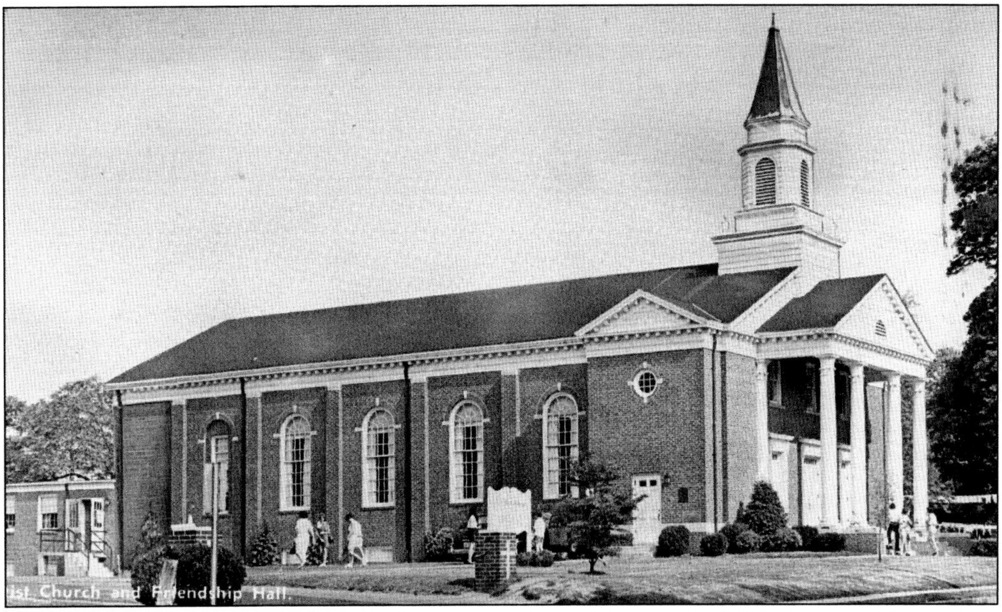

The First Baptist Church of New Market organized on February 26, 1852, drawing 45 members from the Samptown Baptist Church and five from the Second Baptist Church of Plainfield. The congregation built their first house of worship in the summer of 1853 at 461 New Market Road. That church burned on March 16, 1953, and was replaced by this one, which was dedicated June 4, 1954.

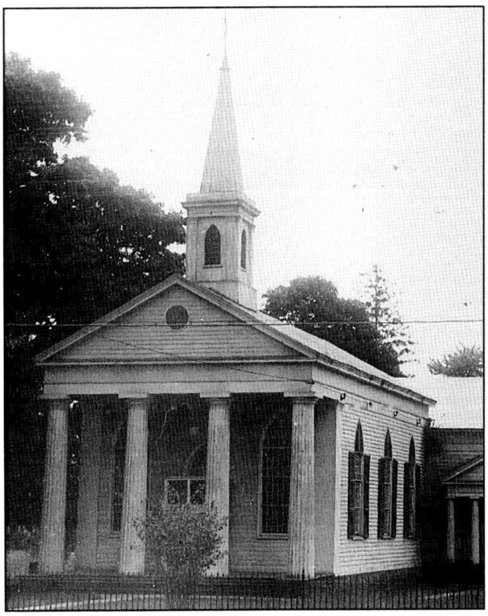

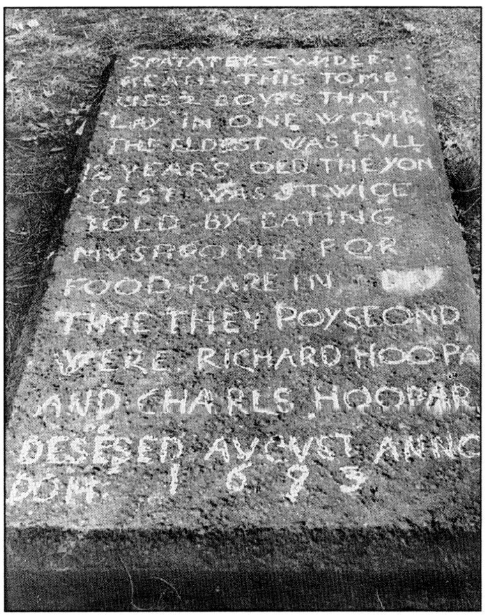

St. James Protestant Episcopal Church of Piscatawaytown was founded in 1704 and built its first church 20 years later. The building was lost in the 1835 tornado that laid waste to much of the village, which is now in Edison Township. St. James then erected this fine, Greek Revival edifice, pictured in 1939. The oldest stone in their ancient cemetery dates from 1733, but it is not as interesting as the pictured one. Presumably most readers know wild mushrooms are still to be avoided.

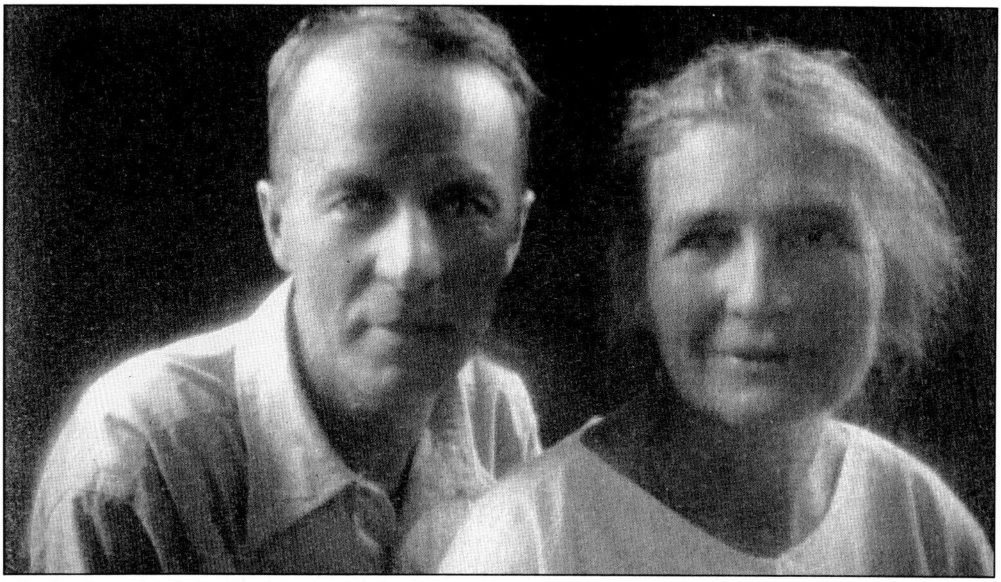

Elizabeth and Alexis Ferm, affectionately called Aunty and Uncle, brought 32 children and four other adults to the Fellowship Farm Colony, a cooperative agricultural community, on May 16, 1915. Elizabeth, born in 1857 in Illinois, began her education in private schools and a convent and graduated from the New York Conservatory of Music in 1885. Alexis, born in 1870 in Sweden, immigrated with his family to America at age two and had to leave school at age 14. He was employed at retail and newspaper positions, became self-educated through reading, and gravitated toward anarchist positions after meeting Elizabeth in 1899. (Rutgers Special Collections and University Archives.)

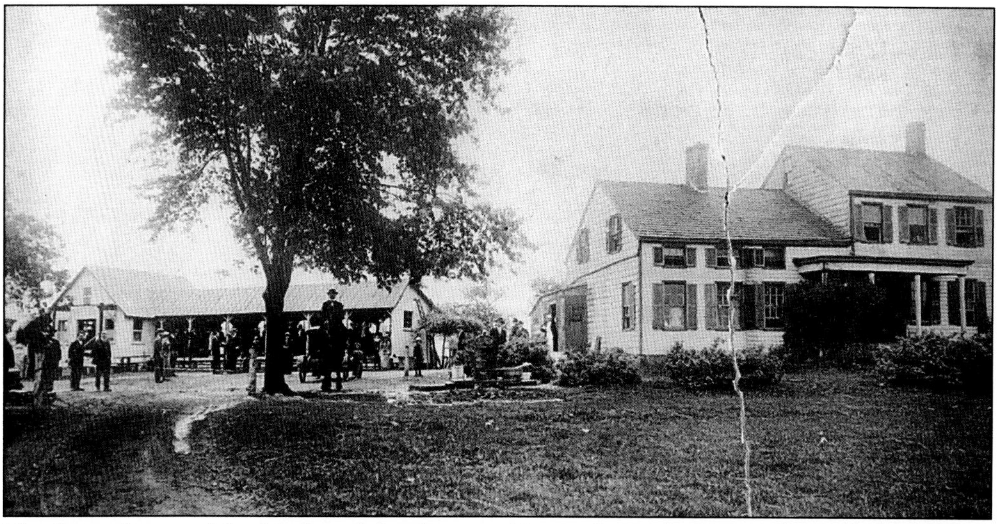

The future home of the Modern School was a 68-acre farm adjacent to the Fellowship Farm Colony. It consisted of an old farmhouse and a barn that Alex Fern indicated was "hardly fit for the cows." The place lacked running water, electricity, and roads. They expanded the settlement, which endured until 1953, by additional acquisitions of 40 and 32 acres. The Living House, pictured on the right in an undated photograph, was initially the center of educational activities; the children of working parents lived there. (Rutgers Special Collections and University Archives.)

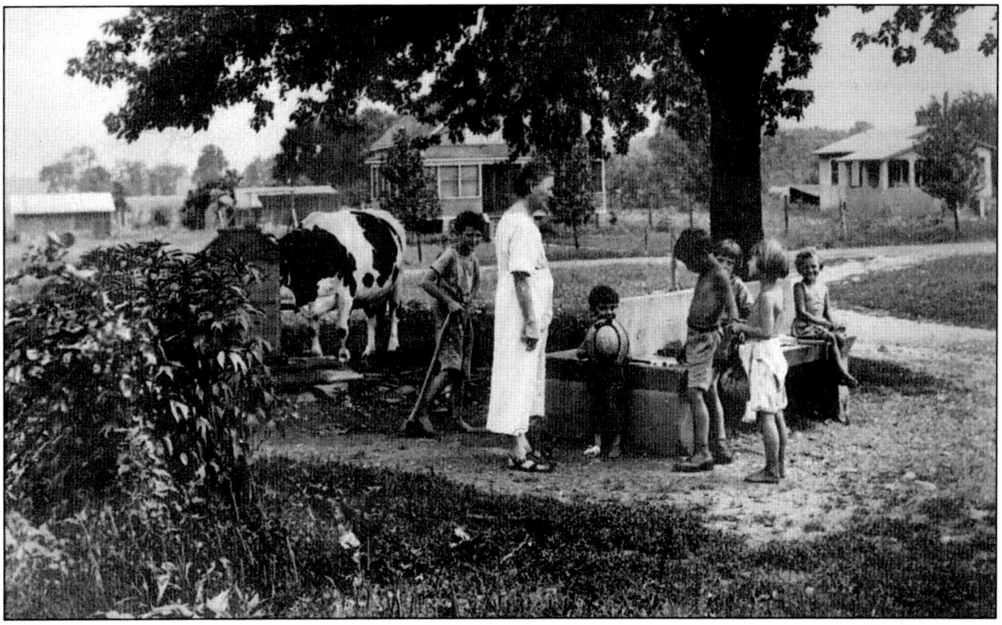

Instruction was given without grading as each child was permitted to learn at his own pace. Self-reliance without conformity were valued over standardized measures of learning. Playtime was regarded as crucial to the development of the individual. Elizabeth Ferm (pictured above) claimed, "Once the play spirit is aroused in man, it should stay with him through his whole earthly experience." Children attended the school to about age 14, when they entered nearby public high schools, where they reportedly performed quite well. (Rutgers Special Collections and University Archives.)

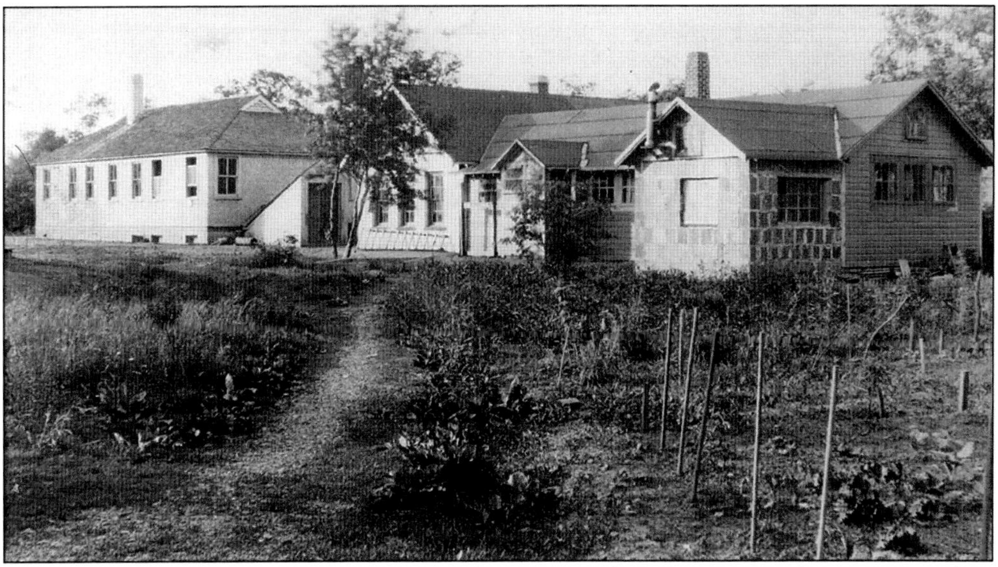

The school building and shops are pictured *c.* 1920. Alexis Ferm started a carpentry shop and vegetable garden to convey his love for handicrafts and nature. The students produced a magazine called *The Voice of the Children* in the printing room. After writing the stories, poems, and other material, they set the type, printed and folded the pages, and distributed the magazine. (Rutgers Special Collections and University Archives.)

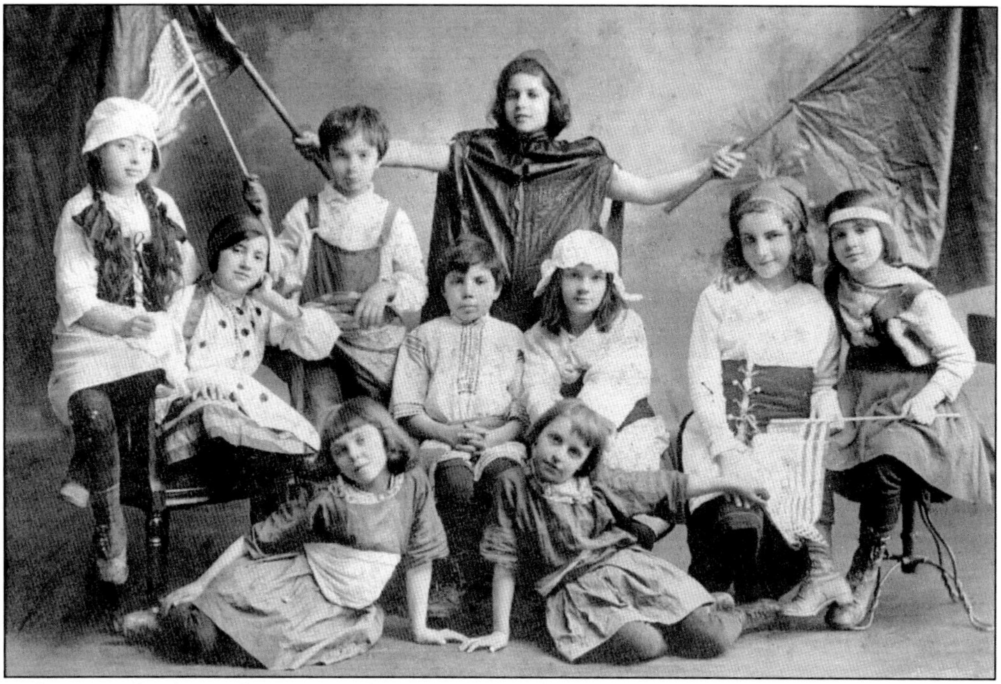

Culture, in the form of a variety of entertainment for grown-ups, came to the Modern School each Saturday night. They included presentations by prominent musicians, dancers, and speakers. Although adults performed most of the theatrical presentations, plays by children, such as this group of unidentified performers, were staged as well. (Rutgers Special Collections and University Archives.)

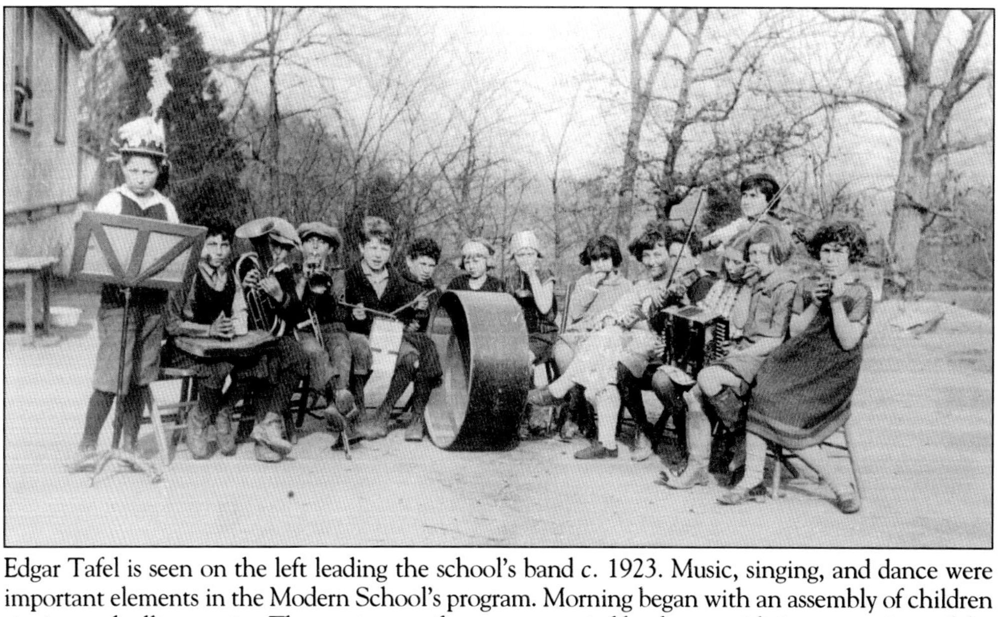

Edgar Tafel is seen on the left leading the school's band *c.* 1923. Music, singing, and dance were important elements in the Modern School's program. Morning began with an assembly of children singing and telling stories. The music was often accompanied by dance, with interpretations of the children's choosing. (Rutgers Special Collections and University Archives.)

Five

Community Service

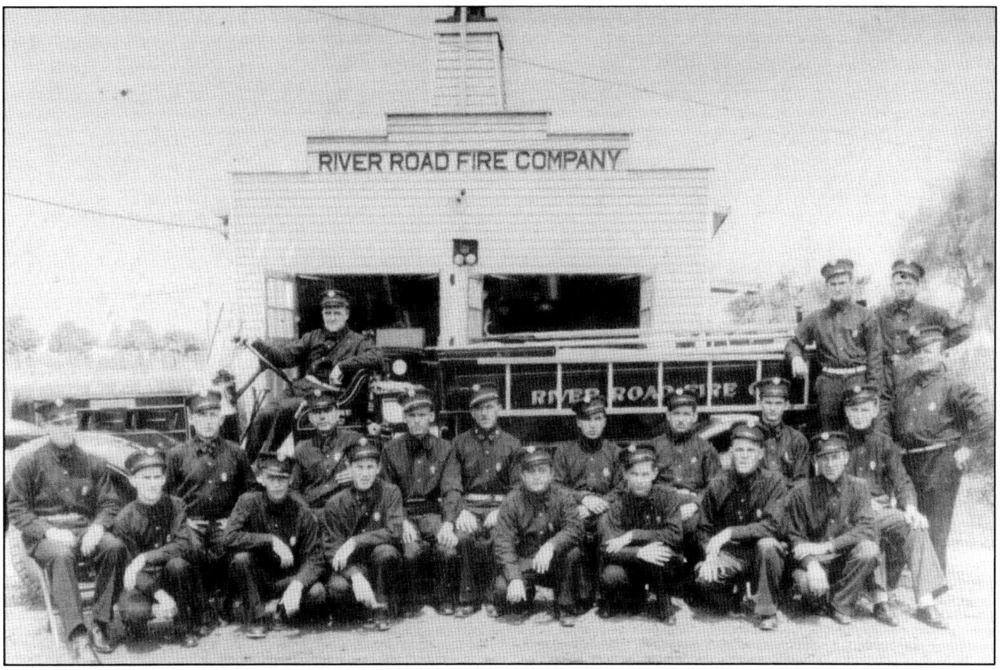

The River Road Fire Company, founded in 1929, was initially housed in this rented garage on River Road. Later it moved to its present Netherwood Avenue site. Dick Bakker claimed that his father provided the impetus for the present home by donating a 50-by-100-foot lot backing a $900 note for material used by volunteer labor to build the new firehouse. The firehouse was sold to the Knights of Columbus in 1953. (Collection of the River Road Fire Company.)

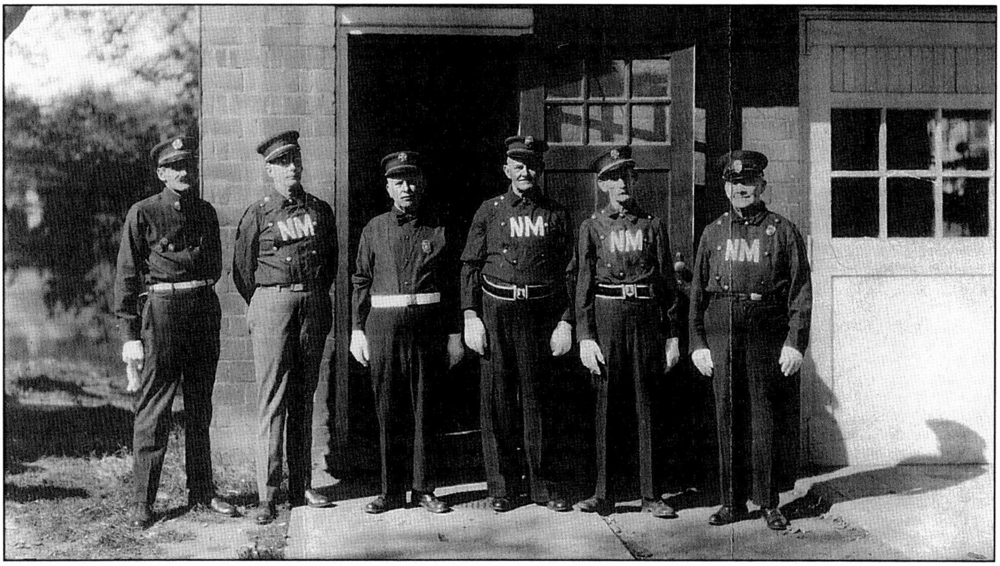

Six early chiefs of the New Market Fire Company are pictured in front of the former two-story firehouse (with bell tower) built in the mid-1920s on Lakeview Avenue. They are, from left to right, Alexander Herrlich, Charles E. Kelly, R.P.F. von Minden, George W. Schenck, Harry J. Piddington, and Clark T. Rogers. The company, Piscataway's first, was founded in 1908 and then covered the entire township.

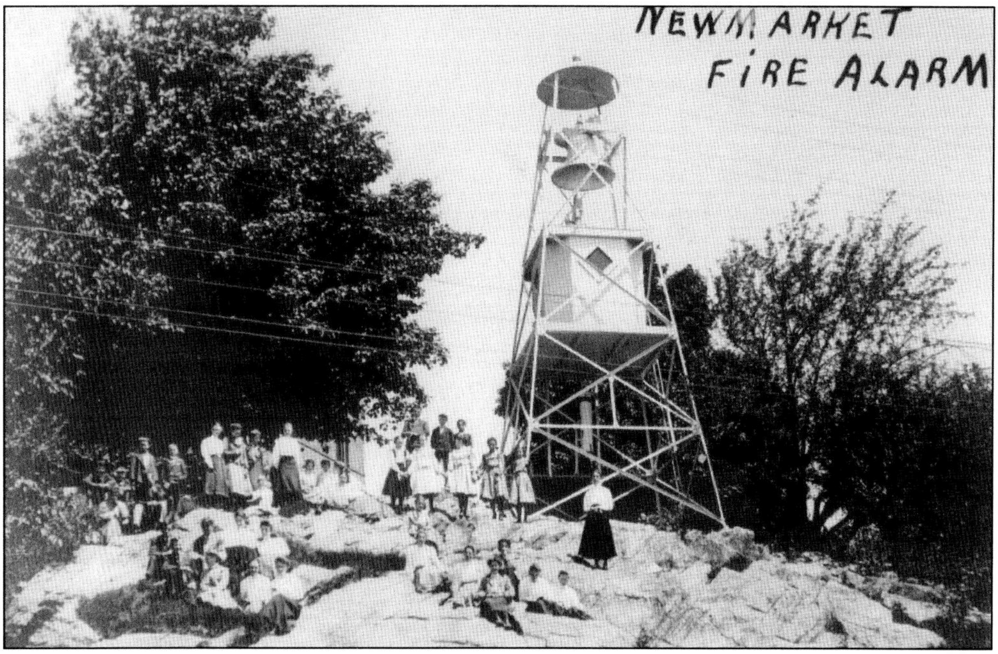

This bell tower, located on the hill overlooking New Market Pond, replaced a locomotive rim as an alarm device in 1912. The steel tower was given to the New Market company by Robert Fairbairn of Fair Acre Farm, who had acquired it about a year earlier with his purchase of the former Joseph Field farm. The bell was later removed to the grounds of the present New Market Volunteer Fire Company building on South Washington Avenue, where it is now a decorative reminder of an early notification system. (Collection of Cynthia Harris.)

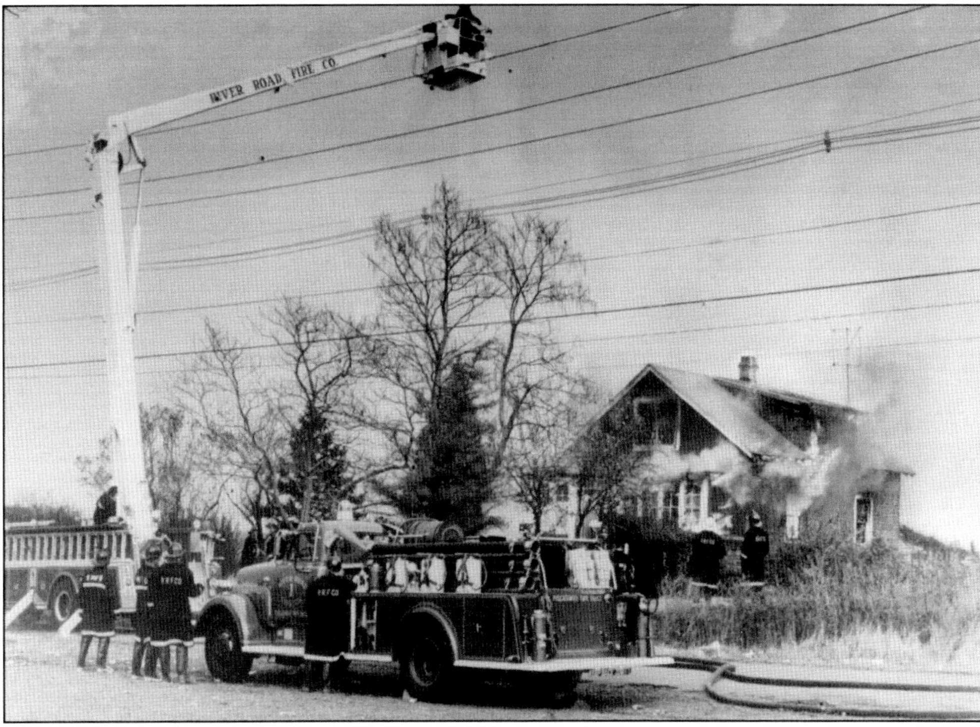

The River Road Fire Company's earliest apparatus, a rebuilt Ford Model T, could be nearly as challenging to operate as the blaze could be to fight. The company is now known for its high aerial ladder equipment, such as this example pictured in 1967. A few years later, the squad was responding to more than 200 calls annually. (Collection of the River Road Fire Company.)

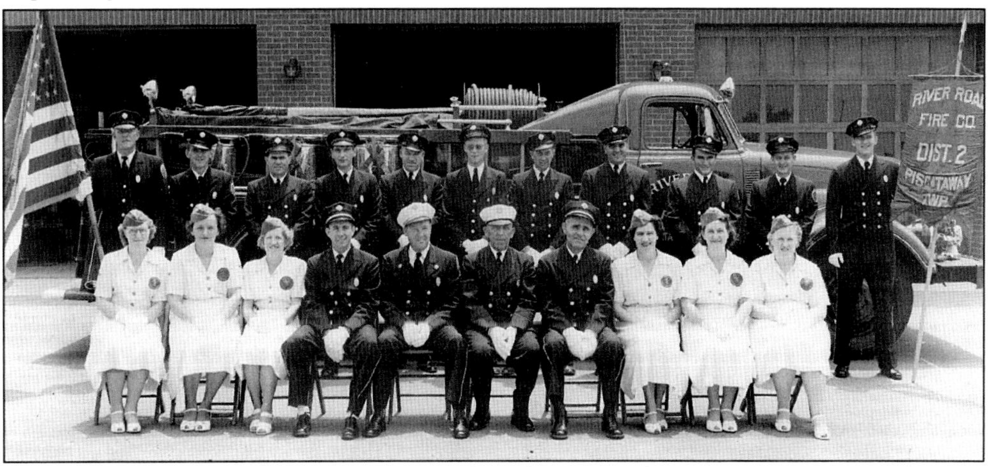

The River Road Fire Company is pictured at the time of a 1955 firemen's parade. The brick firehouse, erected in 1953, was clad with a stone face in a 1990s renovation that also installed an elevator to reach the second-story hall. Posing on site, from left to right, are the following: (front row) Anne Rosenski, Anne Brarens, Helen Kinasky, Chet Trichask, John Brarens, Glenn Butz, Frank Livak, Jennie Krupaki, Helen Gajaiski, and Jean Krupaki; (back row) Jack Butz, John Schaeffer, Walter Krupaki, Pete Tempinara, John Piorkonski, Charles McCann, Al Eledge, Mike Diener, John Lettong, unidentified, and Raymond Rose. (Names were copied from the script on the original.) (Collection of the Piscataway Public Library.)

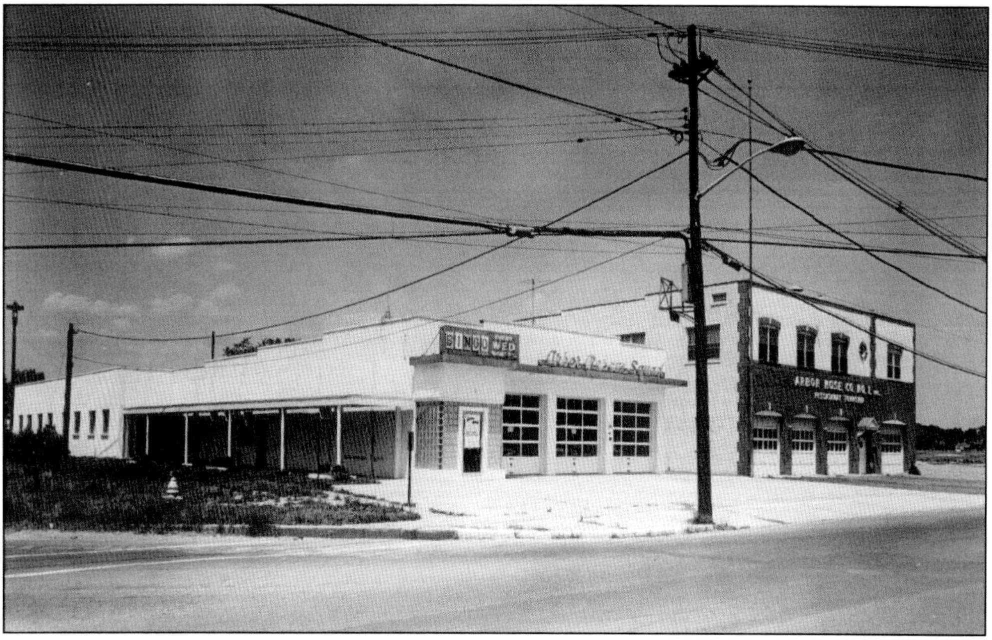

The Arbor Rescue Squad, one of New Jersey's earliest, was founded in June 1931 and incorporated in 1933. Their building at 1750 West 7th Street, at the corner of Walnut Street, was erected with two stories and is believed to date from the 1930s. A September 1963 fire resulted in the loss of the upper story. The building, seen in 1965, retains its Bingo sign and appealing glass block entrance, although modern doors replace the pictured ones. The section in the rear is a later addition. (Rutgers Special Collections and University Archives.)

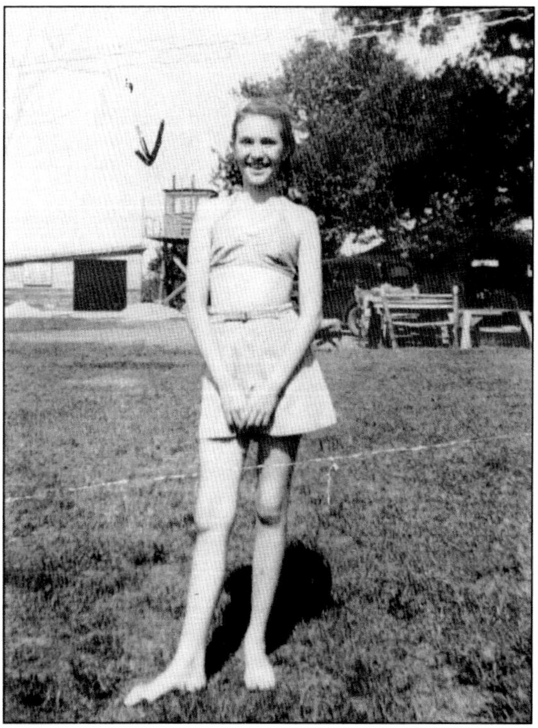

The World War II threat of aerial bombardment was met by an extensive network of citizen aircraft spotters who watched the skies and telephoned their sightings to central locations. A culture and kinship grew among the many volunteers who spent long hours searching for an enemy that fortunately never arrived. Ruth Morris Williams is pictured in 1943 in front of the spotters' tower, then located at Hoes Lane near Sidney Road.

Piscataway, once protected by constables, established a police department by ordinance in 1917. The squad, initially two men, appointed Arthur H. Schlunsen a regular member on April 1, 1930. Schlunsen, known as Pete, became Piscataway's second or third police chief in 1935 after the passing of Elmer Barrett. The sequence varies depending on whether or not one includes the real first chief, Cornelius J. McCarthy, who left when South Plainfield was incorporated in 1926. Schlunsen indicated his biggest case was the Kearny murder, in which two would-be mail truck robbers killed a motorist whose car they sought to take and his young son. Following his retirement on December 15, 1959, Schlunsen moved to Florida. (Collection of the Piscataway Public Library.)

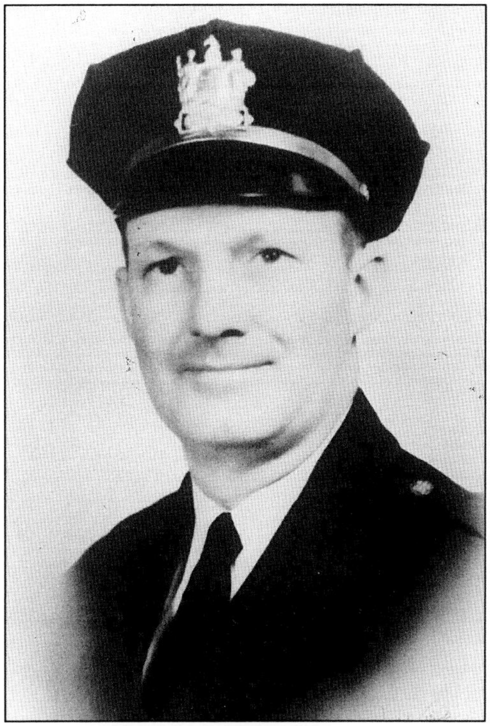

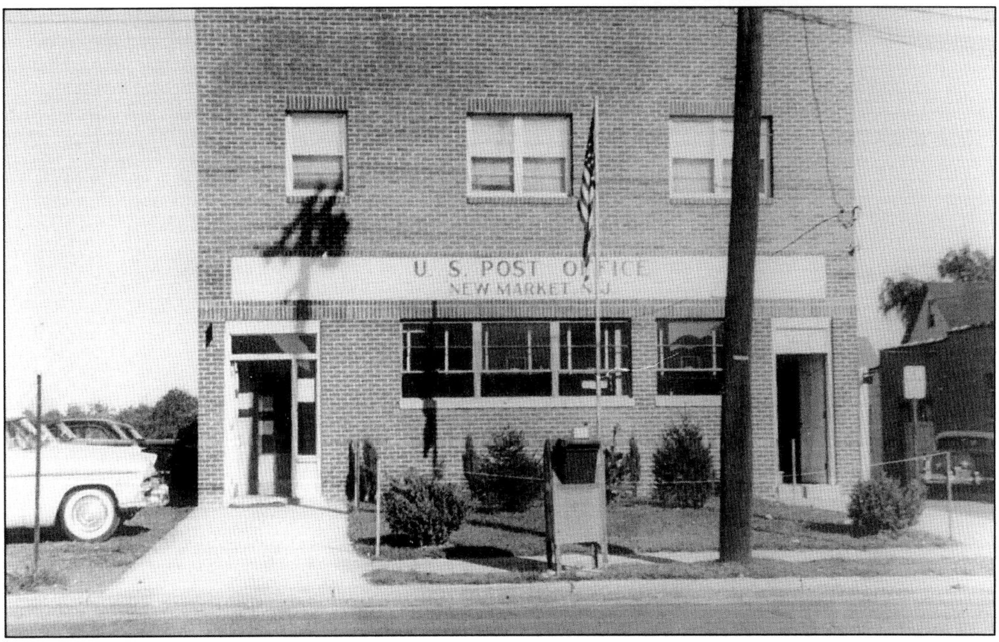

The New Market Post Office, founded in 1804, was located near the town center at Lakeview Avenue and Terrace Court prior to the September 1, 1954 opening of this building at 139 Stelton Road. This post office served until the 1976 opening of the present one at 3 Skiles Avenue. In 1965, the township consolidated mail service under a newly opened Piscataway office. The pictured location, now a dry cleaner, is still readily identifiable, although a one-story addition was built on the left.

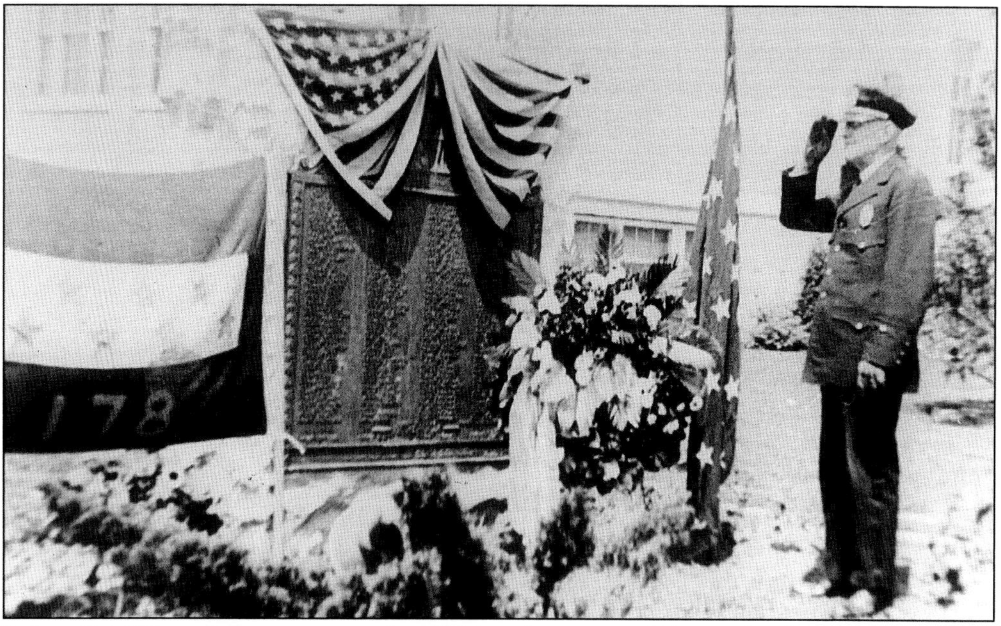

Police Chief Elmer Barrett is pictured in 1930 at the memorial "erected in honor of those from Piscataway Township who served their country in the world war." The bronze tablet quotes president Woodrow Wilson: "In a righteous cause they have won immortal glory and have nobly served their nation in serving mankind." This image shows the monument in its original location in front of the former New Market School (page 77); it was relocated to the front of the American Legion building at 840 Washington Avenue at the northwest corner of Summers Avenue. (Collection of the Piscataway Public Library.)

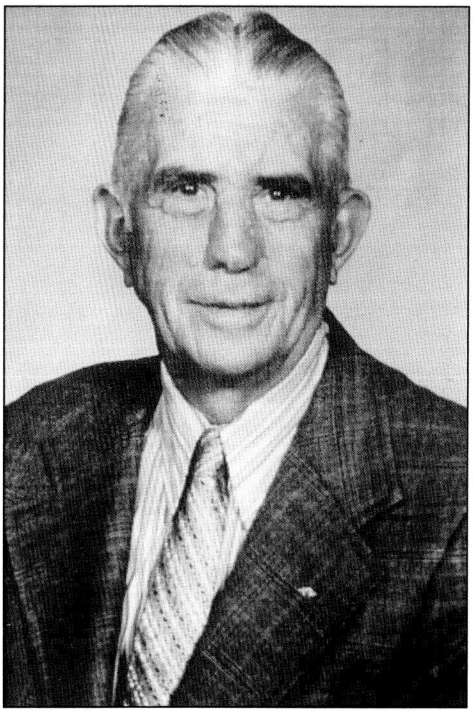

Clarence D. Perrine was born in 1900 at 625 River Road (page 32), a house he occupied for more than 75 years. After farming, he was employed by Mack Trucks for many years, retiring in 1961. Perrine was active in public and organization life, serving on the township committee in the 1930s, including a period as chairman when that position was the equivalent of mayor. He was a founding member of the River Road Fire Company, the Piscataway Historical and Heritage Society, and the Piscataway Library Board of Trustees. He was a ruling elder of the Presbyterian Church of Bound Brook, active in hunting and fishing circles, and a member of various other organizations. Perrine died in 1988 at age 87. (Collection of the Piscataway Public Library.)

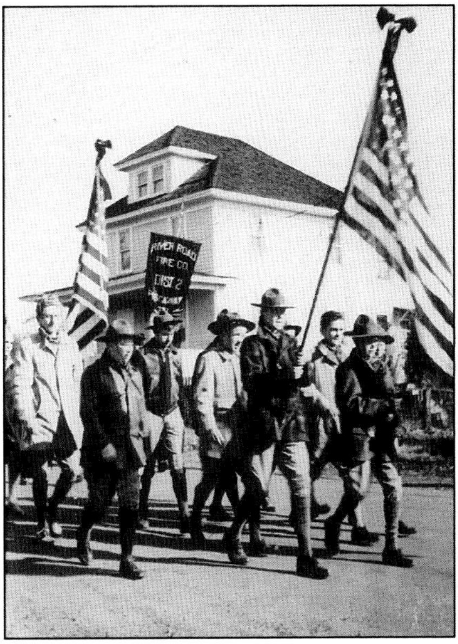

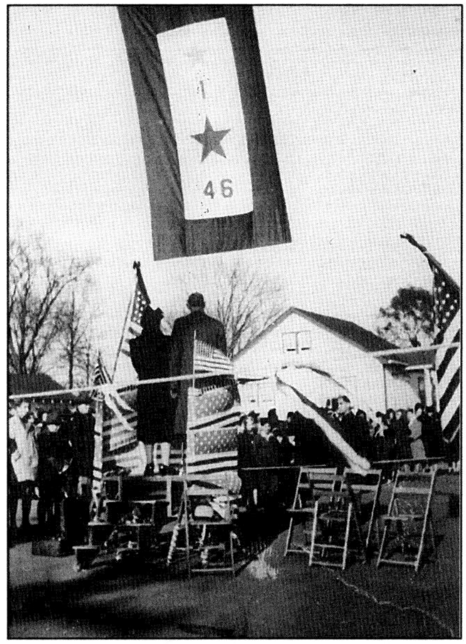

A parade and banner ceremony in 1943 honored Piscataway's military forces. The marching scene on the right is on Plainfield Avenue between Cooper and White Streets. Mr. Artus was the speaker under the banner, which was hung over River Road and Plainfield Avenue. The numeral 1 indicated one gold star for a death; the 46 designated blue stars representing that number in uniform at the time. (Collection of the Piscataway Public Library.)

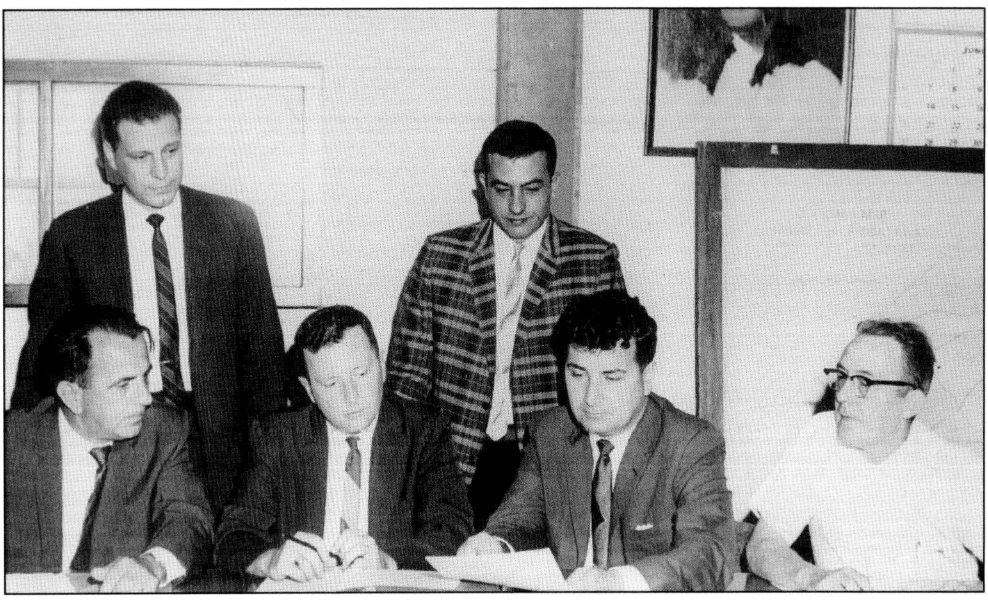

The 1960s sewer program was planned to reduce the number of septic tanks in the township, diminish the number of health complaints, and enhance safety by minimizing water contamination. Industrial and residential building capacity was also substantially increased. Members of the sewer committee, seen *c.* 1965, include, from left to right, George Sheenan, Vic Di Leo, William R. Walsh, Frederick Copolla, Mayor Frank Markley, and William Prudhon. Notice the Gilbert Stuart portrait of Washington. Some readers will recall the time a similar one hung in most New Jersey public school classrooms.

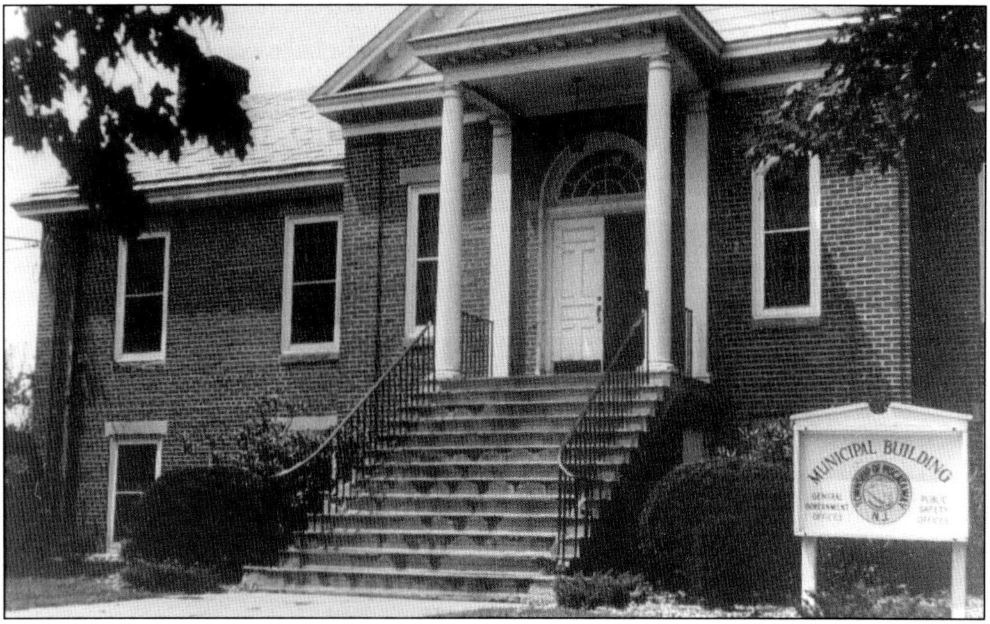

Piscataway built a handsome Colonial Revival–style township hall at 18 Stelton Road in 1939. The hall was erected by local contractor August Morris. The project, ambitious for a sparsely populated rural municipality, was supported by Works Progress Administration funds; it permitted the consolidation of scattered township offices. The building's facade is little changed except for the replacement of the stairs by a small porch supported by ramps from the rear on either side; it is now occupied by the Piscataway Funeral Home. The township vacated the building in 1968 for the present complex at Hoes Lane and Sidney Road.

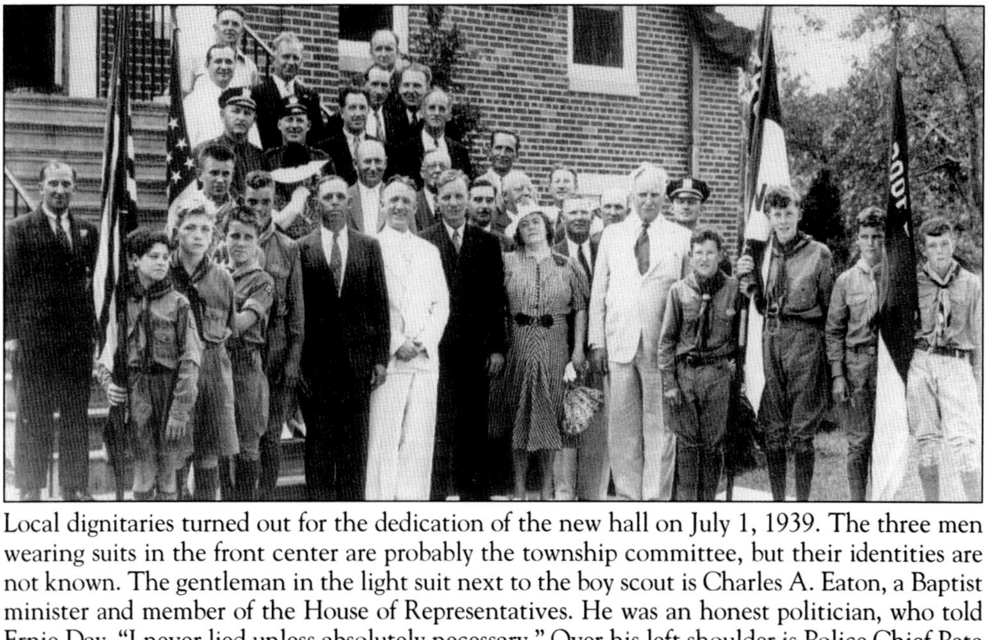

Local dignitaries turned out for the dedication of the new hall on July 1, 1939. The three men wearing suits in the front center are probably the township committee, but their identities are not known. The gentleman in the light suit next to the boy scout is Charles A. Eaton, a Baptist minister and member of the House of Representatives. He was an honest politician, who told Ernie Day, "I never lied unless absolutely necessary." Over his left shoulder is Police Chief Pete Schlunsen (page 91); Officer (later Chief) Matthew Lund is on the right of the American flag. Charles S. Day is the partially obscured man in the center of the three in the second row.

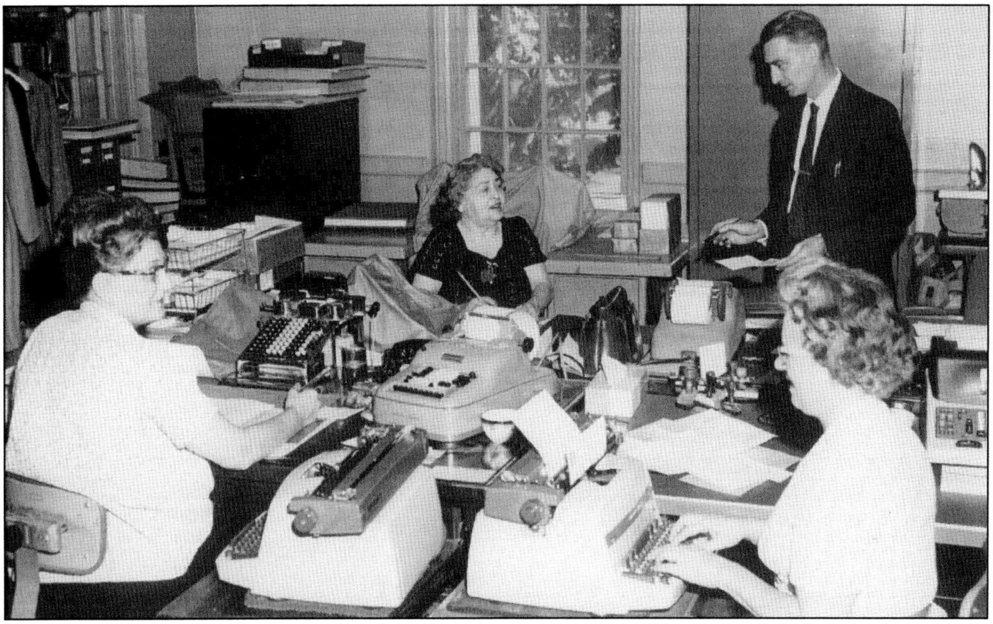

Tax collector Peter Bongiorno is pictured *c.* 1965 talking to Lillian Evans (center), then a 15-year veteran of the tax office, seen in cramped quarters at the old township hall. On the left is Lottie Jurkowski; Helen Prudhon is on the right. Notice the pictured office antiques, including a coffee cup in lieu of the now obligatory mug. Many may remember the 10-button calculator, but you are getting older if you have ever seen the monstrous machine such as the one in front of Ms. Jurkowski. (Rutgers Special Collections and University Archives.)

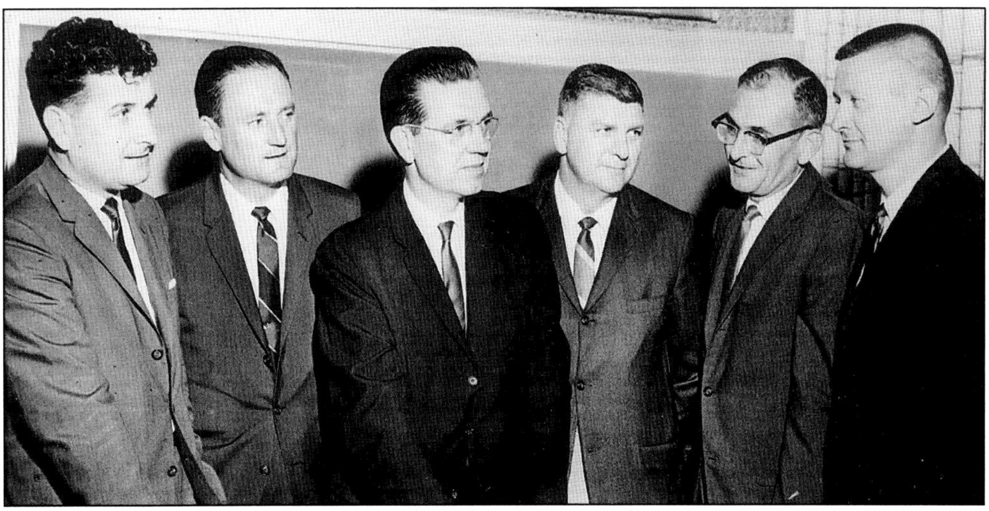

Piscataway officials have long cultivated good business ratables. A number are pictured *c.* 1965 showing their pleasure as Union Carbide announced it was expanding its facility (pages 59, 68, and 69) by constructing a costly synthetic phenol plant at its River Road tract. Shown, from left to right, are Francis X. Markley, mayor; William C. Campbell, committeeman; Charles G. Habenstreit, Union Carbide's manager of engineering and construction; William H. Atkins, committeeman; Henry A. Zanetti, the township engineer; and Ernest F. Schultz, the Union Carbide superintendent of industrial relations. (Rutgers Special Collections and University Archives.)

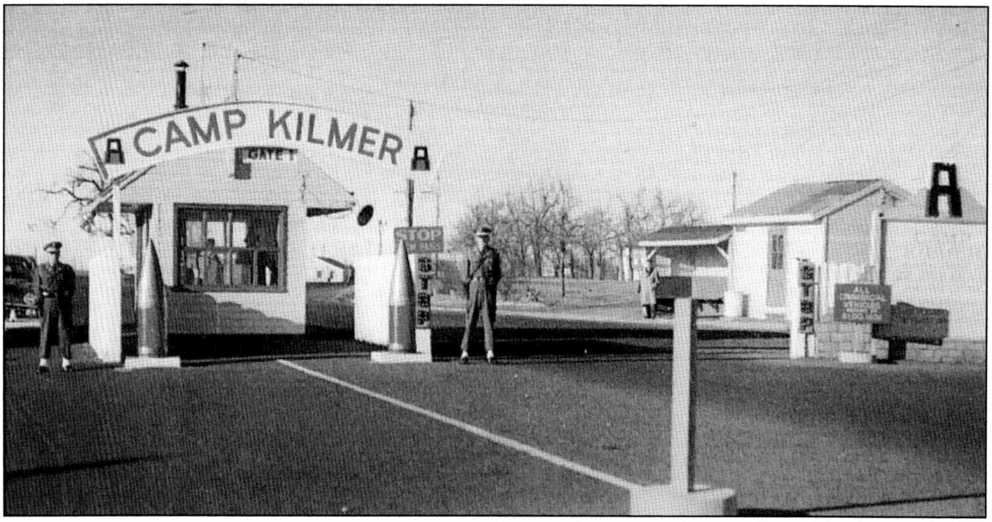

The U.S. Army took an extensive tract from Edison and Piscataway, including the former poor farm in the latter, to build the largest troop staging area in the country and the first to be built solely for that purpose. This installation of the New York Port of Embarkation, part of the gigantic Army Transportation Corps, was named for Joyce Kilmer, the New Brunswick journalist killed in France during World War I; it was activated in June 1942. (Collection of Donald Wayne)

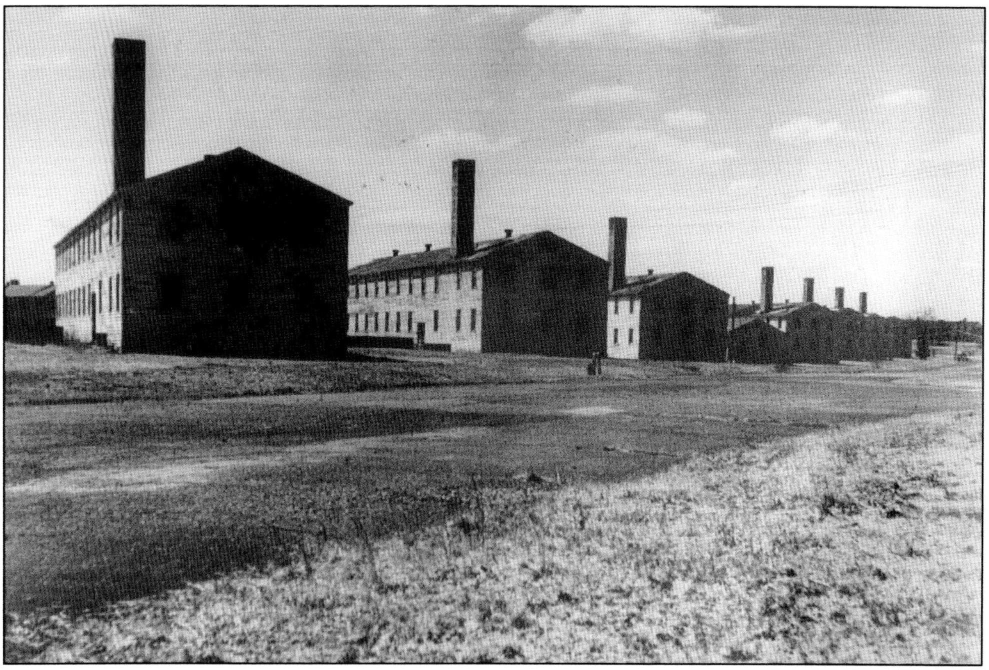

The camp had 10 identical barracks areas. Unit designations were posted on building exteriors, which soldiers were cautioned to mark down, as it was easy to get lost. Chow was a challenge; enlisted men were told to be punctual and to take their knife, fork, and spoon with them. Colored painting schemes later helped distinguish the common buildings. The camp later housed Hungarian refugees, following the anti-Communist uprising there in 1956. Kilmer was deactivated c. 1963 and the grounds returned to the townships for industrial and educational uses.

Six

Changing Landscape and Borders

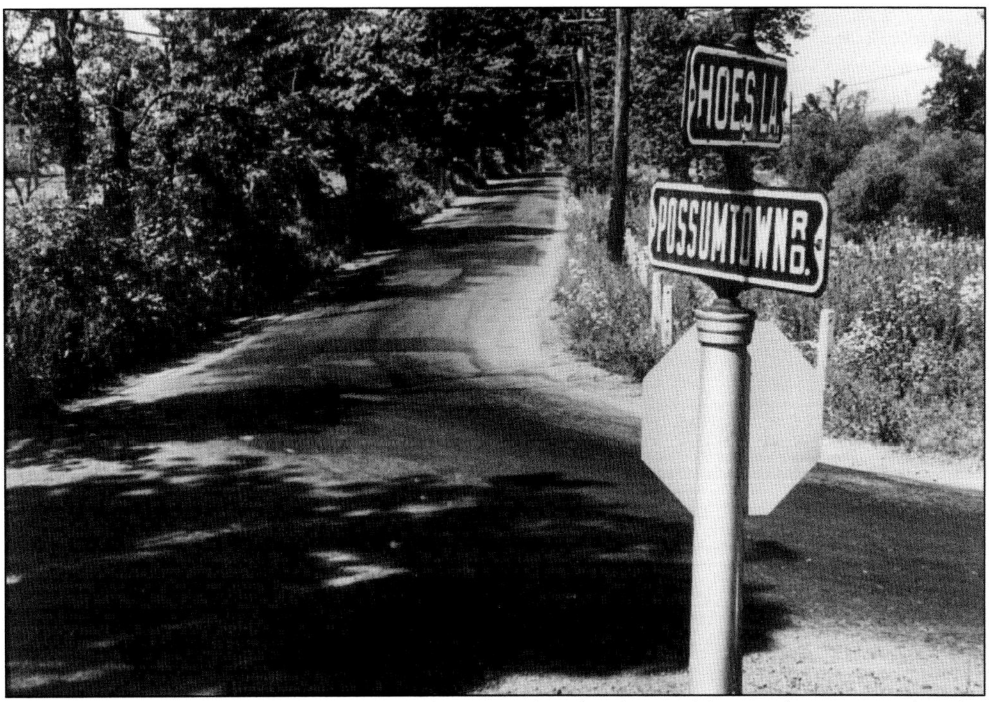

Piscataway's rural character lasted into the 1960s but has been obliterated in recent decades by road widening and development. This juncture, pictured *c.* 1960, is no longer extant. The intersection has been realigned for a construction project. (Rutgers Special Collections and University Archives.)

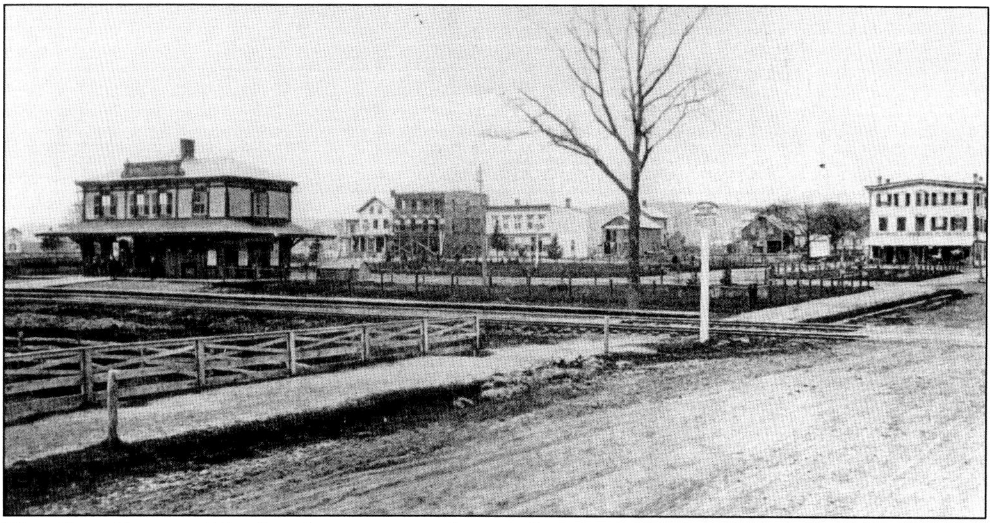

The Dunellen neighborhood grew around its rail station on the Jersey Central line. This development was largely due to the Central New Jersey Land Improvement Company, which began operation in May 1868 with a 300-acre tract. The town was mapped and a new station built; it is pictured in 1873. The improvement company also reserved land for churches, schools, and the future Washington Park. The developing area sought independent governing powers and succeeded in establishing a borough government in 1887. The influence of Dunellen's origin remains in its nickname, the Railroad Town.

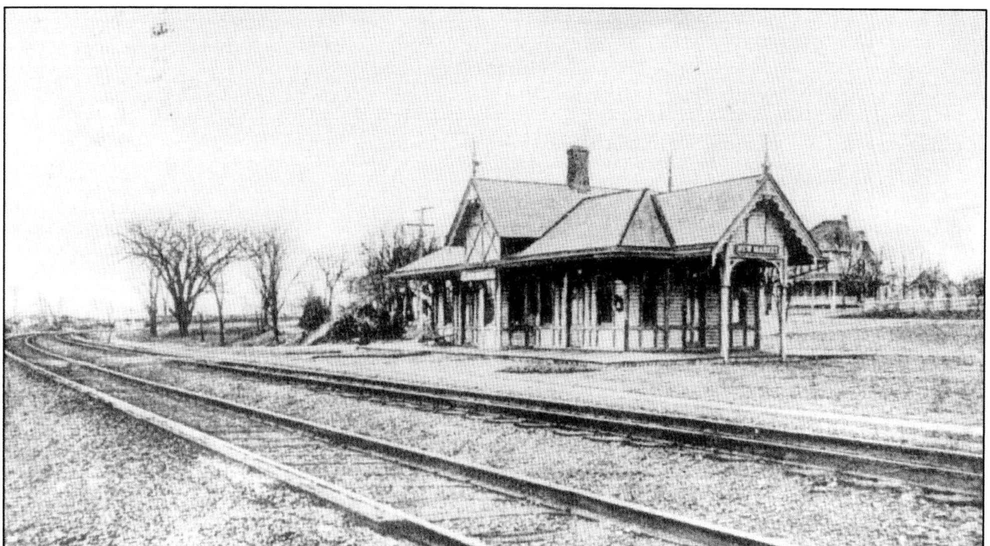

Asa Packer built the Easton & Amboy Railroad across central New Jersey in the 1870s to ship Pennsylvania coal to New York City. The line, incorporated into the Lehigh Valley, terminated at Perth Amboy, where the coal was loaded on barges. The line stopped at Bound Brook, where passengers could transfer to Central Railroad trains to New York. The Carpenter Gothic–style New Market station, pictured on a c. 1910 postcard, was built in the mid-1870s and stood at Union Avenue between Prospect Avenue and New Market Road. It was razed perhaps in the 1940s. A freight line still runs through town, reduced to a single track. (Collection of Cynthia Harris.)

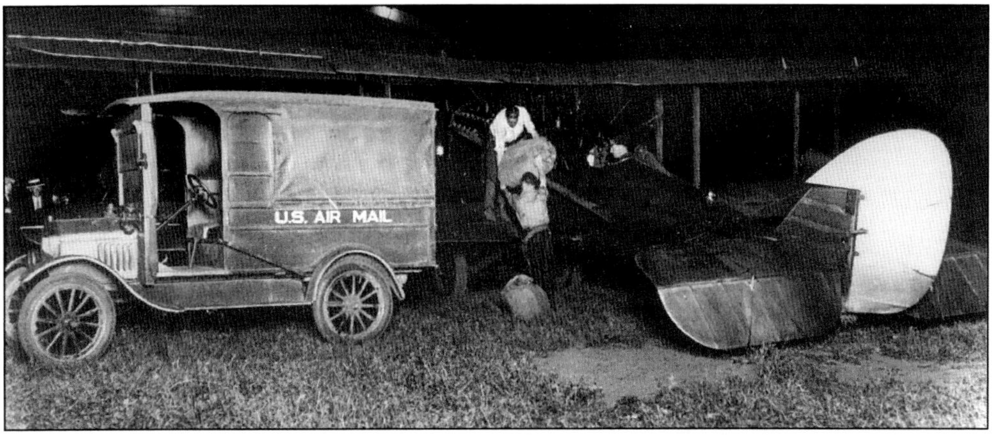

The Post Office Department chose John R. Hadley's farm for its level fields, unobstructed countryside, and "good flying weather" to build an airfield to service airmail for the metropolitan New York area. The first hangar and a single landing strip opened in 1924. Hadley Field was under Post Office Department jurisdiction until August 31, 1927, when contract carriers took over airmail transport, flying many of their routes into Newark. Hadley later became a general aviation field. A Dehaviland, or DH-4, is pictured loading mail. Hadley landed on the South Plainfield side of the border following its 1926 incorporation. The field, which saw a number of aviation firsts, closed in 1968 when the borough sold it for commercial development, including the Middlesex Mall.

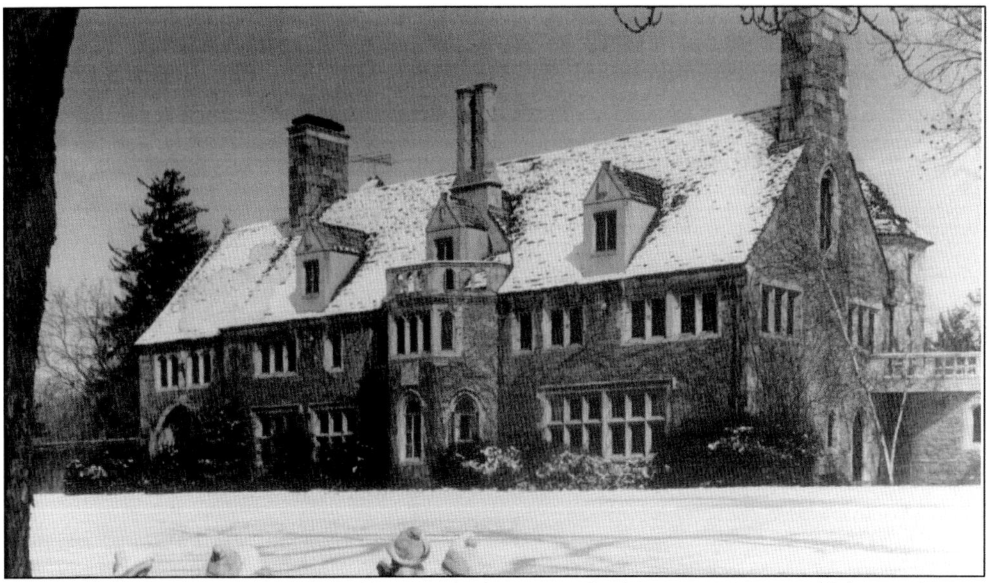

The name of the Tudor-influenced home of John Seward Johnson is Merriewold, but a glimpse conveys its informal label, the Castle. Designed by Thomas Harian Ellert and built in the late 1920s, the house stands on a hill at 433 River Road, just east of the township's border with Highland Park. The house contained a reported 25 rooms, 11 fireplaces, 150 leaded windows, and two secret stairways, one hidden by the obligatory swinging bookcase. Tragedy struck here in 1963 when Barbara Farmer was killed by her estranged husband, Charles. The Castle, a convalescent center in the late 1940s, was sold to Kaplan & Sons Construction Corporation in 1968; their plans to develop the property were unfulfilled. The place is occupied as offices; the south facade, pictured in the 1960s, is virtually unchanged.

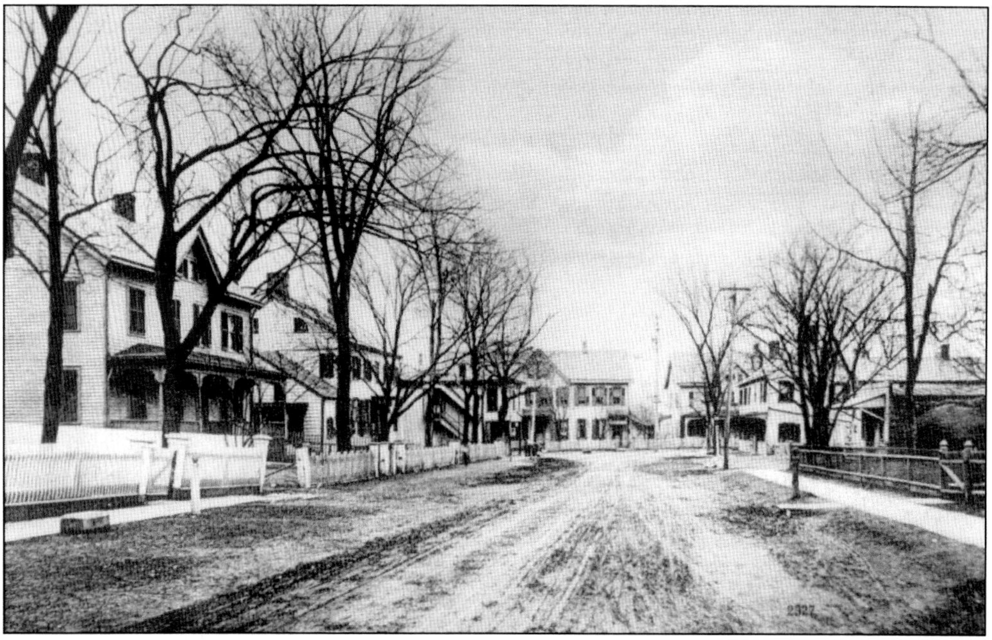

This northerly view of Stelton Road, c. 1910, shows the New Market town center when it looked like a country path. The background buildings are 209 and 211 Lakeview Avenue, the latter still recognizable by its front gabled roof and chimney. However, its facade is now radically altered. The New Market Tavern, also known as the Hotel Nelson (page 70), is visible at the foot of Stelton on the right. The houses at 8 and 6 Stelton Road are the prominent buildings on the left; the latter now possesses a brickface. (Collection of Cynthia Harris.)

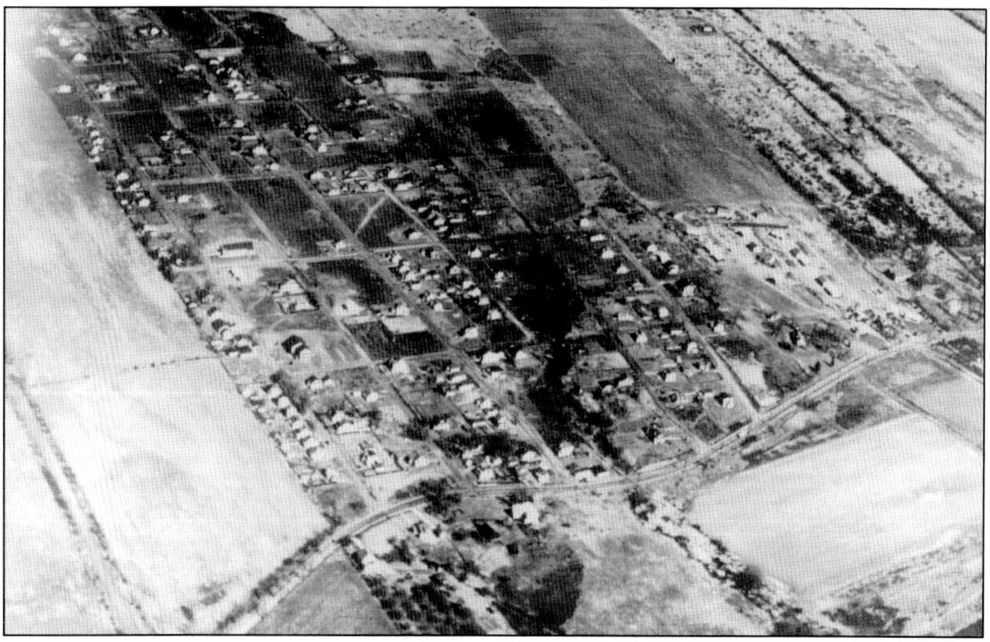

River Road curves along the bottom of this 1954 aerial. Centennial Avenue, in its county road incarnation, is the tree-lined strip at the left. The streets of Bound Brook Heights are to the right of the field adjacent to Centennial Avenue.

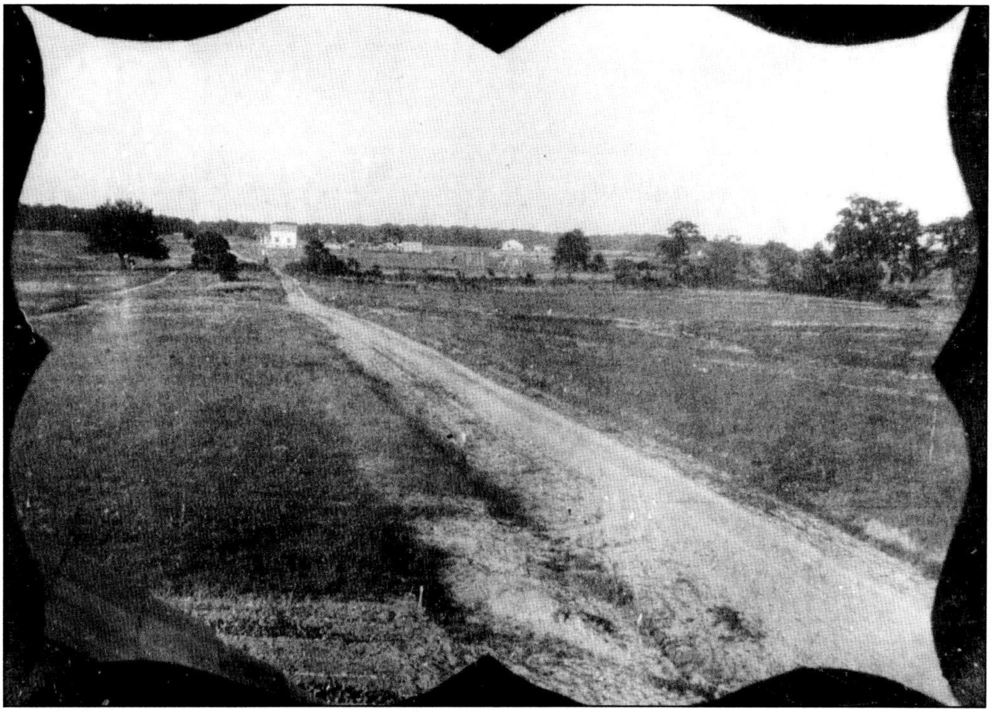

Plainfield Avenue is pictured in a 1910 view looking east. Scant development suggests it is the thoroughfare's distant stem, perhaps in the Hudson Street area. The street, now nearly fully developed, contains a number of pre–World War II houses (typically front-gabled two-story structures) and many others, typically ranch houses, built after the war.

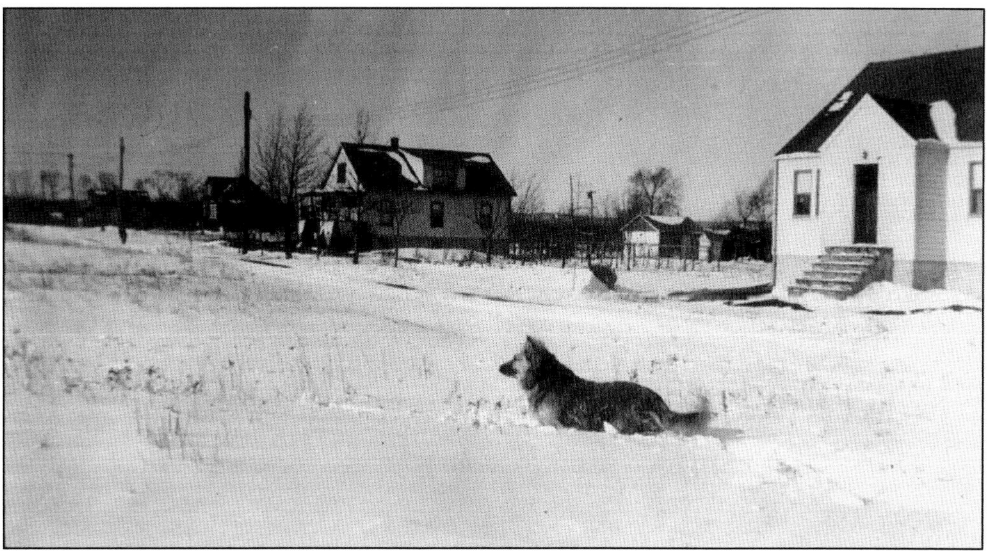

The east side of Spencer Avenue south of Plainfield Avenue is pictured c. 1943. The street, although filled in with post–World War II construction, is recognizable today. The house on the left, No. 2601, has changed little; dormers now penetrate the roof of No. 2605, on the right. Later construction filled the space between them and the west side of the street.

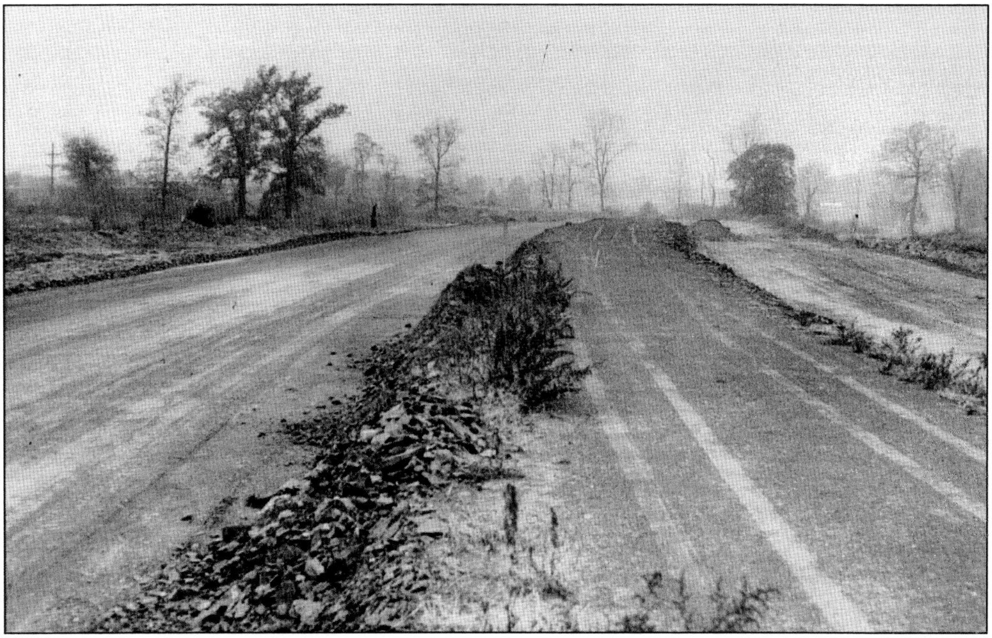

Centennial Avenue, once a rural path, was transformed into a major commercial thoroughfare by the township after the completion of Interstate 287. The street is seen in 1965 after the Piscataway Department of Public Works left new fill dirt from nearby construction projects, a process planned to reduce construction costs for the street's extension. (Rutgers Special Collections and University Archives.)

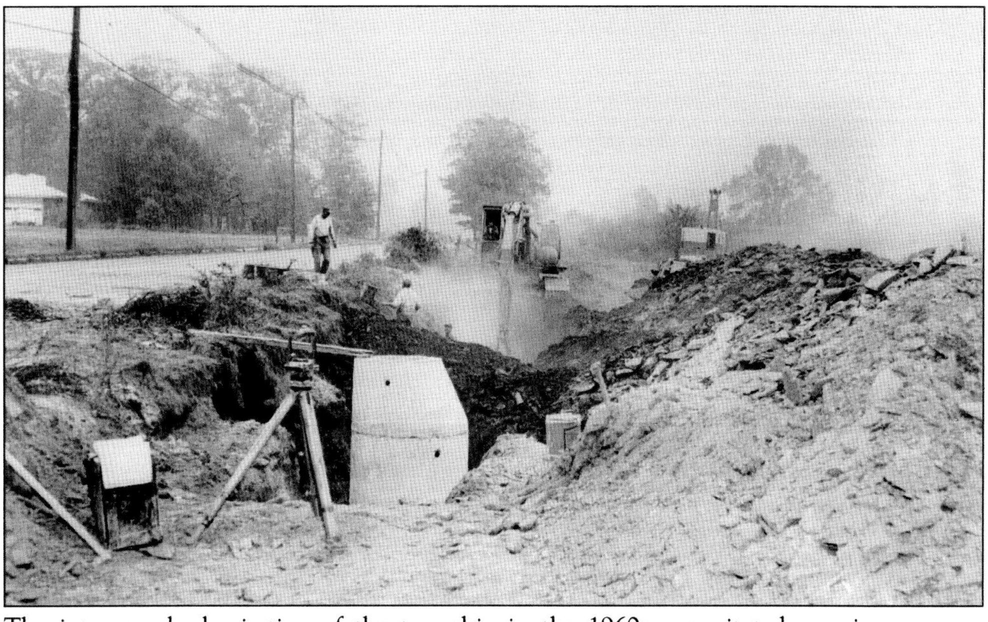

The intense suburbanization of the township in the 1960s necessitated a major sewerage program financed with about $6.4 million in bonds. This 1965 picture shows a manhole under construction on the Ambrose Brook trunk line, which then served about 1,000 houses in the Lake Nelson, Durham Park, and North Stelton neighborhoods near the township's industrial heart. (Rutgers Special Collections and University Archives.)

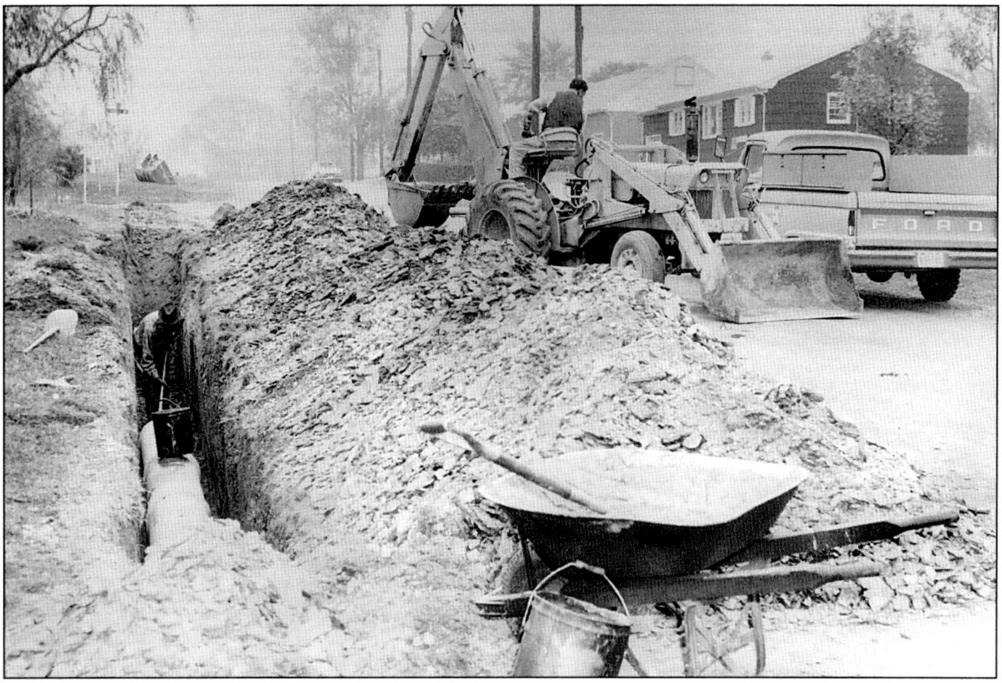

The installation of storm sewers is pictured *c.* 1964 on Dupont Avenue in the New Market section. The man on the left is a reminder that working in a ditch is potentially one of the most hazardous construction tasks. (Rutgers Special Collections and University Archives.)

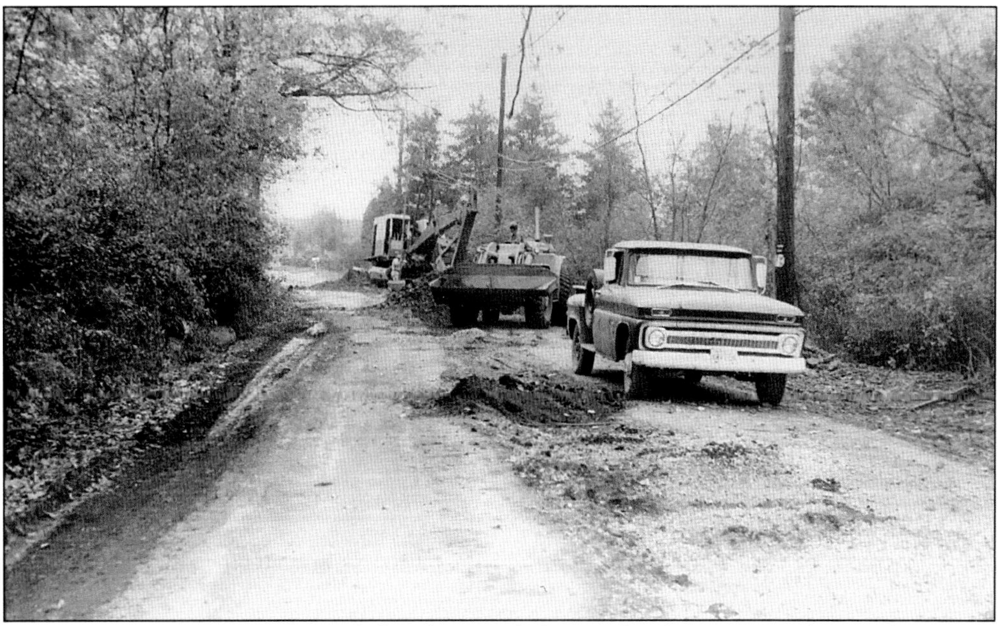

The 1960s sewer projects coincided with a needed upgrade of many township roads. Timing the latter to follow the former was helpful in eliminating the scars of patched roadways. A 1965 *Piscataway Chronicle* review of public works projects labeled this image "the start of drainage projects prior to road improvement" but offered no locale. (Rutgers Special Collections and University Archives.)

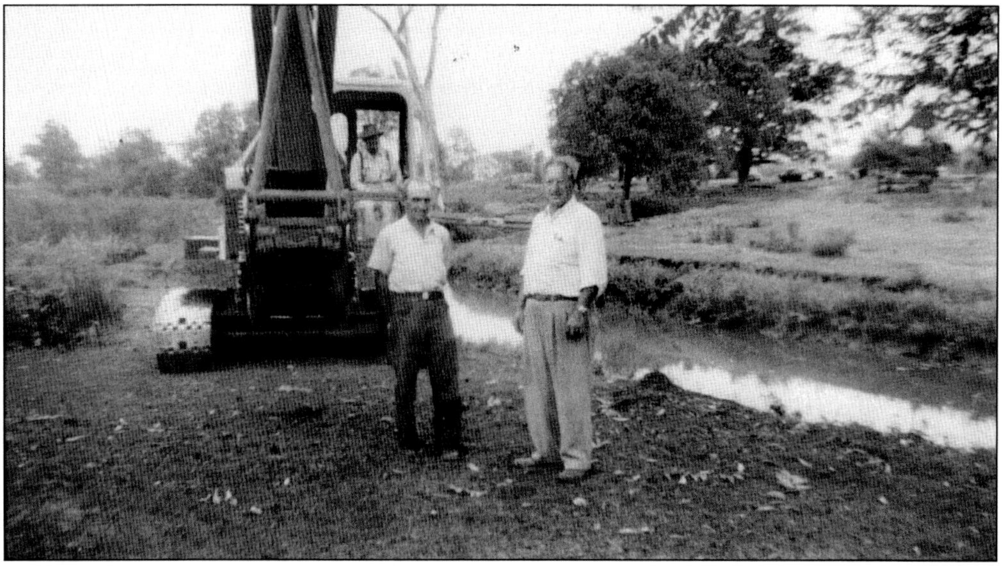

Heavy equipment and a major effort were required to build the pond at Morris Park, near Knightsbridge Road. Much of the pond, pictured under construction in the 1930s, has been filled in.

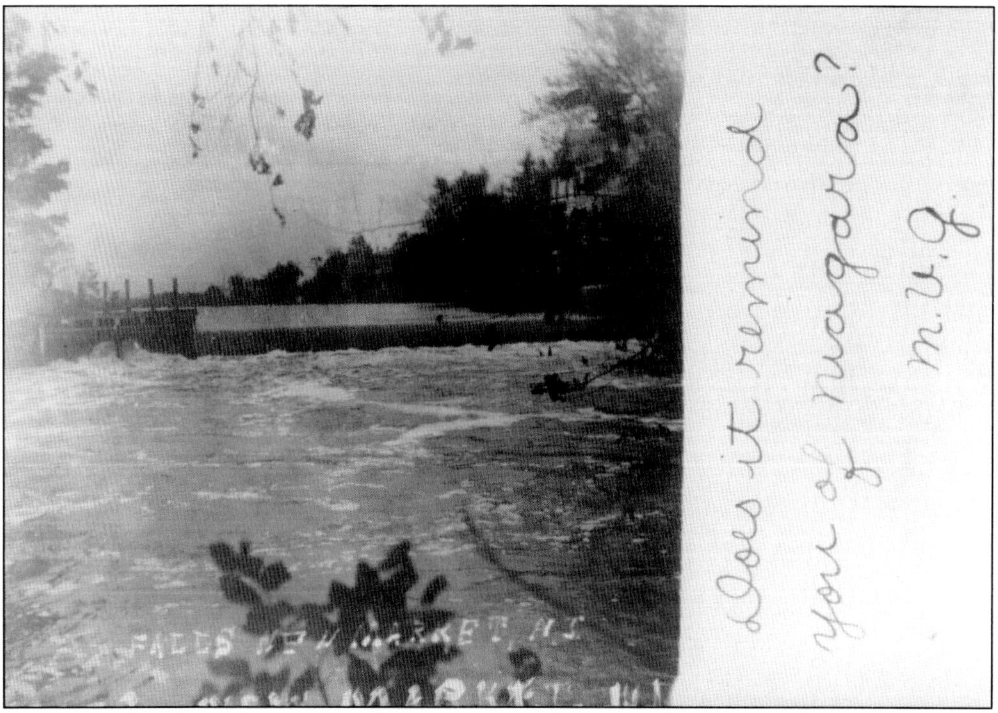

The gentle flow over the dam at New Market Pond may not bear a resemblance to Niagara Falls, but this *c.* 1905 photographic postcard provides a view of the dam wrecked by ice in December 1910.

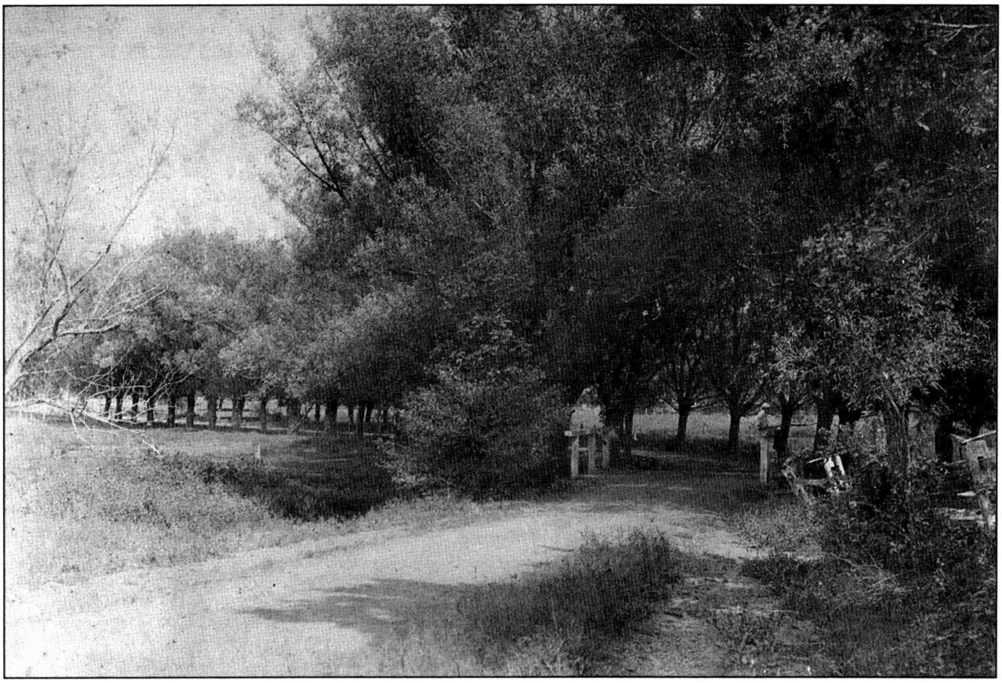

What a difference a century makes for the Sidney Road bridge over Ambrose Brook. The surroundings of this small wood structure about 100 years ago were an idyllic pastoral setting. The present bridge has the feeling of a figurative speed bump on an access road to Interstate 287.

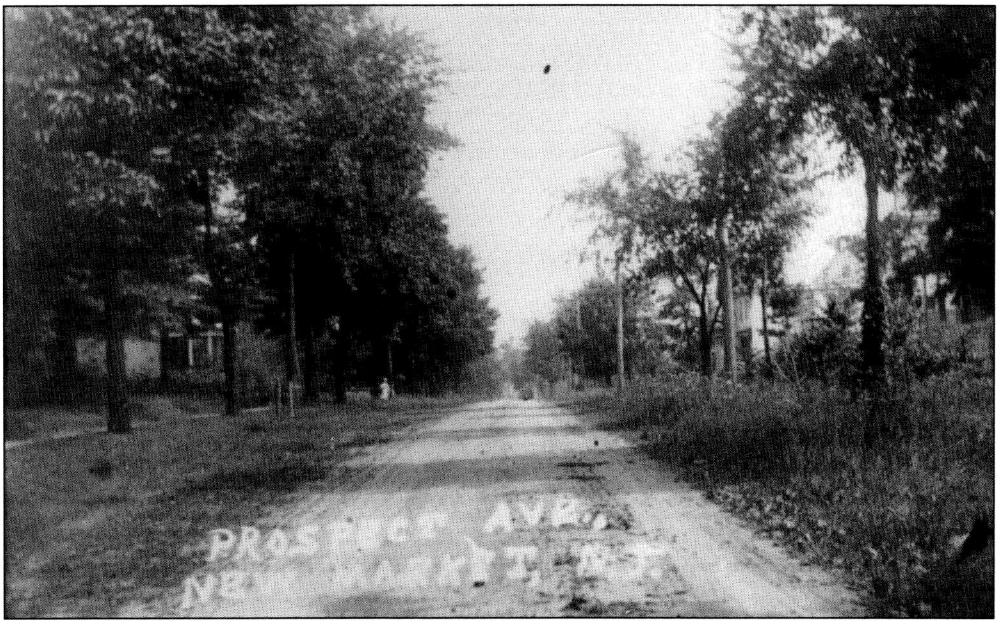

Prospect Avenue is now a main stem running from "downtown New Market" into central Dunellen. This view, from a photographic postcard, is north from near the site of the railroad bridge; Union Avenue is near the right. Lack of pavement gives the scene an ancient character, but many of the still-standing houses were in place by *c.* 1905, the date of the image. The house at 520 Prospect Avenue is visible through the trees on the left. (Collection of Cynthia Harris.)

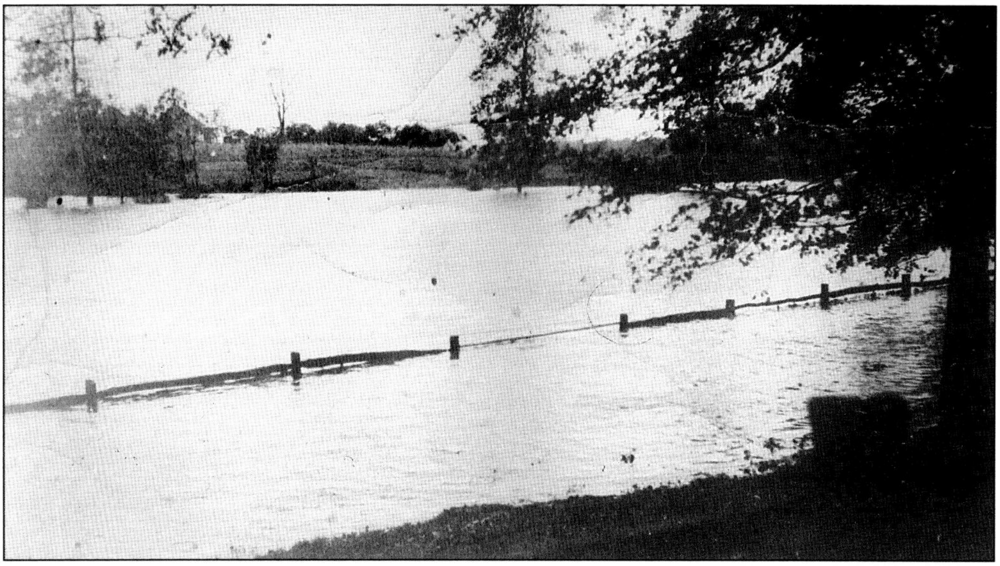

Ambrose Brook, which runs through the Ambrose Doty County Park, is pictured perhaps c. the 1930s, overflowing in the Sidney Road area. Old-timers recalled the once good fishing at the brook.

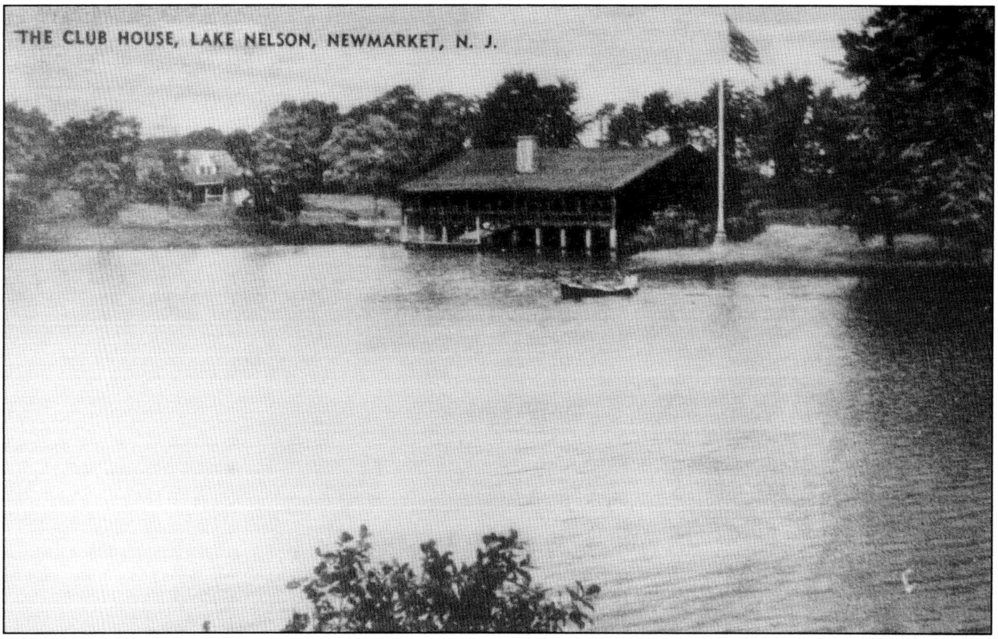

Physician William J. Nelson lived in New Market but owned an extensive tract to the south on Ambrose Brook. He failed three times, but he eventually succeeded at damming his property, using headstones from New Market Cemetery and concrete. He also built an icehouse on the north side of the pond. Nelson's son and two partners sold the land c. 1926 to the SKS Realty Company, which developed the surrounding property. The buyer-homeowners also owned the lake. Their property association built this clubhouse, pictured c. 1930. After a later incarnation as a restaurant-bar (page 72), the building was destroyed c. 1990. (Collection of Cynthia Harris.)

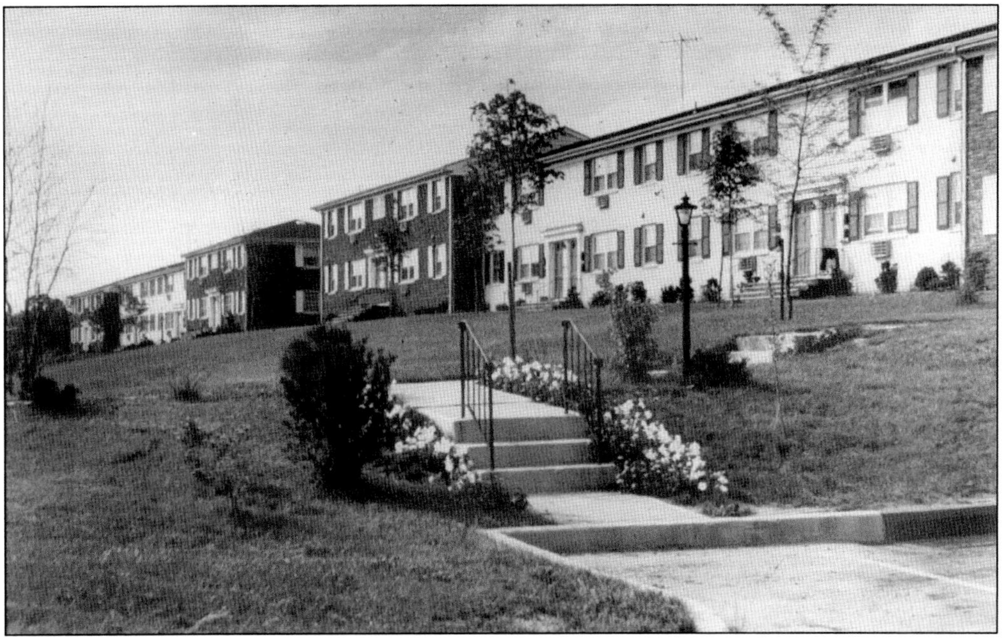

The 172-unit Rivercrest Garden Apartments were located at 280 River Road, north of Interstate 287, and were completed in 1963. It was the first major multiple-dwelling development in Piscataway. Director of public works Henry A. Zanetti claimed that apartments were desirable not only to house workers for the new industrial plants but because their tax revenues exceeded the cost of schools and services for their tenants. His pronouncement of $60,000 per year in taxes for a cost of $10,000 in services likely stemmed from a mix of naiveté, "voodoo mathematics," and misleading statements by the developer. The onset of apartments threatened the character of the township and caused local political ferment, but it obviously continued unabated for decades.

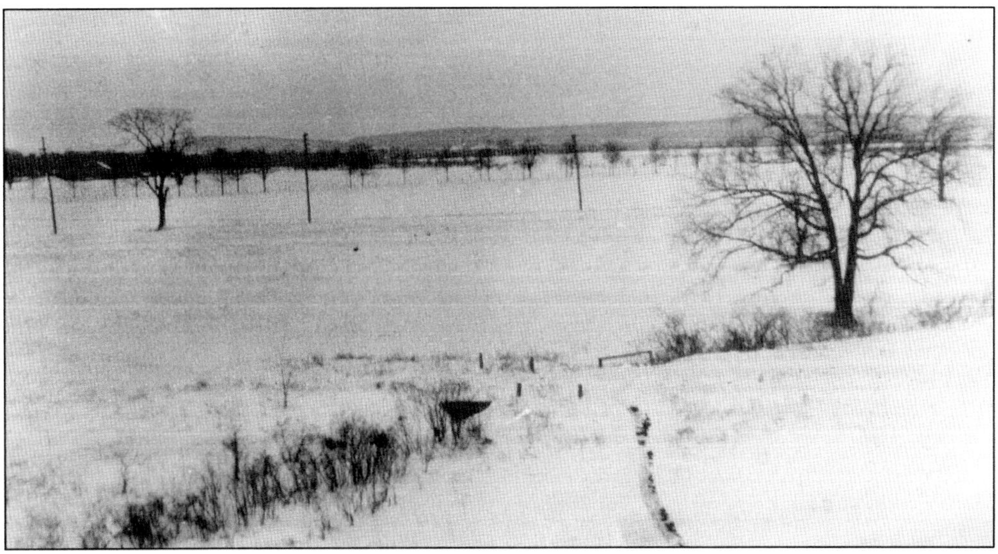

The Watchung Mountains to the north make up the background in this c. 1920 picture taken from Plainfield Avenue. The line of trees depict old Centennial Avenue, prior to its 1960s expansion for commercial construction.

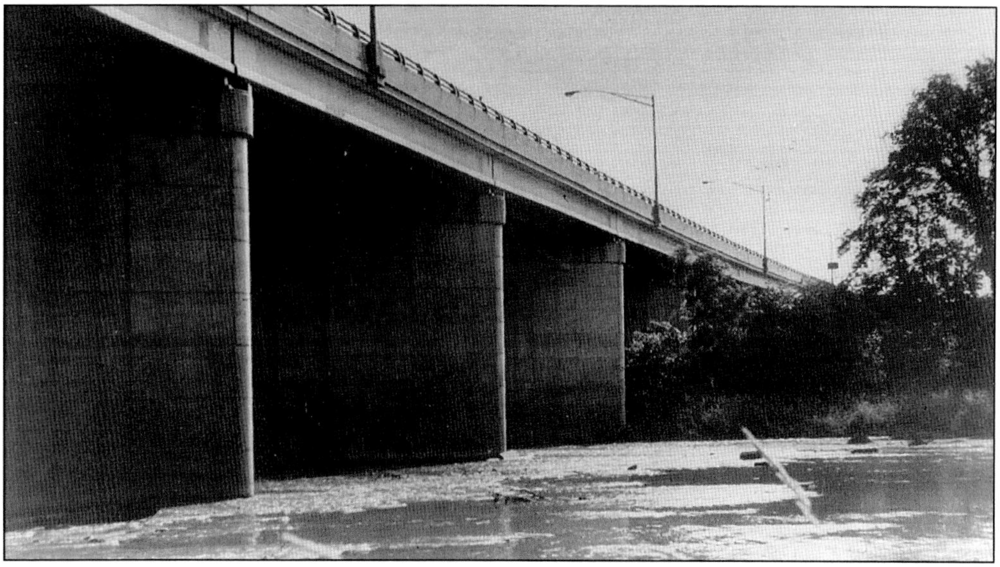

Interstate 287 runs north-south through New Jersey from near the Raritan River to the New York border, but it bisects Piscataway east and west. The highway provided a corridor for extensive commercial development near its course and motor access for the thousands of new residents who followed in the decades after its 1960 opening. The underside of the bridge over the Raritan River is a good perspective for viewing, given the spare new construction standards of the system and the resultant need for maintenance vigilance. (Collection of the Piscataway Public Library.)

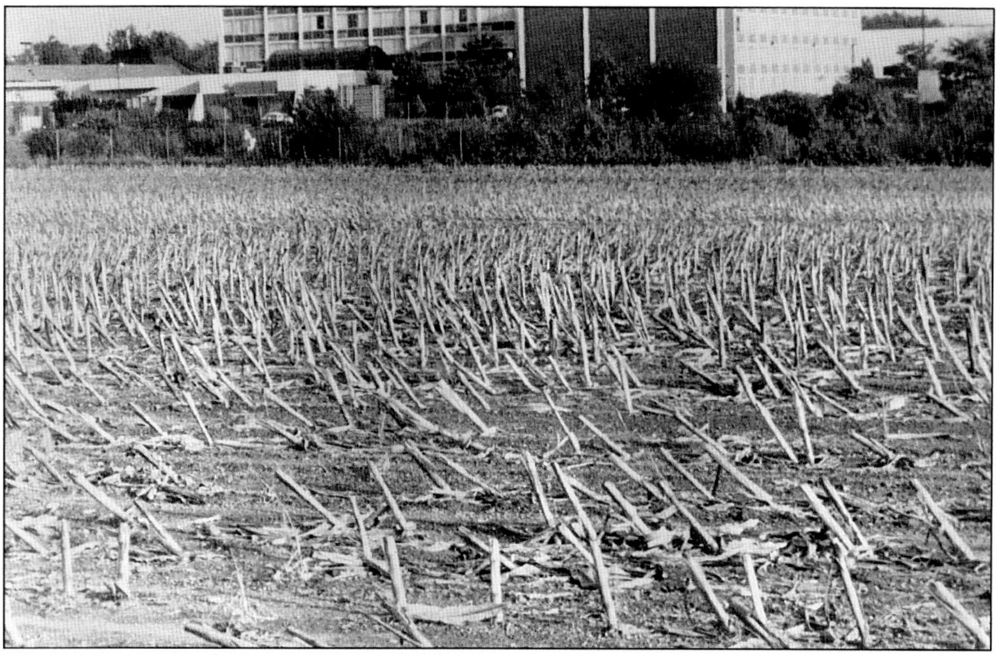

The juxtaposition of a harvested cornfield and new commercial construction on the north and south of Interstate 187 is symbolic of Piscataway's changing character, continuous since the 1960s. The foreground on this 1986 scene was filled in by the Woodfield housing development. The hotel was the Sheraton Inn. (Photograph by Ed Marsh.)

Seven

Rutgers University

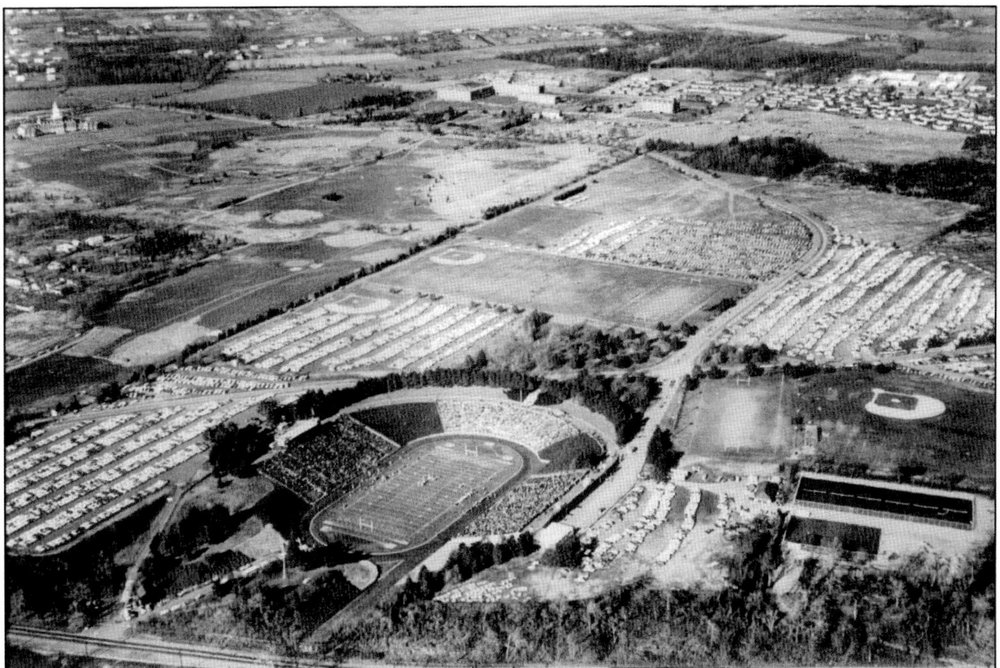

Rutgers University's major presence in Piscataway began with construction of its football stadium on part of the Vermeule farm, which the university bought in 1935 for $98,500. Architect George P. Howell (Rutgers Class of 1919) designed the 23,000-capacity arena, which cost $1.3 million; the Works Progress Administration contributed $1.1 million. The overall facility included eight gridirons, three baseball diamonds, and a parking for 5,000 cars. Another feature was the nearby golf course (page 115). The stadium, which opened on October 4, 1938, with a Rutgers 20-18 win over Princeton, was replaced after the 1992 season (page 114). The 1938 construction of the stadium kicked off a Rutgers presence in the township that now comprises more than 12 percent of township land. (Rutgers Special Collections and University Archives.)

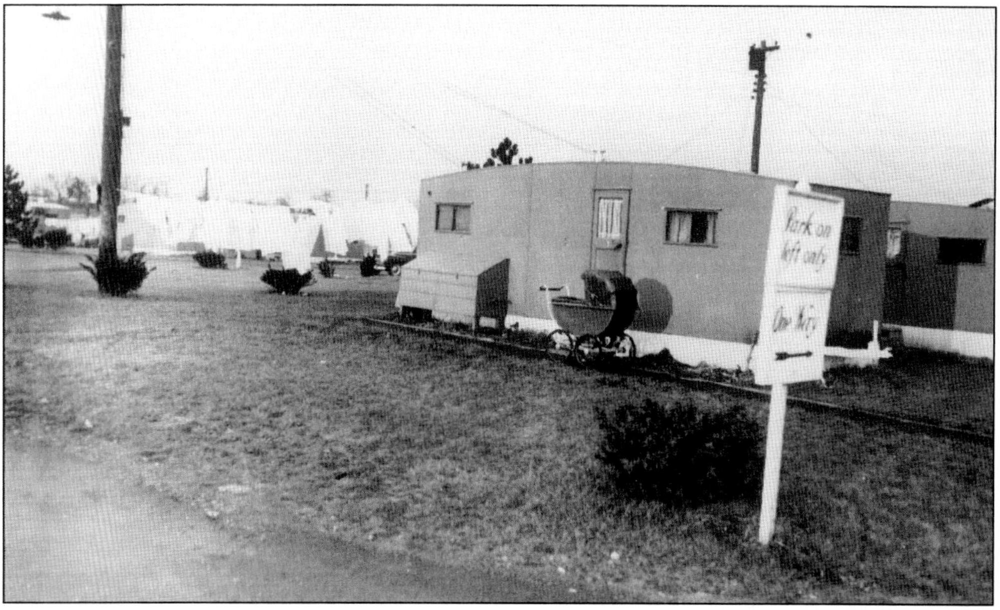

The Rutgers University population exploded in the post–World War II years as returning servicemen took advantage the G.I. Bill of Rights. Enrollment in men's colleges soared from 750 in 1945 to 4,200 in 1948. Residents were housed in a variety of makeshift and temporary quarters, including the Hillside Trailer Camp. The baby carriage shown here is indicative of a second population explosion and the area's nickname of Fertility City. (Rutgers Special Collections and University Archives.)

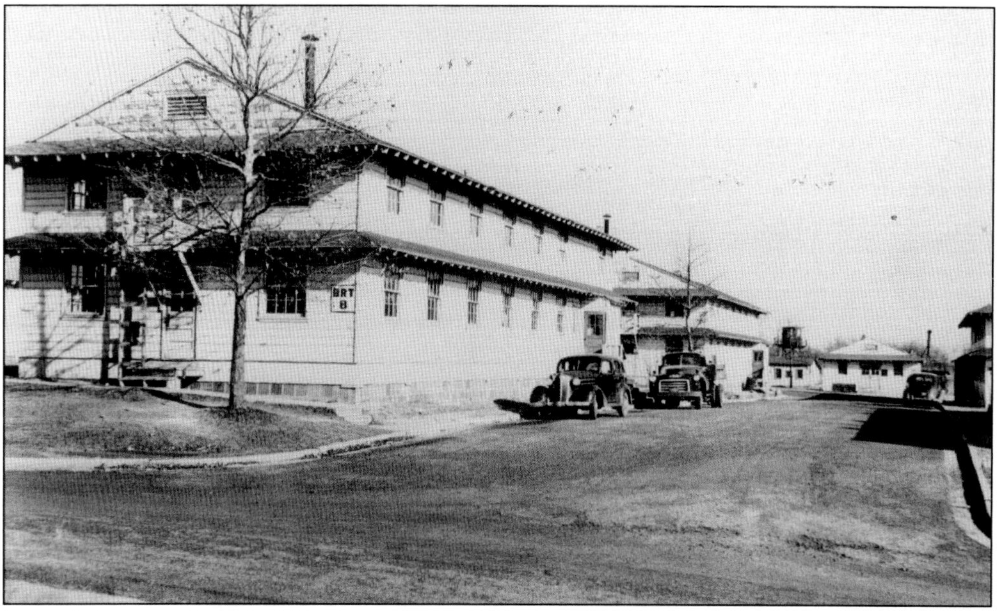

Barracks housing from the U.S. Army's Camp Kilmer was incorporated into the Kilmer campus, since renamed Livingston. Prominent identification on a sign was needed, especially in the era the area was occupied by short-term resident soldiers (page 96). Housing included a variety of semipermanent units that provided fast and inexpensive quarters. (Rutgers Special Collections and University Archives.)

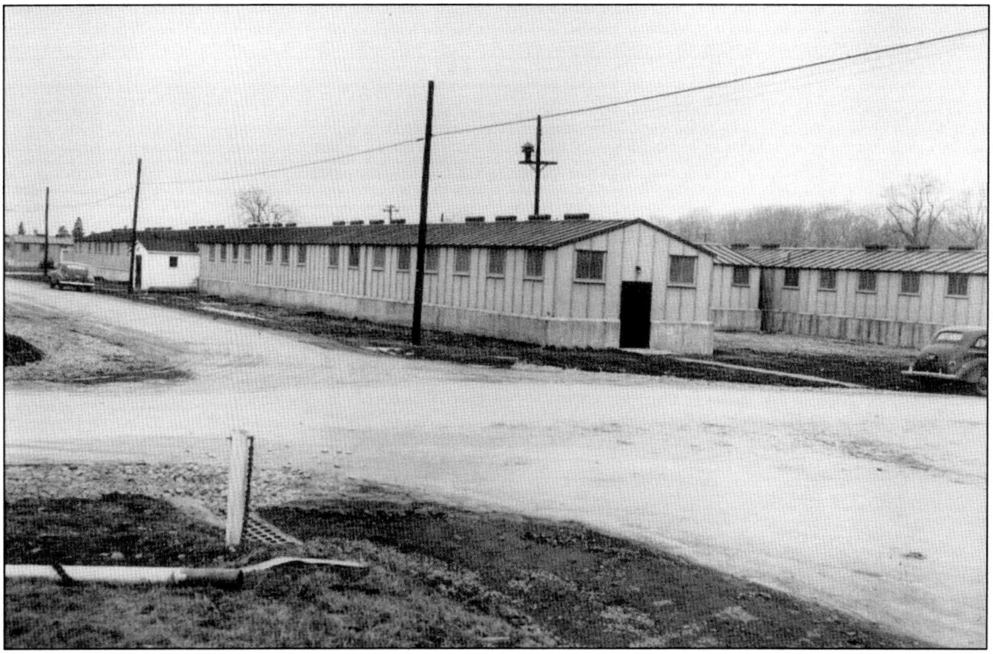

The chemistry laboratories, semipermanent at best, were replaced by the 1950s. This 1948 picture depicts one infrastructure improvement, the recent construction of sewers. (Rutgers Special Collections and University Archives.)

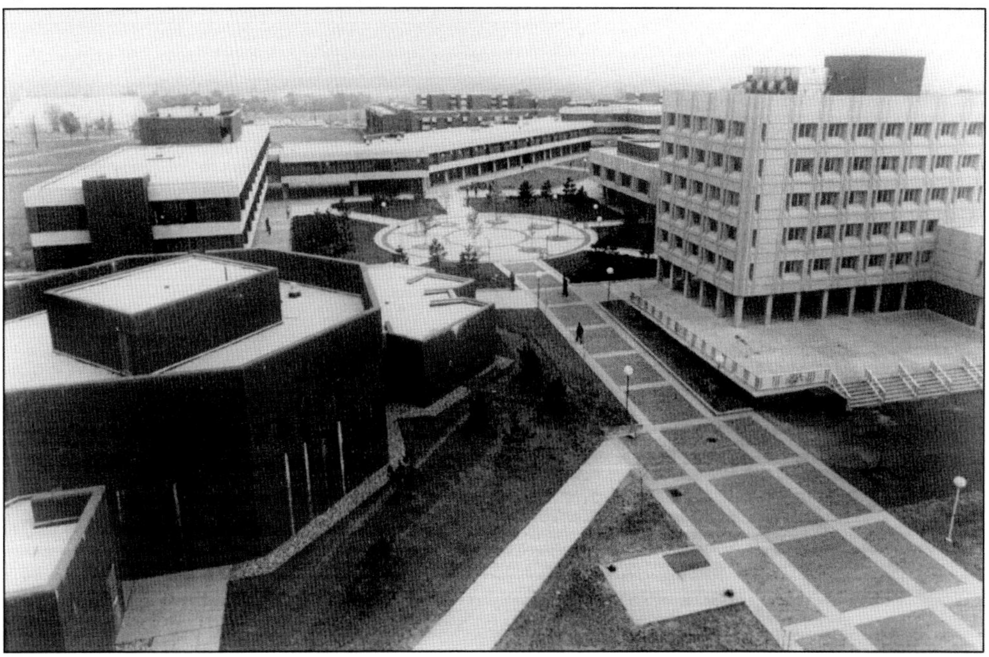

Livingston College, one of three small colleges planned on a former piece of Camp Kilmer, was the only one built; it opened in 1969. Livingston intended to nurture a traditional sense of student community through social relevance. Its initial idealism was marred by student ferment in the early 1970s, resulting in the establishment of more conventional procedures. (Rutgers Special Collections and University Archives.)

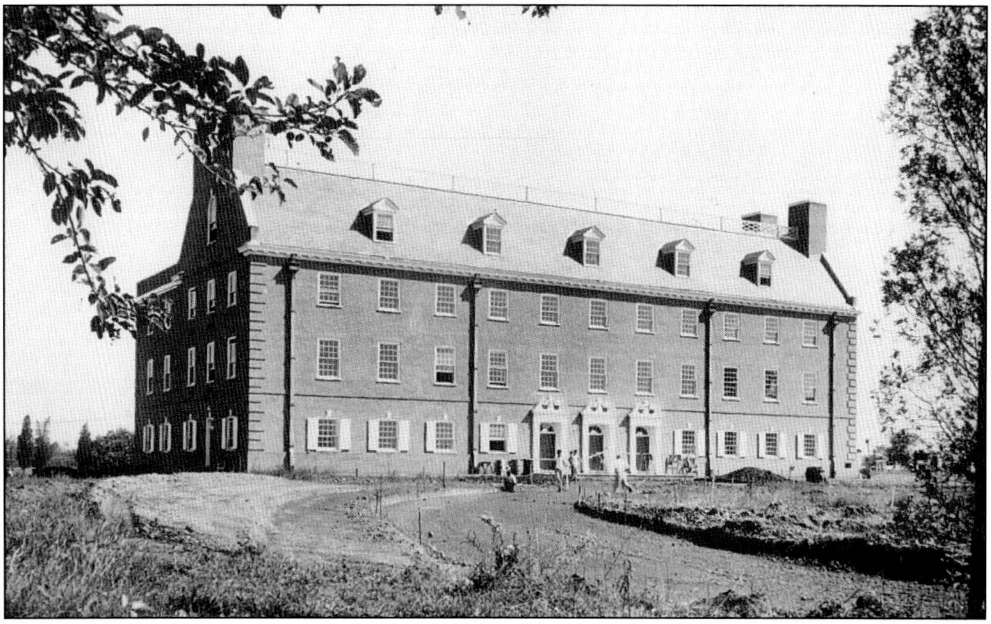

The Rutgers Chemistry Building, or the Wright Labs, was completed *c.* 1949 on Brett Road and named for Dr. Ralph G. Wright, a professor of chemistry from 1907 to 1930. The building is pictured around the time of its completion. A wing was added later and was named for Prof. William Reiman. The two buildings are known collectively as the Wright-Reiman Laboratories. Note the design similarity of this building to the wings of the microbiology building, pictured below. (Rutgers Special Collections and University Archives.)

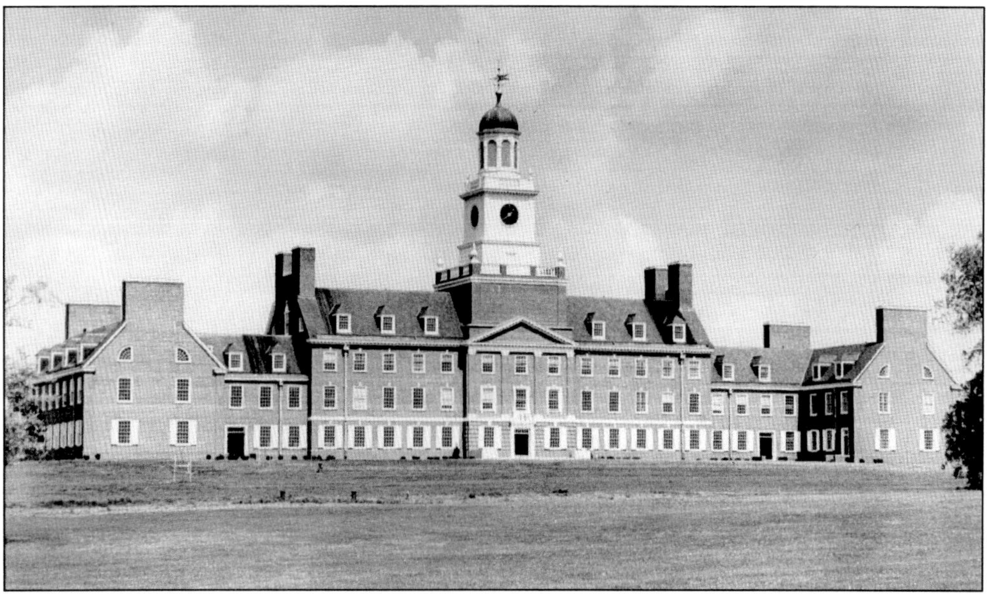

The Rutgers Institute of Microbiology was the research home of Selman Waksman (page 57) and his associates, a team whose discovery of streptomycin won the 1952 Nobel Prize for Medicine. Designed by York & Sawyer, a New York architectural firm with extensive experience in the health field, the building was completed in 1954 and the institute renamed for Waksman in 1974. (Rutgers Special Collections and University Archives.)

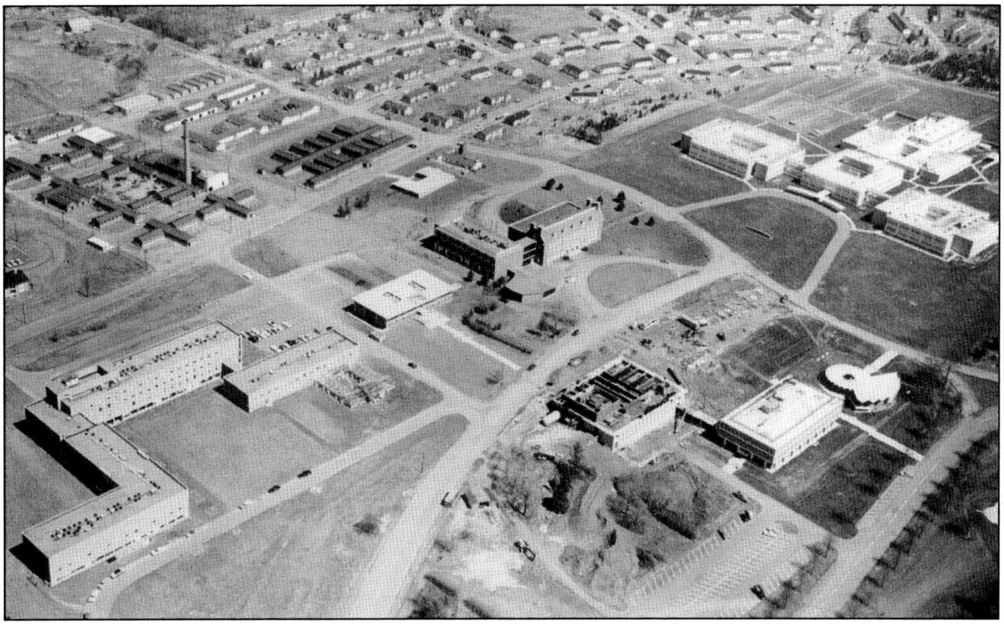

This 1964 aerial depicts both new scientific buildings and older faculty housing (upper left). The Nelson Biological Laboratories are on the lower left, and the construction scene to its right is of the Tandem Accelerator. The Wright Labs (opposite) is detectable in the center and the Alcohol Studies Building is between it and Nelson. The Rutgers Engineering Center (page 116) is on the upper right. (Rutgers Special Collections and University Archives.)

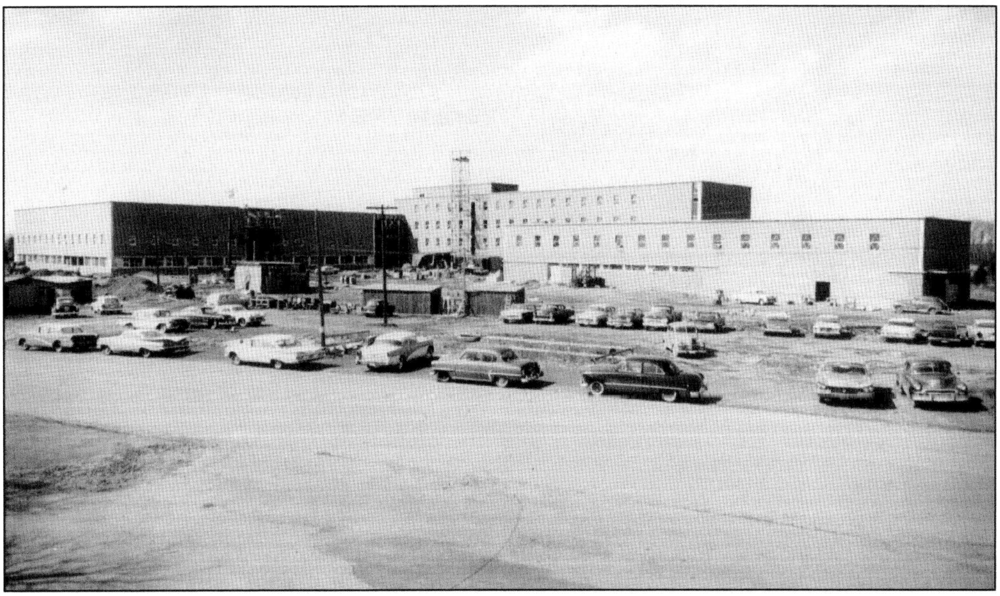

The Nelson Biological Laboratories, pictured nearing completion, opened in September 1961 and were dedicated the next year. The labs are named for Thurlow Nelson (Rutgers Class of 1913), a longtime faculty member who chaired the Department of Zoology from 1925 to 1954. The University Heights campus was renamed in 1972 for Charles L. Busch, a wealthy investor who, in 1971, willed Rutgers about $10 million for biological research. (Rutgers Special Collections and University Archives.)

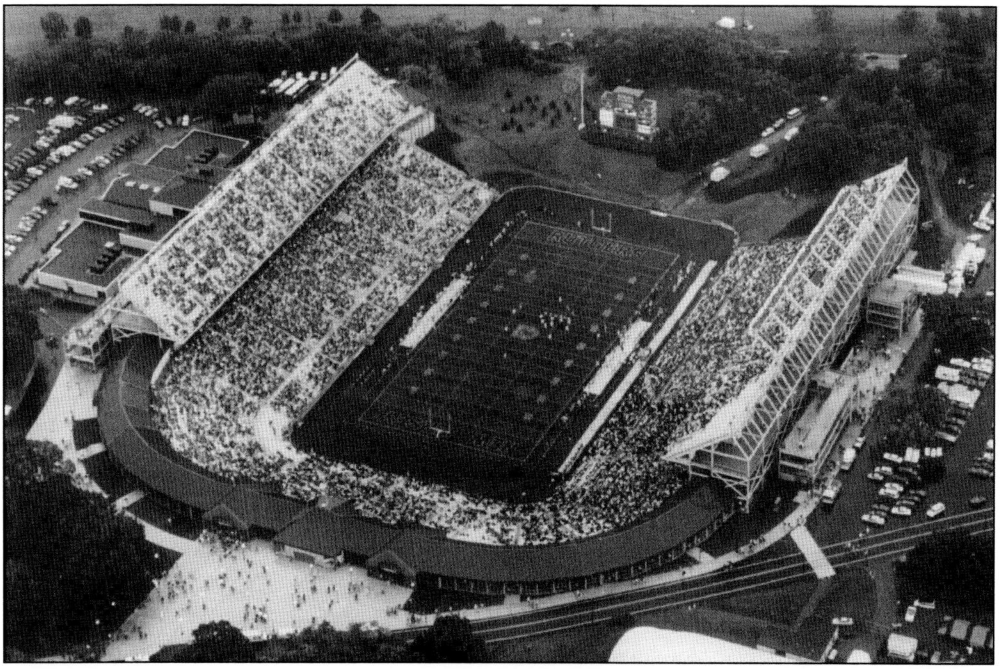

Rutgers, requiring a larger stadium after joining the Big East Conference, built this 41,000-seat arena in 1993–1994. Designed by the firm GSGSBH and erected by the Terminal Construction Company, its siting was moved 25 feet to the west. Rutgers played its 1993 home games at Giants Stadium in East Rutherford. The new field is pictured at its September 3, 1994 opening. (Rutgers Special Collections and University Archives.)

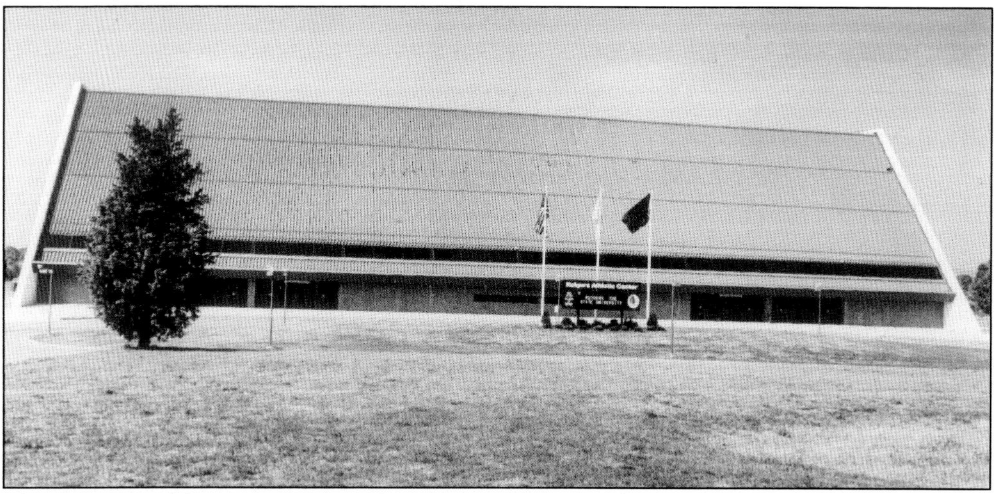

The Rutgers Athletic Center, a multipurpose gymnasium built primarily for indoor spectator sports (with a priority for basketball) opened in 1978. The facility can seat about 8,500 for basketball but is also used for tennis, volleyball, and badminton, among other sports. The largest indoor gym in New Jersey offers parking for 3,000 cars and spacious press facilities. The center was host to the National Basketball Association New Jersey Nets in its early years and is home to both Rutgers men's and women's basketball teams; the latter was nationally ranked in 2001. The center was renamed in 1986 for Louis Brown (Rutgers Class of 1936), a generous Rutgers donor, especially for athletics. (Rutgers Special Collections and University Archives.)

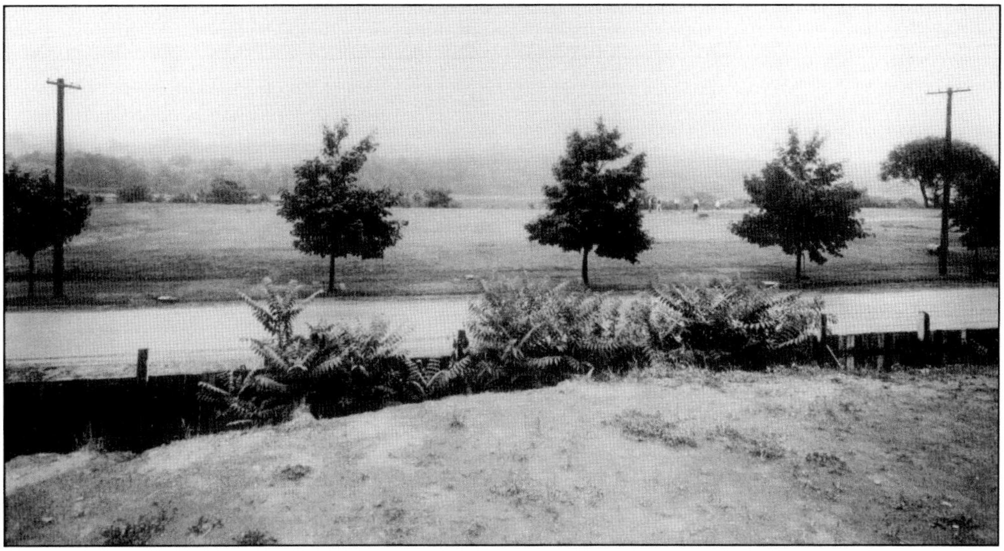

The origins of the Rutgers Golf Course stem from the 1894 private New Brunswick Golf Club, one of the first to join the U.S. Golf Association, which was also founded that year. Their 1897 purchase of 50 acres on the south side of Ross Hall Boulevard permitted replacing an initial six-hole course with a nine-hole, 2,396-yard links. The club purchased an additional 118 acres in 1912, lost its club house to fire in 1925, and became bankrupt in 1933. Rutgers bought club property from its mortgagee and an additional 130 acres in 1935. An 18-hole course laid out by noted golf course architect Hal Purdy, built for under $200,000, officially opened on May 29, 1963, and remains in use. (Rutgers Special Collections and University Archives.)

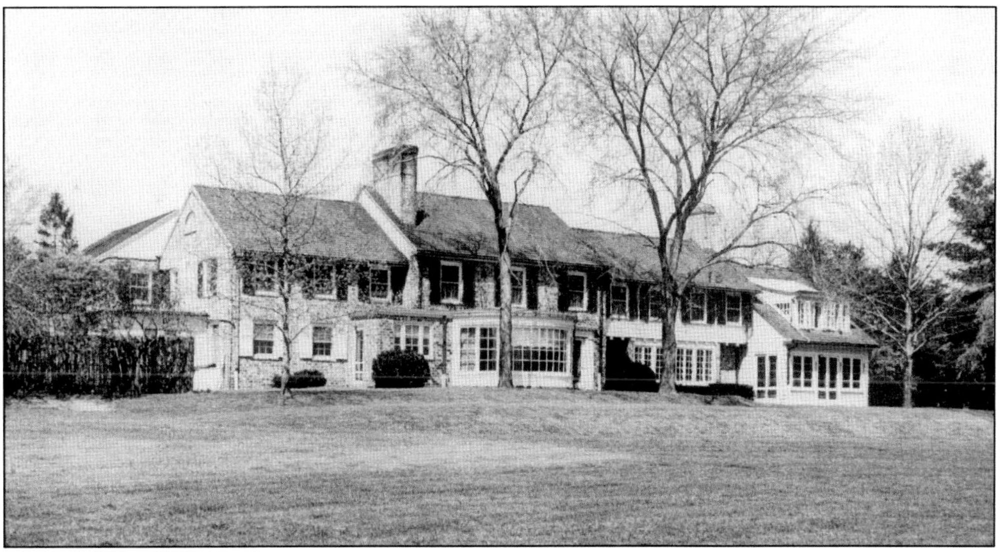

Robert and Roberta Nicholas built their home Glenlybber in 1929 on an extensive hilltop tract at 1245 River Road. Robert was the president of Shirley Industries, a hosiery manufacturer of Shirley, Massachusetts. Roberta was a local Johnson. Rutgers trustees bought the home with privately raised funds to provide a suitable home for the university president. Their 1939 price of $39,000 was well under the reported cost to build new for $125,000. Robert Clothier was the first to occupy the home as university president. An entertainment wing was added in the 1960s and the dining room was expanded. (Rutgers Special Collections and University Archives.)

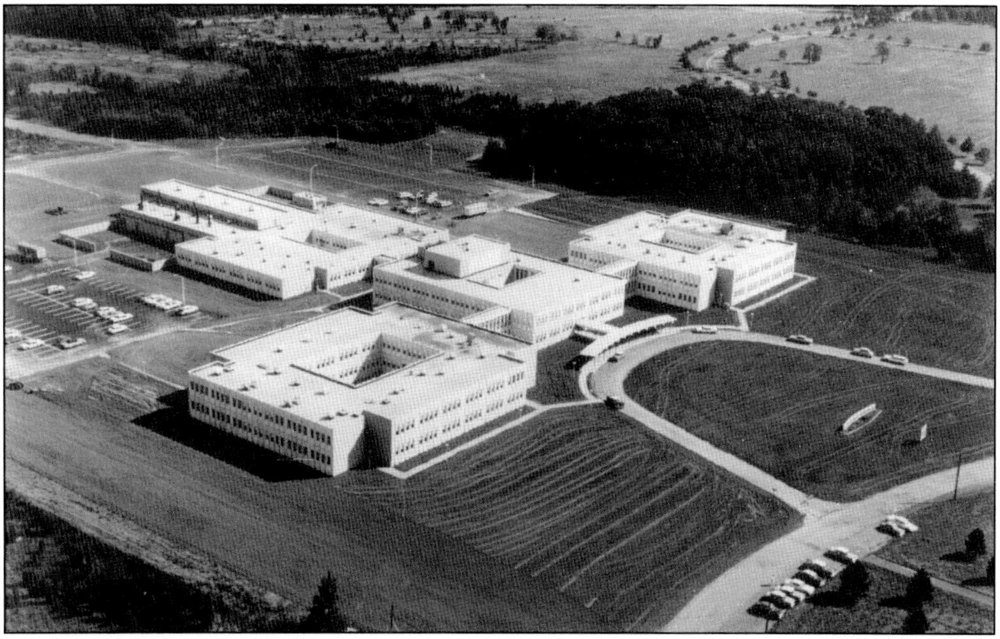

The Rutgers Engineering Center, designed by Frank Grad & Sons, opened in the fall of 1963 but was dedicated on May 2, 1964, at the 100th anniversary of engineering at Rutgers. These four buildings, pictured when new, then comprised about half of the College of Engineering's facilities. (Rutgers Special Collections and University Archives.)

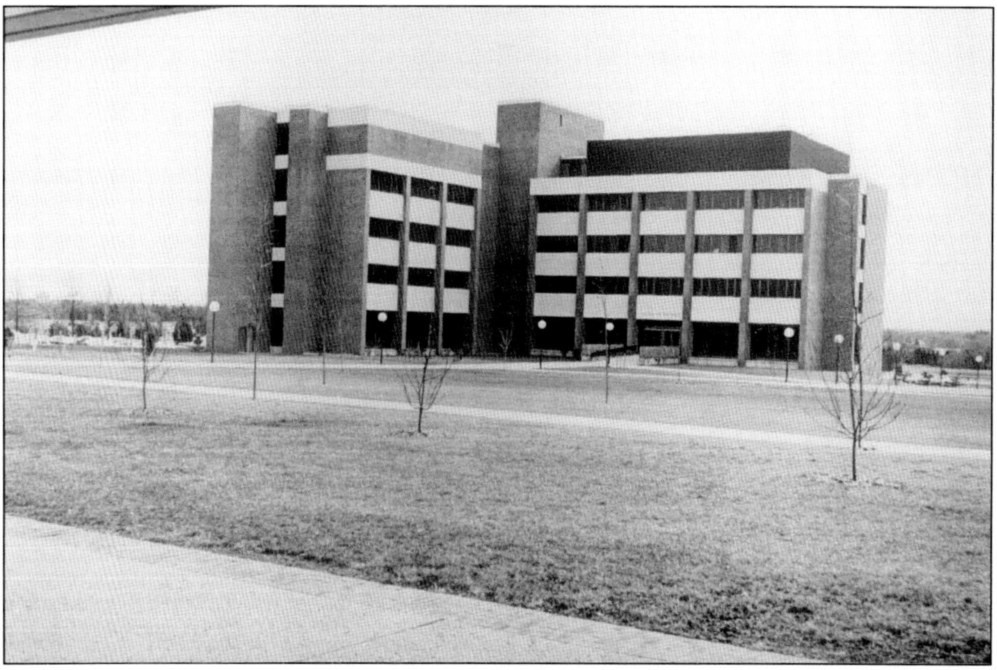

The Rutgers College of Pharmacy, formerly located at the Newark campus, moved to the Busch campus with the construction of this building designed by Drake, Convery, & Cueman of Summit. Ground was broken at the 160 Frelinghuysen Road location in 1968; the school opened in 1971. (Rutgers Special Collections and University Archives.)

Eight

East Jersey Olde Towne

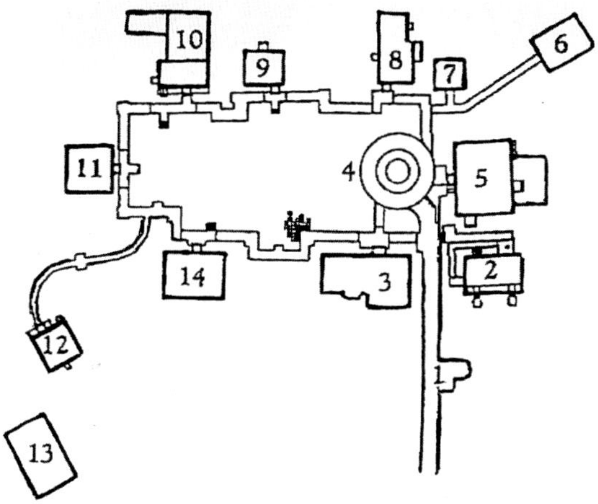

East Jersey Olde Towne

Directory

1 - Directory Area
2 - New Brunswick Barracks
3 - Runyon House
4 - Courtyard
5 - Indian Queen Tavern
6 - Farley Blacksmith Shop
7 - Williamson Wheelwright/ Blacksmith Shop
8 - Six Mile Run House
9 - Smalleytown Schoolhouse
10 - Vanderveer House
11 - Church of the Three Mile Run
12 - Fitzrandolph House
13 - Runyon Dutch Barn
14 - Dunn House

Joseph H. Kler founded East Jersey Olde Towne in 1971 by establishing a not-for-profit corporation in an attempt to save the Indian Queen Tavern in New Brunswick (page 120). He conceived the idea of collecting other threatened buildings, envisioning a living history establishment in the style of Old Sturbridge Village in Massachusetts. The County of Middlesex leased 12 acres at River Road and Hoes Lane to his organization in 1973 for a historic village park. Kler was guided (or, perhaps, restrained) by preservation architect Charles Henry Detweiler Jr. for a 10-year period beginning in 1973. Kler died suddenly in 1983 and the organization foundered. The village was donated to the County of Middlesex in 1989, which undertook a program to meet codes, stabilize and restore the properties, and bring the village into public use. It operates East Jersey Olde Towns as a museum and cultural center. Area No. 1 on this contemporary directory is the entrance.

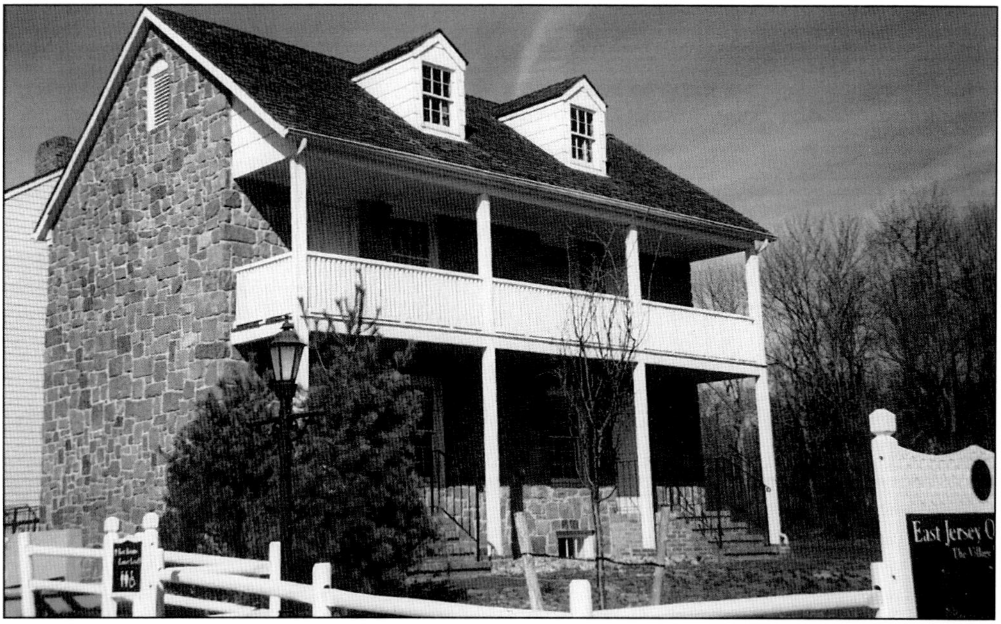

In 1758, the New Jersey Assembly authorized construction of barracks for British soldiers to eliminate the odious practice of billeting them in private residences. Six were built; one is now restored on site in Trenton. The one shown is a reconstructed example of part of the larger barracks that formerly stood on George Street, across from Paterson Street, in New Brunswick.

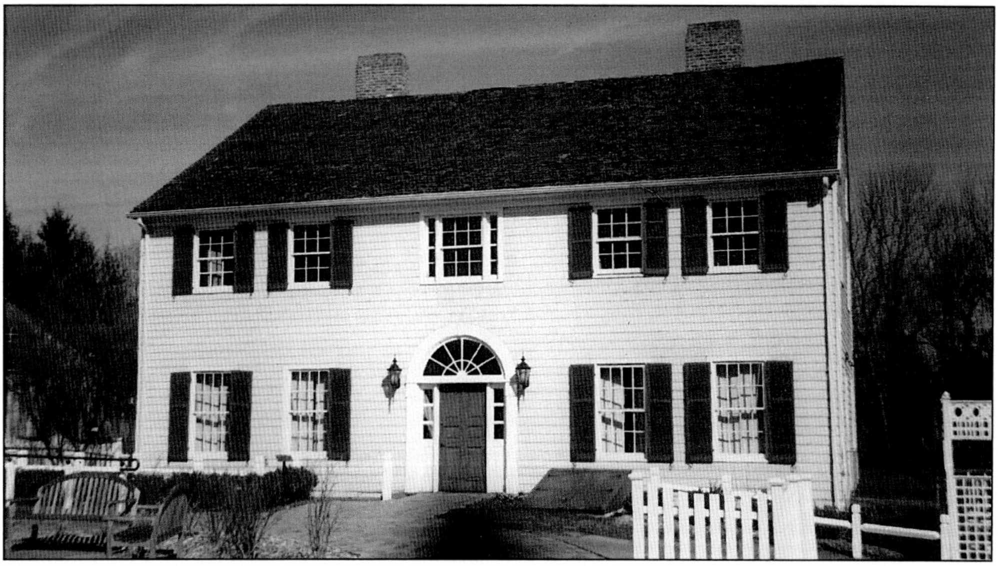

The origin of the Indian Queen Tavern may have been a one-story house built c. 1740 by William Farquhar. Perhaps James Drake was the first to conduct a tavern there, in the Revolutionary era. The place at the northeast corner of Albany and Water Streets was often altered, expanded to three and a half stories and, by the World War II years, was run as Andy's Hotel. In the way of Route 18 expansion, the building was disassembled and placed in storage with plans to reerect it at East Jersey Olde Towne. However, a two-and-a-half-story building more appropriate to the late 18th century was rebuilt there instead. Plans have been made to rebuild a functioning tavern interior.

Needing a church, East Jersey Olde Towne built one, modeled on early-18th-century Dutch church-building principles and an 18th-century example in Massachusetts. Little is known about the original Church of the Three Mile Run, but its construction is attributed to 1703. The church was long mired in controversy within the Dutch Reformed movement. The original church's demise is not known, but speculation early in the 20th century suggested that British troops may have destroyed it during the Revolutionary War. This reconstruction was dedicated on October 30, 1978, the 350th anniversary of the Dutch Reformed Church in America.

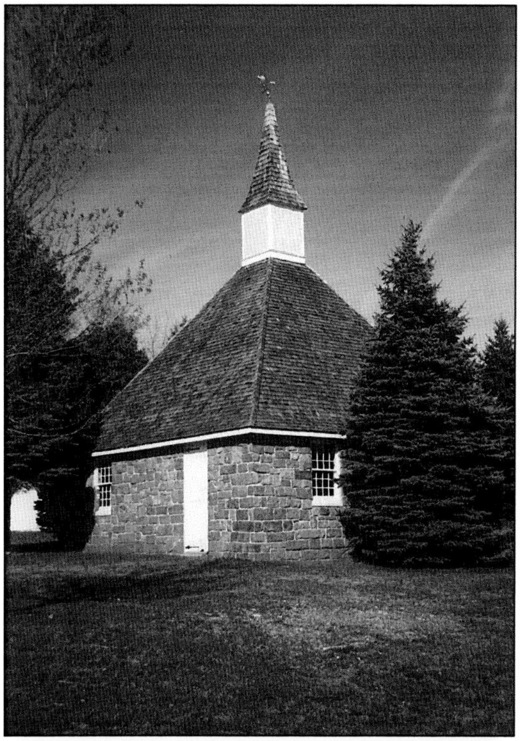

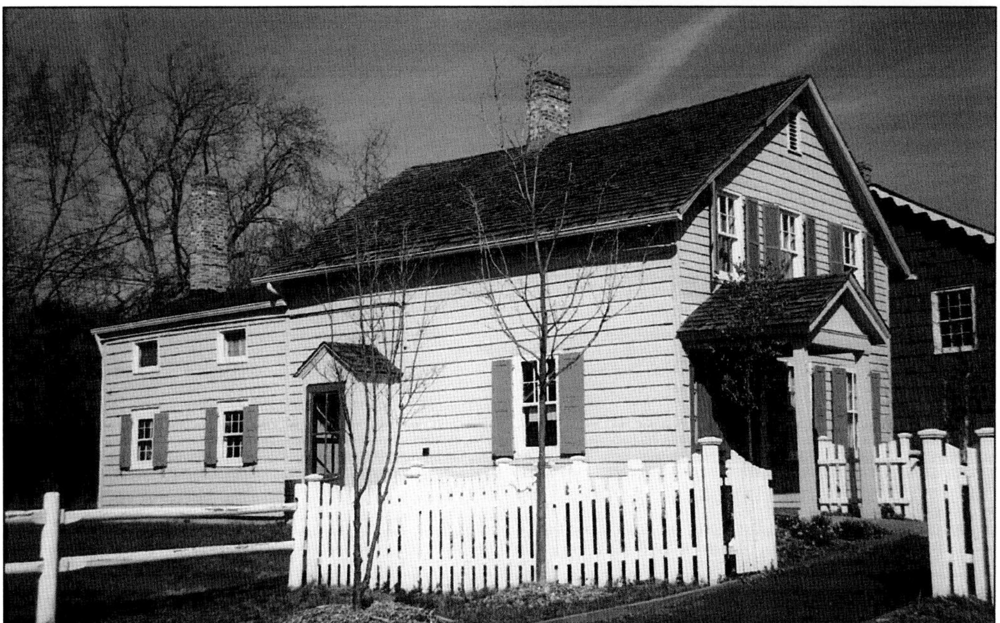

The one-and-a-half-story rear of this building is the *c.* mid-18th-century origin of the Six Mile Run House, a building originally located in the village of that name, outside New Brunswick. The house was a residence until donated to East Jersey Olde Towne by Harry Grossman and his wife in 1979. The two-and-a-half-story, front-gabled main block may date from the second quarter of the 19th century.

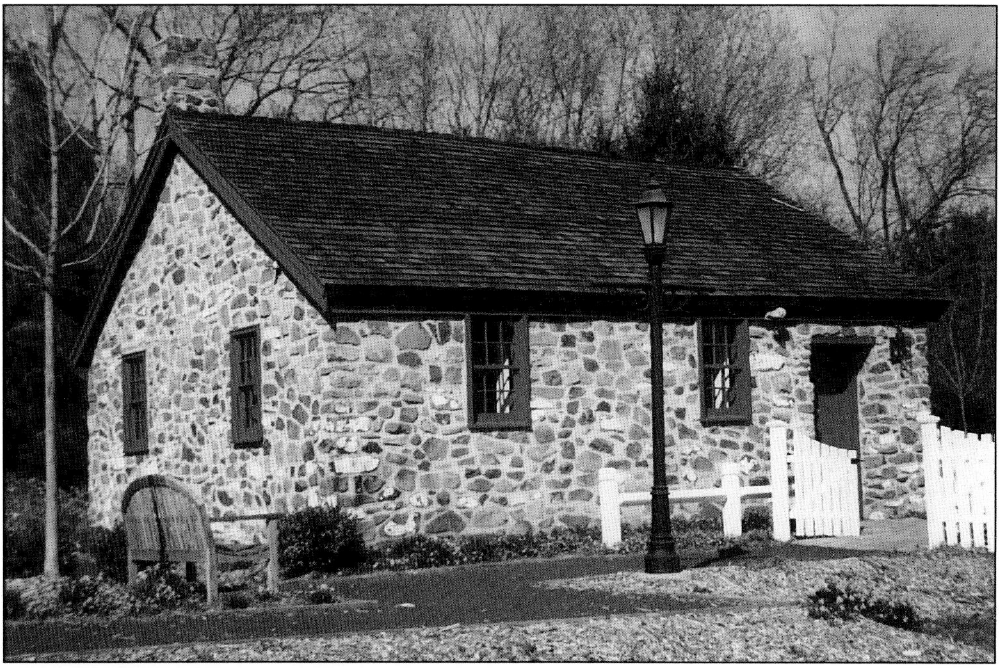

East Jersey Olde Towne attributes the origin of the Smalleytown Schoolhouse to 1803, although a later date seems probable. The one-room stone building stood at Mountain Avenue and Stirling Road in the Smalleytown section of Warren Township, Somerset County. The school was converted to a residence *c.* 1920 and served as temporary home to the Epiphany Lutheran Church, which donated it to East Jersey Olde Towne in 1976.

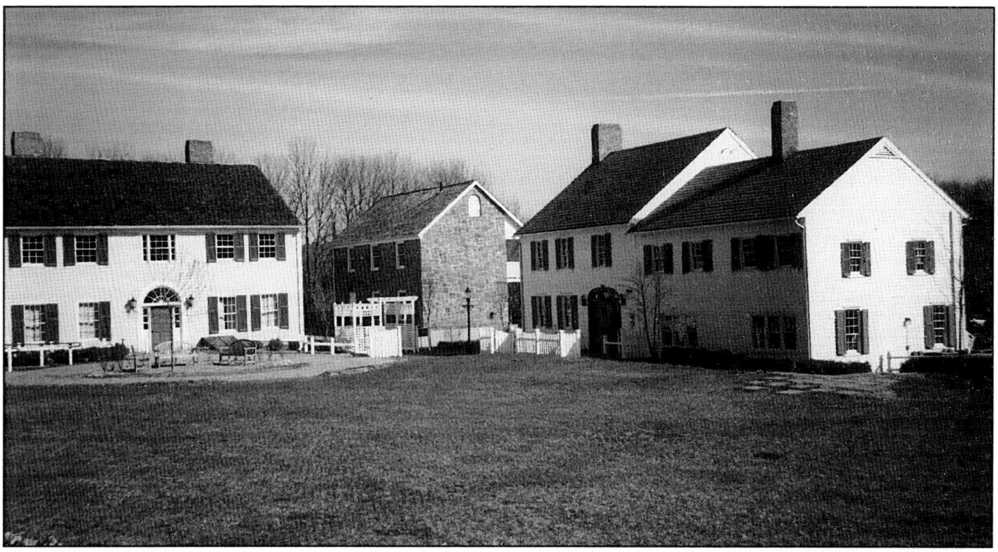

The Runyon House was donated and moved here in 1978 from 175 Possumtown Road following its purchase by Beecham Inc. The Runyons are one of Piscataway's earliest families; the first, Vincent, moved here by 1677 and bought 154 acres along the Raritan River. Benjamin, a grandson, built this house around the third quarter of the 18th century. The house, finely restored after a spell of decline, is used for a variety of exhibitions and meetings. (See page 118 for the Indian Queen Tavern, left, and the New Brunswick Barracks, center.)

Nine

People, Places, and Events

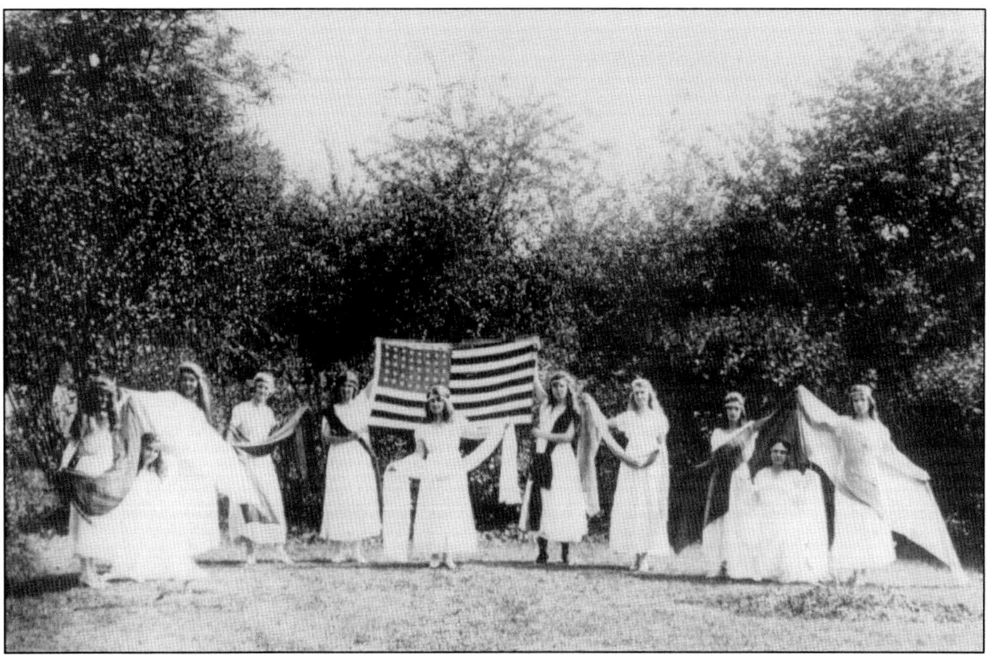

An unidentified New Market celebration c. 1915 presents an image of glamour and fun. The attire and 48-star flag suggest graduation or Independence Day. (Collection of Cynthia Harris.)

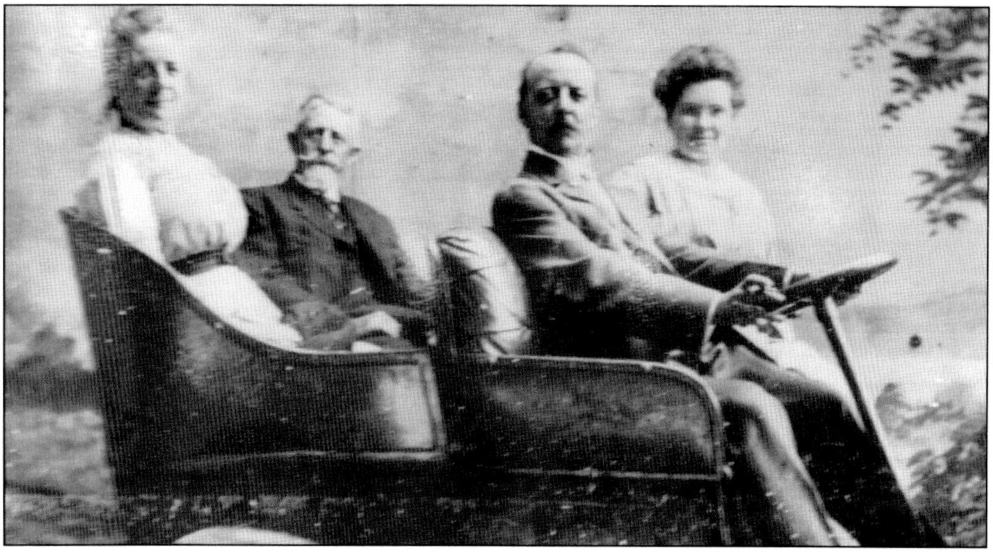

Posing practice of *c.* 1900 and the seriousness of early automobile travel are reflected in the rigidity of the subjects, including Stanley Day at the wheel. His wife, Alice Pierce (known as Allie), shares the front seat. Frank Van Nuis and wife Connie from Randolphville are in the rear. (Collection of the Metlar House.)

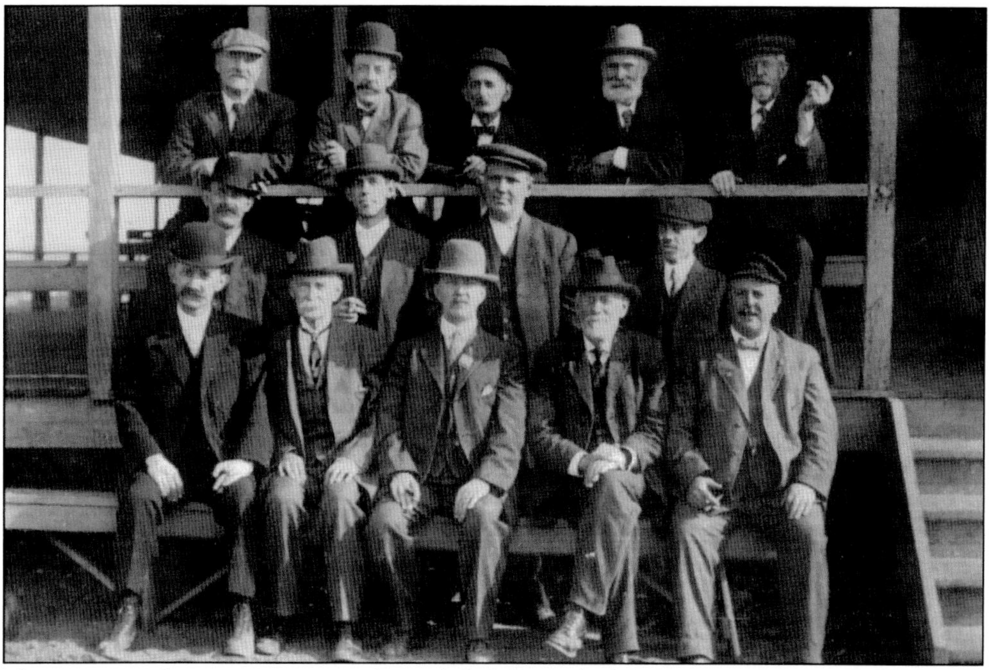

The mystique of a secret society may have eluded the Owl Club. However, they were a men's club that kept their business under their hats. That headgear was perhaps mandatory attire, or sensible protection against the elements, as depicted in this *c.* 1915 image of the men gathered for a fishing trip. Identities (some less than certain) are, from left to right, as follows: (front row) Clarence Haight, R. Pierce, Stanley Day, Charles E. Kelly, and magistrate R. Von Minden; (middle row) unidentified, unidentified, Alex Stillwagon, and unidentified; (back row) Ty Russell, Charles Day, A. Rynd, Phil Jennar, and Frank Van Nuis. (Collection of Cynthia Harris.)

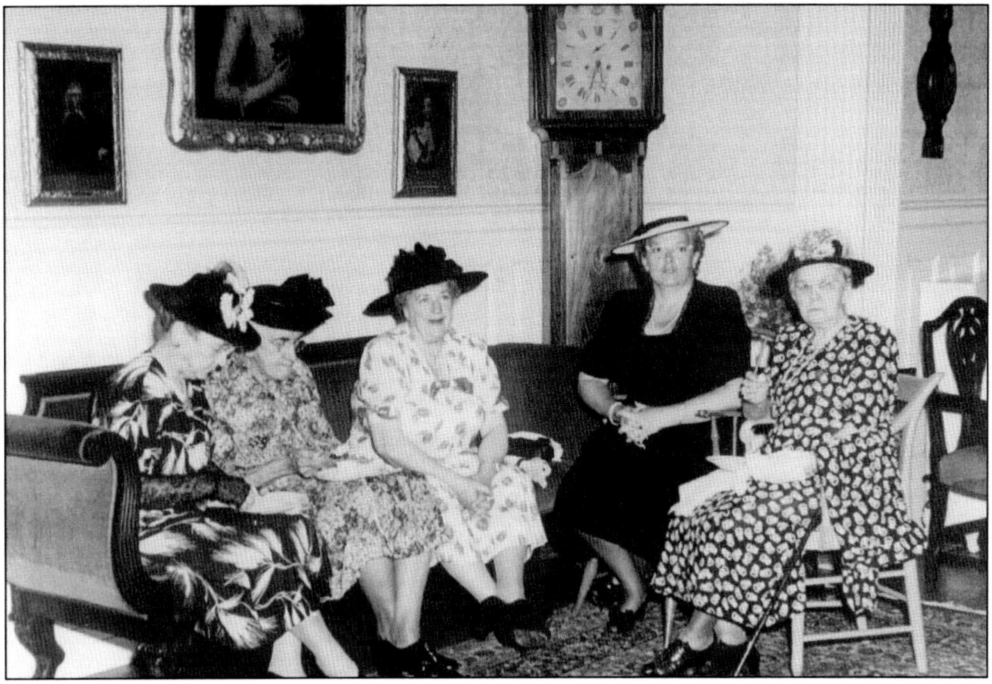

The old, attractive, tall case clock marked a lot of time, appropriate for this quintet, all of longtime Piscataway residence. They are, from left to right, Emma (Mrs. Vandyke) Perrine, Emily (Mrs. David Onderdonk) Perrine, Ede (Mrs. Russell) Perrine, Eleanor (Mrs. Charles) O'Rourke, and Jane (Mrs. Charles) Hoffman Perrine.

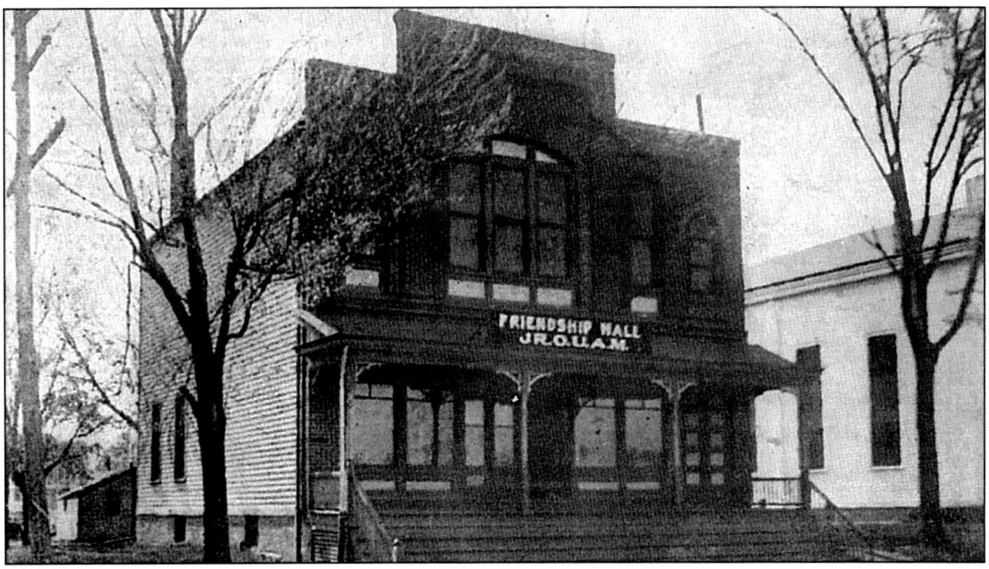

What Friendship Hall lacked in design distinction it made up in an expanse of glass impressive for its day. The early-1890s building, pictured on a c. 1910 postcard, was a lodge for one of many fraternal organizations active at the time—the Friendship Council of the Junior Order of the United American Mechanics, which organized on December 9, 1890. The hall has been remodeled with a gabled front and a Palladian window and is now owned by the adjacent First Baptist Church (page 83).

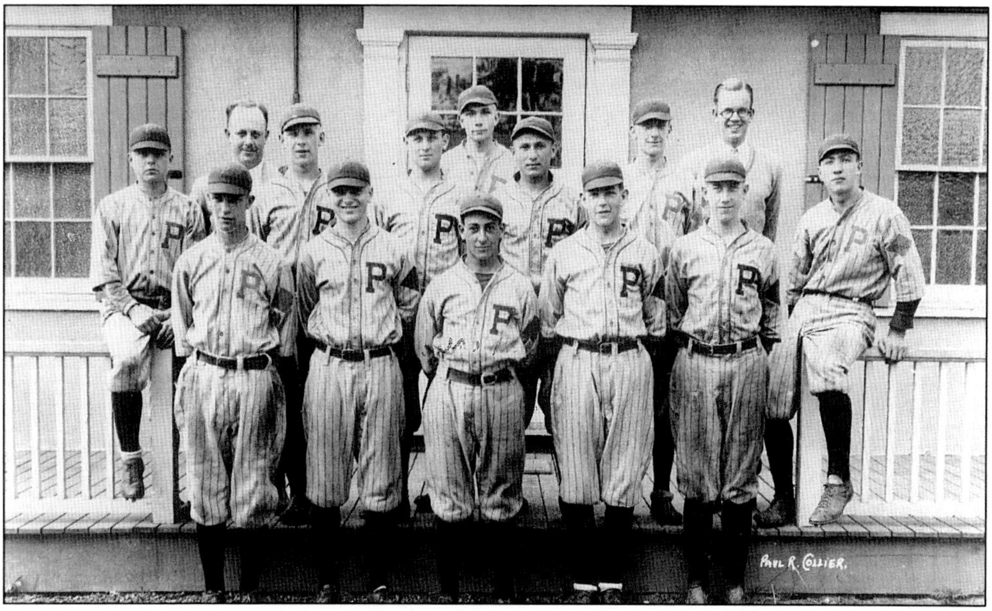

An unidentified Piscataway baseball team (or are they from Plainfield?) appears to be a well conditioned, able squad. They had to be durable, too, with only three substitutes in addition to two managers. Today, of course, retaining only three relief pitchers would not be adequate. This image is perhaps c. 1915, although baggy flannel uniforms lasted past the mid-20th century. (Collection of the Piscataway Public Library.)

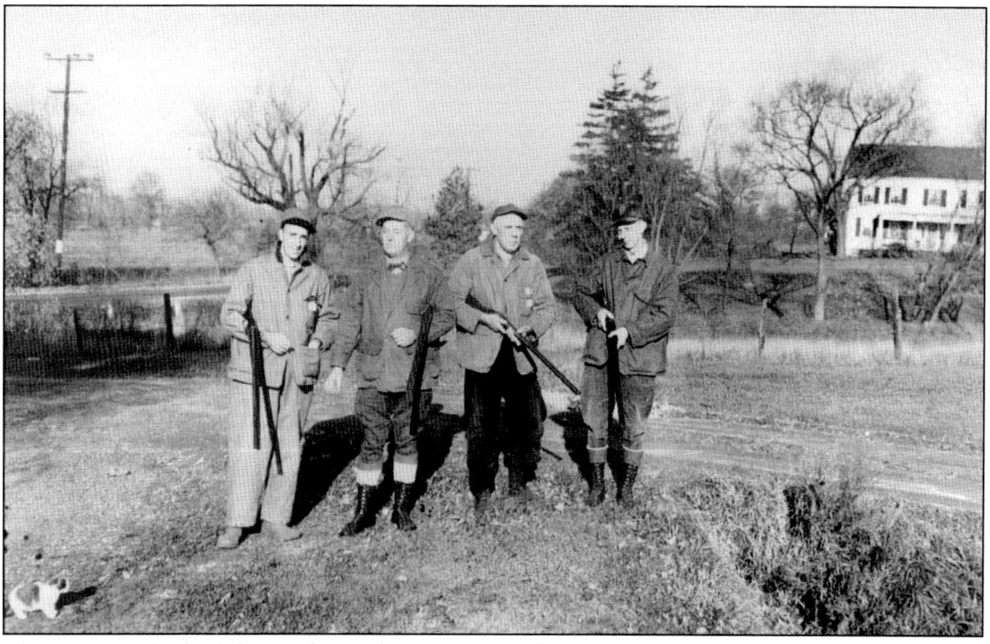

The Isaac Onderdonk house, located at 701 River Road (pages 40 and 41), is the backdrop for four local gunners seen in an undated photograph from a time when River Road (at the rear) still had a rural character. Posing with an unusually round cat in the lower left corner, the men are, from left to right, George Frisch, Russell Perrine, Bob Smith, and unidentified. Piscataway banned hunting within its borders in 1963.

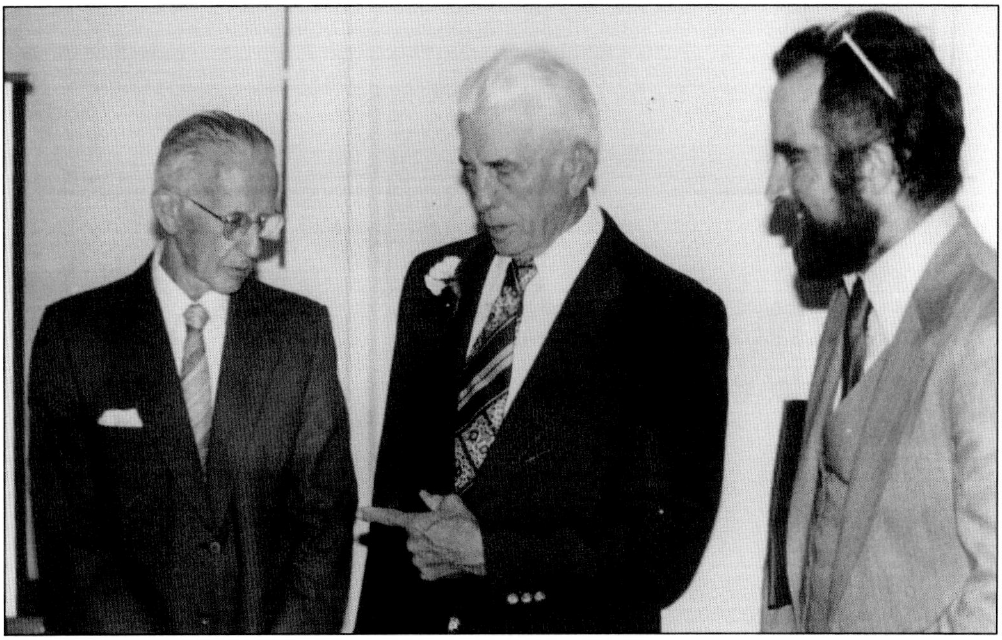

Clarence Perrine (page 92) makes a point literally to Walter Meuly as Joel Grossman, a key archeologist on the first Raritan Landing project, looks on. Meuly, born in 1899 in Switzerland, was a chemist who immigrated to the United States in 1923. Dupont, his employer, sent him to the Piscataway area in the early 1930s. He chaired the 1966 Piscataway Tercentenary Commission, a role leading to a second career as local historian. An avid photographer, Meuly left a rich written and pictorial legacy of Piscataway Township.

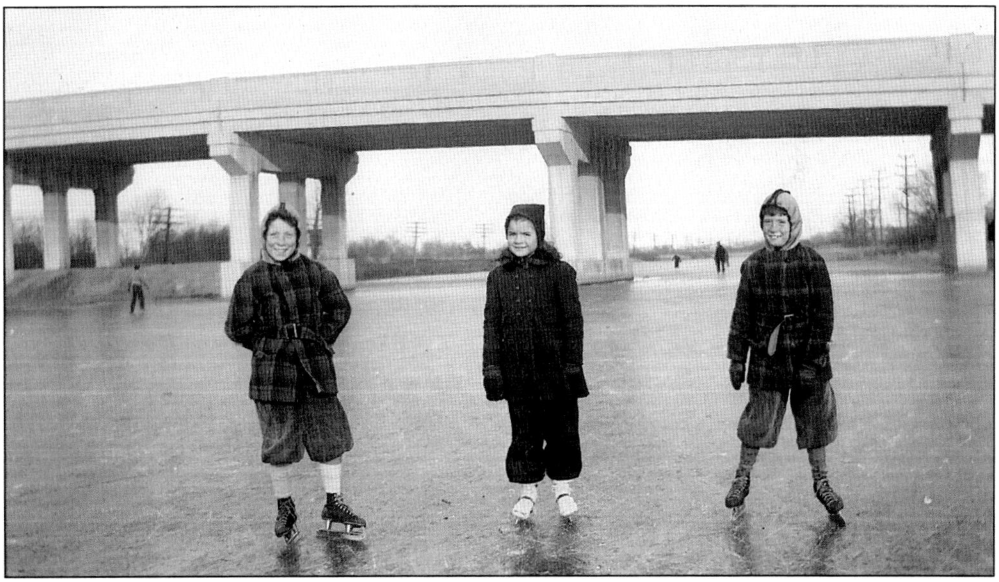

Robert La Costa (right) furnished this photograph. He is pictured skating on New Market Pond in January 1943 with his brother Daniel (left) and friend Doris Hudak. The high-level crossing on Washington Avenue that replaced an earlier one at grade was known as "the white bridge." It also spans the railroad in the background. Robert, a Rutgers graduate and retired dentist, now resides in Holmdel. He recalls the pond in the 1940s as an active recreational site.

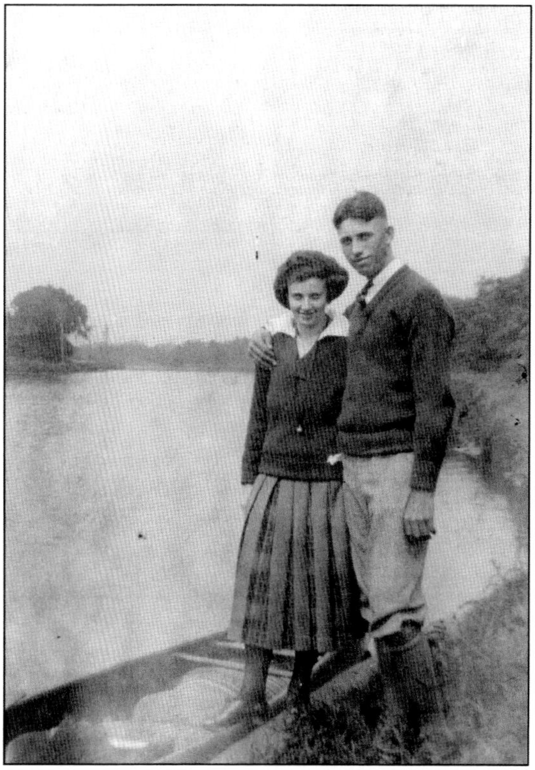

Lydia Tyler, a descendant of Pres. John Tyler, joins a youthful Clarence D. Perrine (page 92), her future husband, in 1923 on the shore of the Raritan River. Lydia, a graduate of Coombs Conservatory in Philadelphia, was music supervisor in the Piscataway school system. The Perrines were married from February 28, 1925, until Lydia's death on December 11, 1984. They had three daughters, including Janice Perrine Kuhn, lender of this and several other pictures.

The game Travo, patterned after Bingo and designed to keep children quiet on motor trips, was invented by a member of Piscataway's Moore family. Different cards had a variety of sites, of varying difficulty to spot, to be found and marked off. Instant nostalgia is inspired by some, such as Burma Shave signs, or milk vending machines on the pictured examples, or miniature golf or a Howard Johnson restaurant on others. Some entries have virtually disappeared from the New Jersey scene, such as the Railway Express truck, wheat fields, drive-in movies, and outhouses. Others are more common, such as squirrels and deer area signs. The Bingo caller retains his numbers and checks the card of the claimed winner, but Travo lacked that control. Imagine the arguments that ensued over whether or not a claimed site was actually sighted. Maybe the game kept the kids occupied but not too quiet. Maybe that is why Parker Brothers never bought Travo.

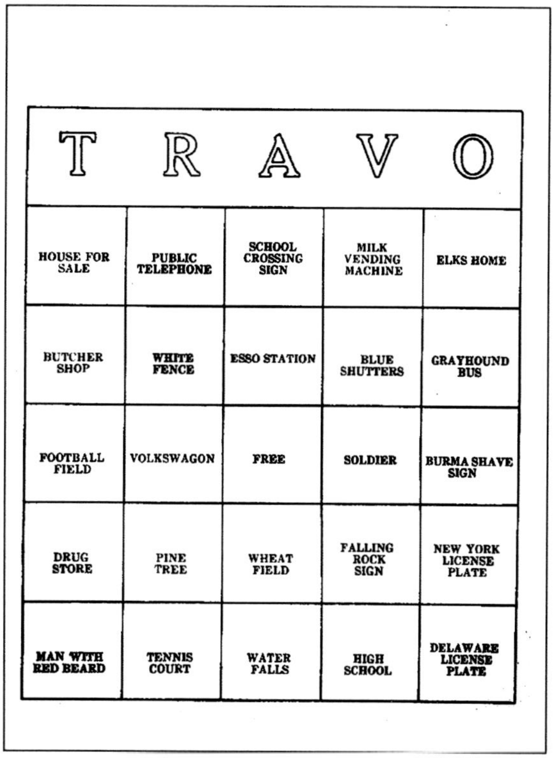

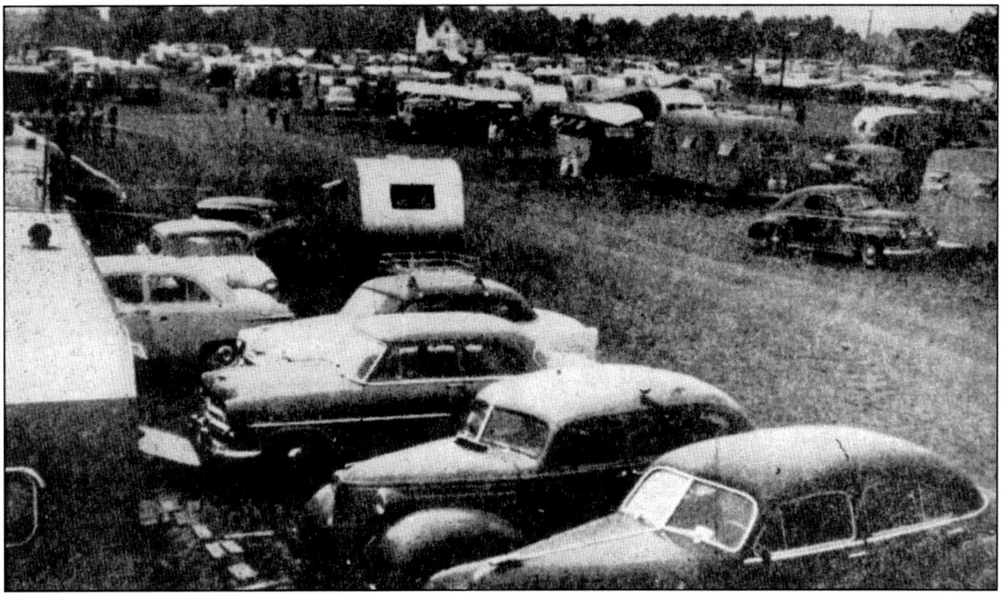

The New World Society Assembly of Jehovah's Witnesses' eight-day convention at Yankee Stadium in New York opened on Sunday, July 19, 1953. Many visitors stayed at a trailer city established on 101 acres of a Piscataway farm, believed to have been on South Washington Avenue. The veritable town, lighted with 23 miles of power lines and 350 street lights, had its own traffic, firefighting, and sanitation departments. Telephone lines carried the proceedings from the stadium to those remaining "at home." (Collection of Cynthia Harris.)

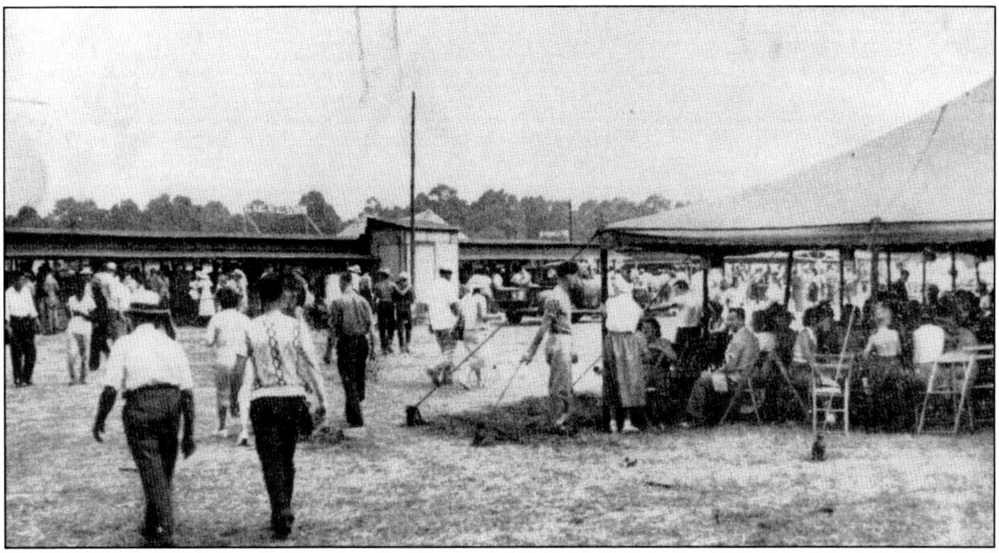

Trailer city drivers clogged the narrow local roads, halting travel to a crawl. Registered visitors numbered more than 44,000, far exceeding the 31,000 expected. They carried their dogs and bicycles, camping in a wide variety of tents and trailers, assisted by about 4,600 volunteers. One report claimed that nearly 40,000 residents of trailer city listened to the telephone hookup. The road jams caused Chief Schlunsen to propose limiting future visitors to a mere 10,000. The trailer city, however, was never replicated. The 10,000 future limit was far exceeded as tens of other thousands merely moved here. (Collection of Cynthia Harris.)

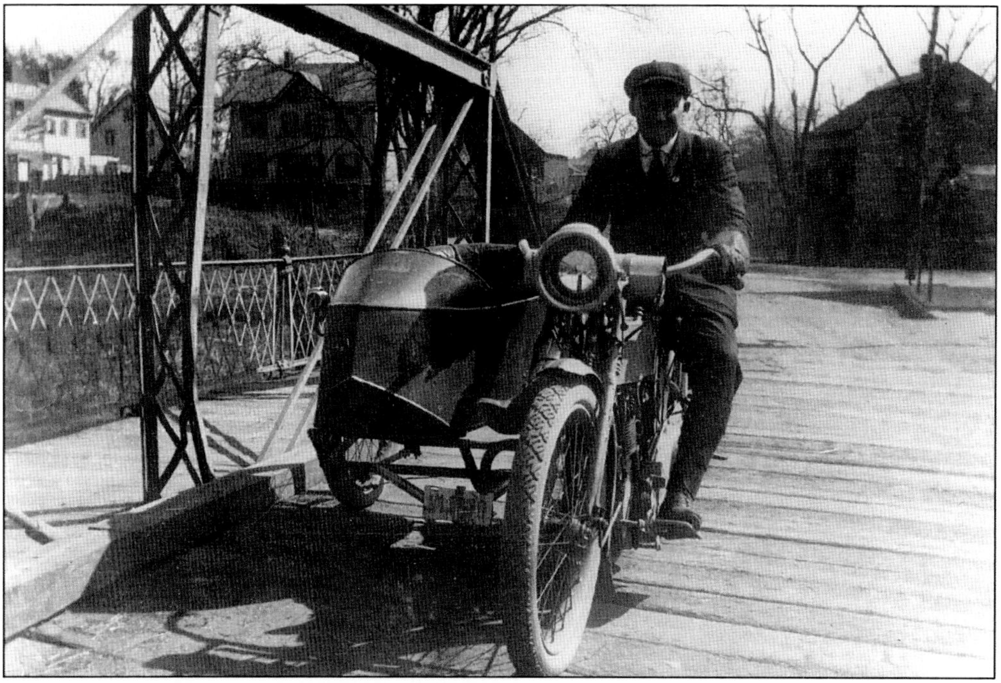

A local motorcyclist is shown with an early sidecar.

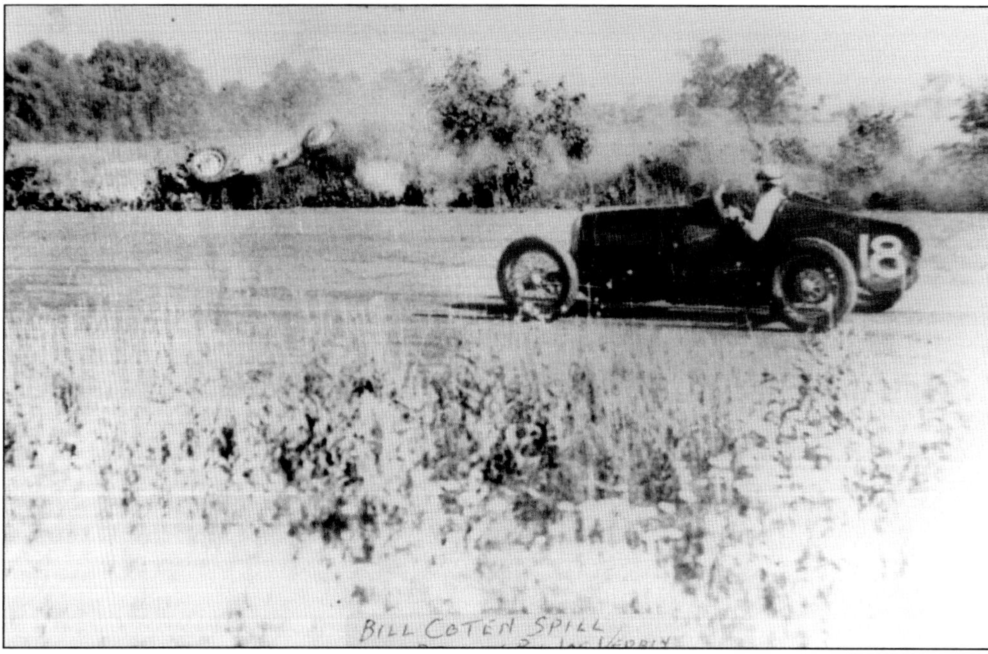

The short, fast life of the short, dangerous New Market Speedway ran from 1927 to 1934. Death was a regular visitor, accidents having claimed seven lives. The half-mile course, originating as a horse trotting track, was located on Lausten's farm on New Brunswick Avenue, near Stelton Road. Fire, acrimony over Sunday closings, and small purses for big risks were merely three of the hazards of rural racing. Drivers numbered locals and regulars over the eastern racing circuit. Bill Coten is pictured in July 1933, crashing in the background as Joe Verbly in No. 18 looks on.